Nāma-Rūpa and Dharma-Rūpa

Nāma-Rūpa and Dharma-Rūpa

Origin and Aspects of an Ancient Indian Conception

by
Maryla Falk

JAIN PUBLISHING COMPANY
Fremont, California

jainpub.com

Jain Publishing Company, Inc. is a diversified publisher of college textbooks and supplements, as well as professional and scholarly references, and books for the general reader. A complete, up-to-date listing of all the books, with cover images, descriptions, review excerpts, specifications and prices is always available on-line at **jainpub.com**. Our booksPLUS® division provides custom publishing and related services in print as well as electronic formats, and our learn24x7® division offers electronic course and training materials development services.

FOREWORD

Ever since that epoch-making event, at the dawn of ancient Indian philosophy, which based the future speculative endeavours on the discovery of a peculiar apex-form of conscious experience and by the same act gave rise and scope to the specifically Indian soteriology – later to be evolved in a homogeneous series of movements during the course of centuries – the characteristic *structuralness* of all the pertinent trends of thought came into prominence in the resultant patterns and persisted deeply ingrained in all the ulterior developments. Its main feature, the constant co-ordination and effective fusion of the anthropological and the cosmological outlook, is determined by the very nature of the basic datum – the experience of cosmic consciousness of self, equating the reality of the psyche with the reality of the cosmos, and, in the speculative issues, investing the latter with the constituent laws of the former. The prototype and nucleus of those structural patterns, the triadic scheme which like a scarlet thread runs through the ideological constructions of the connected religious systems, is determined by the notion of the process which *psychologically* effects that supreme form of experience transcending and superseding all the other forms of conscious life – and which, hence, is held to produce *cosmologically* the transition to the corresponding transcendent sphere of existence. Deduced from an analysis of mental states, this process of the translation of being through the transformation of consciousness is methodically reproduced in a practice known, along with the relevant psycho-physiological and cosmological theory, under the name of *yoga*. In several writings previous to the present (*Il Mito Psicologico nell'India Antica; Un Inno Yoga nell'Atharva-Veda; Upāsana et Upaniṣad;* etc.), and even after it (mainly in my Madras lectures on *The Unknown Early Yoga and the Birth of Indian Philosophy*), I have shown that accepted opinion by far underestimates the antiquity of Yoga as a definite theory and technique and its importance for the evolution of the ancient systems of thought; that, as a matter of fact, its emergence and earliest diffusion go back to the end of the Ṛgvedic period, and that it was organically and fundamentally inherent in the speculation of the Upanishads, becoming the determinant factor in the filiation and formation of several subsequent currents of thought. To this common substratum was due the continuity of the structural schemes, unimpaired by the growing boundaries of schools and systems.

The triadic scheme connected with that basic ideology underlies the conception of *nāma-rūpa*, the most current item in all contexts of ancient Indian construction of reality. Its implications and its developments form the kernel of a coherent complex of theories and doctrines, whose interconnection has remained unnoticed and whose origin has as yet been to a large extent unexplained. This partial shortcoming of research in their regard seems due to the fact that attention has been hitherto far too exclusively concentrated on their systematic classification and their metaphysical interpretation in later dogmatics, while far too little consideration has been given to the modes of their genesis. The present work is intended to fill in this lacuna both methodologically, by drawing attention to the structural factor in the genesis of ancient Indian soteriological systems and the relevant dogmas, and at the same time evidentially, by pointing out the solution of several outstanding problems and preparing the ground for further study of cognate questions on similar lines. The validity of the method may be tested by the evidence of the concrete solutions it affords.

In the present treatment of the subject any extensive collation of material pertinent to single points has been purposely dispensed with and the examination of illustrative details suppressed, or, in few cases, relegated to the footnotes, with a view to maintaining the compendious character of a schematic survey. This has demanded the sacrifice of some matters of interest which I hope to present elsewhere. For the same reason the number of the texts of reference has been reduced to the necessary minimum. Each of the points treated is liable to extensive elaboration; each element of evidence to far ampler documentation.

This essay in the study of ancient Indian structural ideologies was written in 1937 and was placed before the Polish Academy of Science (Oriental Commission) in February 1938, when its publication in due course under the care of that body was decided upon. The customary summary in Polish language was published in the Reports of the Academy for February 1938 (vol. XLIII, no. 2, pp. 35-40). Owing to accumulation of work on hand the printing of this book was delayed and its eventual publication was at last frustrated by the war. It had for sixteen months shared the fate of some of my other writings whose publication was due in 1939, when in January 1941 the generous offer of Dr. B. C.

LAW, the well-known Maecenas of Buddhistic studies in Bengal, to finance its publication at Calcutta, and the almost simultaneous suggestion by Dr. B. M. BARUA, Professor of Pāli, Calcutta University, to place it before the Publication Committee of this University renewed the prospect of its seeing the light of day in the near future.

My thanks are due to Dr. SYAMAPRASAD MOOKERJEE, ex-Vice-Chancellor, President of the Councils of Post-Graduate Studies, Calcutta University, for sanctioning the immediate publication of the work, and for the encouragement to further efforts I have thereby received at his hands.

For the sake of celerity it was decided that an outside press be entrusted with the printing; but a series of unforeseen interruptions resulted instead in an additional year's delay, so that the publication is finally nearing completion four years after it was undertaken for the first time. However, as far as I can ascertain with the limited amount of up-to-date bibliography at my disposal under the present circumstances, no other study of the subject has been attempted during this interval.

The vicissitudes of the publication account for the fact that the work, which had been partly perused in provisional sheets by some European scholars, has been cited in papers published in 1938 with the date of that year, Cracow having been indicated as the place of issue.

The appearance of this study at Calcutta was facilitated by its having been written originally in English, thanks to the valued suggestion of Dr. STANISLAW SCHAYER, Professor of Indian Culture at the University of Warsaw, who rightly objected to almost all my previous works having been written in languages less diffused among students of Indology (mostly in Italian, in French and German). I take this opportunity of recording my sense of deepest gratitude to this elder colleague and true friend, whose entire dedication of himself to the cause of developing and spreading the knowledge of India in Poland has during these last years been subjected to such a grievous trial. The keen interest evinced by him in this particular line of my research work, at a time when I was alone among students of Indology to attempt this line of genetic reconstruction, has more than once provided a stimulus to my pursuits. On his advice I decided to condense my ample survey of the subject in the form of a short monograph, whose moderate claim to the reader's time may in part compensate for the specific weight of its unadorned technical presentation.

I am grateful to Dr. B. M. BARUA, for taking the initiative of reporting on the present study to the Publication Committee, and to Mr. SHAHID SUHRAWARDY, Professor of Fine Arts, Calcutta University, for his kind assistance in proof-correcting. I also desire to express my thanks to Mr. J. CHAKRAVORTI, M.A., Registrar of the University of Calcutta, for the trouble which he has taken over the publishing of this book.

Calcutta,
February 1942.

CONTENTS

	Page
Foreword	v
Chapters :	
I	1
II	15
III	41
IV	48
V	56
VI	68
VII	97
VIII	107
IX	138
Index	191
Errata	221

I

The definition of worldly reality as *nāma-rūpa*, "name-and-form", expresses a conception peculiar to ancient Indian thought, widely current already in the first period of the Upanishads and further developed in the successive periods as well as throughout the stages of Buddhist speculation, but going back in its earliest evidence to the Ṛgveda. In modern research only few, and rather cursory, attempts have hitherto been made to interpret the import of that binomium, mainly with a view to reducing it to familiar denominations, on the lines of free comparison with apparently similar – but essentially quite heterogeneous – conceptions. They were based on two contrasting types of a priori evaluation of ancient Indian thought as a whole: on the one hand, ethnological generalization in the light of "primitive" standards of thinking; on the other, philosophical generalization from points of view of Western thought, considered as universally valid. Interpretations thus obtained[1] are not verified by the data of the contexts. The emergence of the *nāma-rūpa* conception cannot, in fact, be understood as a shadowy approach to the categories of matter and form, yet verging on the range of primitive magic lore: not only because

[1] See esp. H. OLDENBERG, *Die Lehre der Upanishaden u. d. Anfänge des Buddhismus*, p. 68; *Vorwissenschaftliche Wissenschaft*, p. 103f.; *Buddha*[7], p. 256 n. 2; P. DEUSSEN, *Allg. Geschichte der Philosophie*, I, p. 260.

it appears, even in the oldest records, with such a wealth of ideological implications and in a speculative structure so highly specified as to prove the very contrary of an undeveloped and groping notion, but also because the intrinsical criterion of the co-ordination between its two component items is quite incommensurate with the Platonic dualism of *Eidos* and *Hyle* from which the Western binomium ultimately descends. Nor can it be adequately explained as an anticipation of Spinoza's *modi* of Godhead, *extensio* and *cogitatio,* since the import of this dual category – which can be critically accounted for only if viewed against its historical background of abstract Scholastic speculation – is equally incommensurate with the Indian conception, in which the unsensuous character of *nāman* does not preclude its having a kind – even a twofold kind – of spatial existence, and the dimensionality of *rūpa* does not preclude its genetic connection with *nāma.* As in so many other cases where the *ab extra* approach to problems of Indian thought has proved a hindrance instead of a help in the search for a satisfactory solution, the only practicable way is that of approach *ab intra,* a method of historical exploration of the inherent substrata.

The source of the Indian binomium is in fact to be found in the specific ideology which underlies a cosmogonic myth elaborated in several speculative texts of the Ṛgveda. It hinges on the idea that before the beginning of things, before the manifestation of multiplicity, all rūpas were one rūpa, *viz.* the unmanifest shape of the universal *Puruṣa,* and all *nāmas* were one nāma, *viz.* the unuttered universal *Vāc.* The negative valuation implicit in the notion of *nāma-rūpa* is due to the fact that it was laden with the sense of the differentiation of the original infinite unity. I have pointed out elsewhere[2] that

[2] *Il Mito Psicologico nell' India Antica,* pp. 35ff. *et*

Vāc was hypostatized as the female aspect of Puruṣa, who was conceived as androgynous. At the beginning of the process of manifestation the Androgyne splits into the male and the female : this is the primordial event frequently described in the cosmogonies of the Brāhmaṇas and of the Upanishads. Older specimens of this cosmogonic conception are found in a group of Ṛgvedic hymns, among which the Puruṣasūkta supplies its most genuine formulation. Here it is said (5) that from Puruṣa emanated Virāj; then of Virāj Puruṣa was born,[4] a cosmic being. This Puruṣa (=Nārāyaṇa), son of the hypercosmic Man and of the Waters, i.e. of the primal heavenly Light-ocean Virāj who is the hypercosmic Vāc (ṚV. I, 164, 41f., etc.; X, 189, 3), was immolated in a sacrifice performed by the demiurges (gods or Ṛṣis) and dismembered into the multiplicity of the contingent cosmos.

In III, 38, where this peculiar cosmogonic conception is wrapped up in elements of the traditional symbolic imagery of the Ṛgveda, the Androgyne is represented as "Bull-Cow" (the current image of the cow is applied to the primordial female Aditi-Virāj in her character of supernal Light-ocean, fountainhead of all life and source of its continued sustentation, I, 164, 41-2). His Name[5] is great, his Form is universal: thus he remained on the plane of Immortality (st. 4cd.; cf. X, 90,3d *tripād asyāmṛ-*

passim, see Index s. vv. Vāc, Virāj, Androgino universale, Macrantropo. *Origine dell' Equazione Ellenistica Logos=Anthropos*, pp. 191ff.

[4] According to X. 72 – a hymn adapting the names of ancient mythological figures to the new myth – Dakṣa was born from Aditi, who had been born from Dakṣa (4-5).

[5] This *nāma*—which as yet embraces in its unity all the nāmas (cf. 7)—is his transcendent Self-Light, hidden by the cosmic light-manifestation (*tad...nāma* in c refers to *svarociḥ* in b).

taṃ divi). But the *ṛṣis* or *kavis* as "artificers" of the cosmos were all busy around him as he came hither (cf. X, 90, 4b *pādo 'syehābhavat*), so that the self-luminous now moves clad in the splendours (ab). The Puruṣasūkta provides the explanation of this difficult stanza. Evidently the two conditions of the primeval being as father and son, hypercosmic archetype and cosmic ectype, are alluded to (cf. 5a). The 7th st. speaks of the son as victim: of this Bull-Cow they measured out the essence with names, while, assuming ever new divine forms, they measured out the Form in him.

From the collation of these texts it appears that the existence of nāma-rūpa is due to two consecutive acts of division: first the separation of the two aspects of the universal Being, then the dismemberment of its twin-and-one cosmic manifestation.

The diversification of the primordial cosmic unity is also a concealment of its original nature. The self-luminous moves about clad in the splendours of cosmic light, which are not his own forms: "it is his (form, cf. 7cd), not mine, the golden brightness which Savitar has diffused" (8ab). But the inspiration of the seer penetrates beyond (cf. 1c) the cosmogonic achievement of the kavis to the primal essence, the *dharman* (2); this indeed is the secret reality by concealing which they arranged for their rule heaven and earth, and which they inserted between the two worlds (3): the current conception of the cosmic Puruṣa as Skambha, the world-pillar, is alluded to.[6]

Analogous facts are related about Vāc: she was the first sacrificial substance (X, 125, 3b)—not indeed her secret three quarters which are immovable, but the quarter

[6] Further developments of this conception in the ṚV. and in the AV: *Il Mito Psicologico*, pp. 27ff.

of Vāc which is spoken speech (I, 164,45). This manifest Vāc the gods divided in many a way, so that she has many abodes and many revelations (I, 125,3cd). When those who founded name-giving set about their task, the first and topmost portion of this manifested Speech, which they found most excellent and pure, was hidden by them (X,71,1); the higher names were hidden by the kavis who watch the seat of *ṛta* (X, 5, 2cd; X, 117,2cd says that in the seat of ṛta they watch the radiant sounding — i.e. uttered — Wisdom, Vāc). They formed seven boundaries, so that the quarry should step into one of them: thus the Pillar of the supernal Life, which abides where all ways end, came to stand on the ground (X,5,6).[7] For us Agni is the first-born of ṛta, but in the prior age it was the Bull-Cow (7).

In its cosmic division and concealment the primal Being's own transcendent reality ("the all-knowing but not the all-pervading Vāc" I, 164, 10d; the *dharman*, III, 38,2d) cannot be perceived by common consciousness: only the seer in his ecstasy[8] may perceive it: "I have no discriminating consciousness when I am, as it were, this (all): I live in secrecy and ready-hearted: when onto me comes the First-born of ṛta, then I attain the inheritance of Vāc" (I, 164,37). Henceforth he is silent for ever

[7] The cosmogonic Skambha grows upside down into the cosmos as a tree rooted above the firmament (cf. I, 24, 7: King Varuṇa keeps its summit upright in the Bottomless, but below the Bottom—the firmament—it was turned with its branches upside down). In human shape the cosmic Skambha is represented as the Uttānapad, the figure whose legs are stretched upwards (X, 72, 3-4). In the Upanishads it is conceived as the Saṃsāra-Tree, with its roots on high, its branches hanging downwards (KaṭhaU VI, 1, Śvet.U III, 9c, MaitriU VI, 4; cf. BĀU III, 9, 28, Gītā XV, 1-5).

[8] The term is understood in the most literal sense; see the ff. pp.

about his visions, lest he lose her by utterance; (X, 71,4-5 :) he to whom Vāc has thus given her form as a lowing wife – by a spontaneous miracle, for otherwise she cannot be won (4ab) – is firmly guarded in this union, not even in the singing-matches is he incited (to give her out): he lives in barren (i.e. silent) autonomous power (*māyayā*), having heard the fruitless and flowerless (i.e. unuttered) Vāc.[9] This union actualizes in his inmost being the all-embracing cosmic unity of the primal mate of Vāc, who knew her in the unuttered state (cf AV V, 1,2): "Let the Lover (*Vena*) perceive the highest Being in the secret place (in the innermost heart, equated with the uppermost – hypercosmic – heaven[10]) where all becomes *of one form*" (AV. II, 1, 1); this supernal Light, in its hidden three quarters, is the all-knowing Father, the One origin of the nāmas of all the gods[11] (2-3; cf. ṚV X, 90, 3d; X, 82,2-3 : the One is the "supreme aspect" of the creator and resides beyond the seven Ṛṣis; 3cd = AV. II, 1,3cd). The Vena knows the immortal (hidden) names (cf. above, p. 5), while the *vipras* cognize and desire only the contingent rūpa of the *amṛta* and follow its perceptible sound (X, 123,4). Having in one instant embraced heaven and earth[12], the seer has attained the First-born of ṛta as Vāc within him who speaks (AV. II, 1,4). And in him the fourth quarter, which in the act of utterence he disjoins (*vi-yunakti*) from the great three quarters as (spoken) Speech, is again joined to them : for in him is effected the union (*yujyate*) of the One (VIII, 9,3).

[9] Cf. BĀU III, 5 *munir amaunaṃ ca maunaṃ ca nirvidyā 'tha brāhmaṇaḥ . yena syāt tenedṛśa eva.*

[10] Cf. *Il Mito Psicologico*, pp. 31, 46f.; below, pp. 18f., 20ff.

[11] So he who invokes the gods only "invokes the name with the name" (AV. X, 7, 31a).

[12] Or: "having encompassed all beings," *ibid* 5a.

It is thus, evidently, a second descent of the supernal Being that restores its original reality in the soul of the seer. In fact already in the Ṛgvedic texts two forms of the descent of Vāc are distinguished, divergent in their modes and opposite in their effects : one is the cosmogonic event – the cosmic division ensuing upon the cosmic generation – , the other is the process of enlightenment, whose most appropriate time is set in the nightly intervals between the daily reproductions *in effigie* of the cosmogonic process – of the descent, dispersion and alienation of the supernal light-fluid – : in fact during those intervals this process is inverted. According to the Vāc-hymn I, 164 the light-wielding factors of creation, the attainments of the sacrifice performed by the Ṛṣis, are distributed in various *dhāmas*, "light-abodes", and manifested in diverse *rūpas* (*teṣām iṣṭāni vihitāni dhāmaśas sthātre rejante* – they blink in the fixed place, on the vault of the sky as luminaries – *vikṛtāni rūpaśaḥ*, 15) while the light dwells in the cosmos. But "along the black path (the path of night) the bright birds investing the waters (the *madhvadaḥ suparṇāḥ* on the world-tree mentioned in 22 : the rays or particles of light, the many "names" of the one Garutmān, 46; the many utterances of the spoken quarter of Vāc, 45d) fly up to heaven : they had come hither from the seat of ṛta (47 ; for night and day are like two tracks within the cosmos – one hidden, the other visible : the former is the path of convergence, the latter that of divergence : III, 55, 15). Thus "the birds join with their melodies the (silent hymn) of the unwinking heritage of Immortality (where the light never sets), Wisdom" (21ab) ; the dhāmas return to their common source, to the "third" light beyond sun and moon (and alternating with them), "whose force does not manifest any form" (44). This hypercosmic abode of Wisdom, the unuttered three quarters of Vāc, is the "highest" and "secret" *dhāman* (*dhāma paramaṃ guhā yad*, AV. II, 1,2b; cf. ṚV. X, 181, 2b; *amṛtasya dhāma* IX, 94,2a; 97,32b; also *paramaṃ nāma* X, 45, 2 opposed to the many dispersed *dhāmas; tṛtīyam, apīcyam, nāma* I, 155, 3; IX, 75, 2cd). The active essence of the cosmogonic differentiation as the basis of cosmic existence is designated by the plural term *dharmāṇi* (with the specification *prathamāni*: X, 90, 16b; I, 164, 43d, 50b; but see also e.g. IX, 97, 12c, AV. V, 1, 1a), the "sustaining factors" of being. Midway between these two opposite aspects of reality is structurally placed the substratum, or victim, of the cosmogonic sacrifice, the cosmic Puruṣa, the cosmic Bull-Cow (cf. I, 164, 43 and III, 38, 7), the son of Vāc whom she held suspended at her foot "below the yonder and above the nether", herself having retired to the hypercosmic beyond (I, 164, 17, cf. III, 55, 13b); the "beautiful bird" which is also the Skambha[13] (7), the heavenly Bird, the one Being which on earth the *vipras* utter in many names (46, cf. X, 114, 5ab). By night the *dharmāṇi* are inoperative, the *pūrvo 'rdha* beyond the cosmos is disclosed, the *dhāma* of the great primal god is sent forth (AV. IV, 1, 6ab, d); now, while "he (the *vipra* active by day, cf. 5) who is born together with the many" (*jajñe bahubhiḥ*

[13] In fact "the cows draw the water from his head, while the inhabitants of the (world-)veil (see below, p. 9) drink the water by his foot (on the earth-level) (7). The many "cows," the life-giving waters, though similar (*sarupāḥ*) or different in shape (*virūpāḥ*), are ultimately of one shape (*ekarupāḥ*), since they derive from the one above, from the ocean of supernal Life; Agni knows their many names by the agency of sacrifice. As they have yielded their form to the gods (in the shape of soma, which is the essence of the immortality of the devas), soma knows all their forms (X, 169, 2, 3ab).

sākam : *sākaṃjāḥ* are the six Ṛṣis, opposed to the seventh who is *ekaja* I, 164, 15a) sleeps" (cd) – now it happens that Vāc again emits her own undivided light-essence. This third, nocturnal light, which to the unseeing is only darkness, and which is revealed when every contingent light has disappeared – a favourite topic of a group of Vedic hymns (e.g. ṚV. X, 189; AV. IV, 1; VIII, 9)[14], later laid down in a famous stanza recurrent in three Upanishads (Kaṭha V, 5; Muṇḍ. II, 2, 10; Śvet. VI, 24) and paraphrased in the Gītā (XV, 6) – is the Fullness of the immortal world (X, 149, 3b; cf. ChU VII, 24-25), the original Dharman of the Bird Garutmān to which Savitar's beautiful cosmos has succeeded (a, cd)[15]. But Savitar, who has called forth the manifestation of this multifarious world, also regularly suspends it, by rising upward (II, 38, 1; 4c) and extending aloft his arms with expanded hands (i.e by directing the light-rays back to their source, cf. I, 164,47, above, p. 7): then, according to Savitar's vow, the "releaser", Night, comes (3). The Weaver has rolled up again the extended world-veil (4; cf. I, 115, 4). This is when "the Mother bestows on the Son the supreme inheritance (the pre-cosmic *dharman*), according to his tendency promoted by Savitar" (5). Such is also the sense implied in the statement I, 164, 17cd, that Vāc who has gone away to the unknown part still comes to dwell in her son, but not in the herd (in the "many"). Thus below the

[14] Cf. *Il Mito Psicologico*, pp. 40-53.

[15] As opposed to *dharman*=*ṛta*, the cosmic order of Mitra and Varuṇa (then also of other deities), this is their precosmic *dharman*, which is the radiance of their great *dhāman* (X, 65, 5c), whereby they maintain their secret ordinances (*vratā* – sc. *guhyā*, cf. I, 163, 3b; III, 54, 5d; X, 114, 2d – contrasted with *ṛta*, V, 63, 7), which renders their abode immovable (V, 72, 2ab).

yonder and above the nether the father of the cosmos is regenerated as the divine manas is born (18). "I call hither the well-yielding Cow, that the milkman with the blessed hands may milk her; may Savitar have incited us to the most propitious tendency; the light-glow is enkindled; may I have well announced this" (26). The Cow who longed after her Calf has come hither by the gift of manas; she uttered her voice towards the winking Calf, into the head[16] (cf. X, 125, 7a *ahaṃ suve pitaram asya mūrdhan*), and thus imparted that voice to it, she roared into the mouth the milk of her light-glow (27, 28; cf. III, 55, 13-14). This communion in her essence raises the "winking", mortal manas to her plane (that of the "unwinking inheritance of Immortality") and to the dignity of a nuptial union: "he utters the roar in whose embrace the Cow produces the sound when she alights on lightning[17]; by plural consciousness she brought down the mortal, but by becoming lightning she has torn off the veil" (the "veil" is the light-texture of the cosmic manifestation [above, p.9], to weave which the kavis stretched seven threads across the calf [5cd, cf. X, 5, 6] and which is inhabited by the earthly creatures).[18] This is the earliest instance of the image of "lightning" as applied to the event of instantaneous enlightenment produced by the union with the transcendent principle of

[16] According to BĀU II, 2 the "calf" as abiding in the head (cf. 3) is *prāṇa* (1) as the "puruṣa in the eye," regarded also as cosmic Skambha (2). Concerning the alternations of *manas* and *prāṇa* as mate of *vāc* see *op. cit.*, p. 415ff.

[17] For *dhvasani* cf. I, 140, 3-5.

[18] So the humans have been prevented from finding him from whom creation derives, since another reality has been placed closer to them — while the authors of the ukthas (the Ṛṣis) who appropriate his life act under cover of mist and utterance (X,82,7).

universal wisdom, which in the later centuries of the history of this image[19] will be again called *dharma*. Thus the seer's enlightenment and ecstasy (whose description in 37 forms the conclusion of the connected sequence of stanzas 15-37, interrupted by the obvious glosses 25, 35), his union with the transcendent Vāc, fulfils the psychic apocatastasis of the cosmic Puruṣa. As by this union with the "formless" dharman-essence the Skambha—whose unique form is that of the Unborn (6)—is restituted to his transcendent androgynous nature,[20] the cosmic veil which encompassed him is torn off: released, he attains his primal abode, the inheritance of Vāc. This

[19] See BĀU II, 3, 6; V, 4 7; ChU VIII, 4, 2; KenaU 29-30; KaṭhaU VI, 2; Śvet. U IV, 4 (*pataṃga taḍidgarbha*); MaitriU VII, 11; Nṛsiṃhottaratāp.U VI; Mokṣadharma (Bomb. ed.) 203_{23}; 241_{20}; 307_{20}; Laṅkāvatāra-Sūtra (Tokyo ed.) p. 42 (*vajrabimbopamasamādhi*). Cf. *Il Mito Psicologico*, pp. 95, 123, 139n. 3, 141, 182, 223, 242, 254, 267, 394, 399.

Concurrently with the psychological criterion of the image—the flashlike character of ecstatic intuition—its cosmological criterion is obvious in this early context: lightning appears as the typical evidence of an instantaneous descent of the hypercosmic Light-essence into the cosmic structure outside the normal channels of the cosmic order.

[20] The seven Ṛṣis, called "seven *ardhagarbhas*" in st. 36, are 3½ *ardhanārīnaras*. The *leit-motiv* of the introductory stanzas of the hymn, emphasizing the recondite connexion of the three and the seven, prepares the final disclosure in st. 15: the god-born Ṛṣis are six twins, the seventh is called the one-born. (Cf. also AV. X, 8, 5b *ṣad yamā eka ekajaḥ*). The three couples represent the three worlds, while the seventh is the Skambha, "the One propping asunder these six spheres", "the One sustaining the three mothers and the three fathers" (10). As contrasted with the many rūpas of the realm of the six, the form of the one is "that of the Unborn"; this form is not sensuous: it is "the boneless sustaining him

supreme reintegration is brought about by the "divine manas," whose birth (18) is the second – soteric – birth of the Skambha. Thus instead of the one Bird (co-extensive with the world-pillar, 7), diversified in the many light-birds, there are now *t w o* Birds coalescent with the same (world)-tree" (20 ab): the divine manas and the mortal. Only one of them "knows"[21] the Father (realizing the transcendent aspect of androgynous being[22], the son – who is father of the world, 18 – becomes the father's Father, the original Puruṣa: 16), and so attains the fruit of immortality, Wisdom, at the top of the tree (20cd-22).[23] The mortal is unaware of his supernal origin, for, "having been wrapped up in the matrix to multiply in the many beings, he was precipitated into calamity" (32cd. Cf. AV. V, 1, 2: the Sustainer, who had known the un-uttered Vāc, was the first to enter the matrix; and ṚV. X, 177, 2: the Bird, as Gandharva, has uttered Vāc in the matrix). So "he knows no more Him who has made him (the transcendent Father), He who has seen him is

who has bones (the sensuous living being), the life, the blood, the breath of the earth" (the micro- and macrocosmic Skambha); it is invisible (6). But in him the androgynous nature of the Unborn is incomplete: it is integrated by the nuptial union with the soteric Light-essence of *Vāc*, which has no form (44), in the lightning whereby the veil which had enclosed him is torn off, so that he can perceive, and join, his transcendent origin.

[21] Cf. *infra*, p. 16.

[22] The transcendent Puruṣa is the supernal archetype of the three androgynous world-beings: "I am told that they are women and likewise men... the sage as the Son comprehends *these* things (this 'nether' aspect of androgynous existence); as he who may descry *those* (the transcendent aspect of this reality) he shall be the father's Father" (16).

[23] The meaning of the stanza is modified in the context of Śvet.U (IV, 6) and of Muṇḍ.U (III, 1, 1) under the influence

now far away from him" (32ab).[24] When by the descent of the divine manas (26, 27b) the way to enlightenment is laid open, the "immortal" and the "mortal" are together in the same individual (30d, 38b); they are not separate, but there is no simultaneity between them: the one moves while the other is asleep and immobilized[25] (30); the ways of the two, the autonomous and the prisoner, are opposite, their directions are always in contrast: one of them is known, not known is the other (38). Thus the "herdsman" (of the thoughts) goes up or down the tracks according as he invests the converging or the diverging ones (31, *id*. X, 177, 3). The "diverging" or manifold thoughts (the differentiation of thought, discriminating consciousness) are in fact the "descent" of the "mortal", as had been stated immediately before (29); whereas concentration – as the context of this st. in X, 177 implies – leads to the supernal common abode of the

of the new conception of the *bhoktar*, coupled with the notion – amply recorded in the Aggañña-Suttanta – that "eating" is the cause of the degradation to cruder forms of existence. The "Tree" is here understood as the *saṃsāra-vṛkṣa* (above, n. 7).

[24] See also AV. V, 1, 3: "He who gave up to suffering thy body, the liquid gold (cf. X, 7, 28), his pure (sc. forms: the pl. of the preceding *tanū* is meant, as the one shape has become manifold when the pure Life became subject to the *dharmāṇi* and as Skambha entered the matrix, 1-2) – in him both put the immortal names; as for this one (the Skambha), let the (cosmic) abodes come to him as vestures."

[25] The activity of the discriminating manas is at a standstill while that of the divine manas, the enlightening ascension, takes place. St. 30 brings out quite clearly the notion that the two are but contrasting functions of the same psyche: "The swiftly proceeding moves while it rests; breathing, the immobile live entity moves within the abodes (world-spheres and organisms); the living proceeds by the self-power of the dead – the immortal and the mortal are born in the same being."

light-rays. There the Bird by manas carries (back) Vāc whom he had uttered in the matrix. Thus the effect of concentration is to "join together that which had remained united and that which was to be re-united" (*tvaṃ hi yuktam yuyukṣe yogyaṃ ca,* AV. VIII, 9, 7b), through that agency of Virāj (*ibid.,* c) which is enacted by night (cf. 2, 6, 8 with 7).

So the second descent of Vāc in the divine manas effects the process of enlightenment in the unification of the differentiated manas and in the ascent of regenerated consciousness to its hypercosmic source; the consummation is sung in I, 164, 37, the development of the soteric process in the preceding set of stanzas, describing the secret inner transformation and upward voyage to the top of the world-tree where its transcendent fruit is attained, the heritage of Immortality. The fruit is the *akṣara,* the "static", undifferentiated essence of Vāc-Wisdom in her highest heaven (34d, 39a – cf. AV. VIII, 9, 8d – ; the *akṣara* is the unique archetype of all forms of chant, 24d). Thus the psychic process of enlightenment implies an ascent to the summit of the cosmos and beyond, the intuition in which it culminates tears off the cosmic veil; the illumination of individual consciousness – simultaneously reflected in its extension to universal totality – is conceived as an apocatastasis of the cosmogonic event: of the descent and the differentiation of the original universal unity.

II

In the Upanishads we are faced with the parallel microcosmic formulation of the ancient mythical conception: the motif of the Puruṣa's dismemberment at the dawn of cosmic becoming reappears in these texts as the differentiation of the ātman (the latter term being adopted ever since the Atharvanic stage as the chief designation of the psycho-cosmic Puruṣa) into the vital functions or prāṇas. In this condition, that is to say in the common conscious existence of man, the ātman cannot be realized because he is non-total (*asarva*), reality being differentiated (*vyākriyate*) in names-and-forms (BĀU I, 4, 7). But in a particular state of "knowledge", in the ecstatic unification of man's being in which the prānas become steady and melt into one (in the later texts this state is called *samādhi;* similar wordings are already met with in the oldest Upanishadic texts: cf. *samastaḥ samprasannaḥ* ChU VIII, 6, 3, hence *samprasāda*=ātman *ibid.* 3, 4 and 12, 3; the psychic exercise by which this unification is enacted in the waking condition – namely the discipline of yoga – is already practised since at least the Atharvanic period (as I have repeatedly pointed out), and is known in the AV. under the verbal forms of the later technical term[1]), the reconstituted ātman, having left the bodily differentiated existence and reached the supernal Light

[1] *Il Mito Psicologico*, pp. 40ff.

(the highest sphere of the transcendent brahman), comes forth *in his own Form* (*svena rūpeṇābhiniṣpadyate*), *viz.*, the one-and-total *rūpa* of the universal supreme Puruṣa (*sa uttamaḥ puruṣaḥ*). (ChU VIII, 12, 3).

So his supersensuous reality is hidden in the prāṇas which are his "functional names" (*tasyaitāni karmanāmāni* BĀU I, 4, 7): his true name is ātman. Therefore one must not realize him under those single aspects in meditation producing identity with the object (*upās* – *upāsana*[2]), for in this way one does not "know" : one must indeed realize him as ātman" : "there all these (prāṇas) become one".

Knowledge of names is in fact knowledge of things, for according to the ancient Indian conception names are nowise fortuitous designations, but are expressive of the innermost essence and power of the things named. We already met with the notion that the real names are hidden, and only the seer discovers them. As "knowledge" is identification with the thing known, the more one "knows", the greater one becomes; by "knowing the all", or, in the terms of this conception, by effectuating the redintegration of all names in the unique and universal name, Vāc, one "becomes the All", becomes identified with the universal Puruṣa. This state of universal knowledge (styled *pratibodha* in the Upanishads [BĀU I, 4, Kena 12], *bodhi* or *sambodhi in Buddhism*[3]) takes place in the ecstatic vision, the Upanishadic description of which (BĀU II, 3, 6, cf. V, 7; Kena 10-12[4];

[2] See *Upāsana et Upaniṣad*, RO XIII (1937), pp. 129-159; *Il Mito Psicologico*, passim, v. Index s. vv.

[3] *sambodhi* in verbal formulation Maitri U VI, 4.

[4] Grammatical construction of the passage, *op. cit.*, p. 121f.

29; ChU VIII, 4, 2; Kaṭha VI, 2; etc.) – as a lightning-instant of illumination whereby immortality is attained in brahman through extension to universal existence – had already been anticipated in the Ṛgvedic seer's description of his cosmic transfiguration through the reception of Vāc in lightning-form, and in the Atharvanic seer's words on the instant in which he embraced heaven and earth, attaining the First-born of reality as Vāc within the speaker, i.e. realizing Puruṣa in his own heart, which is the seat of Speech.

Alongside with such psychological descriptions of the unification of reality in consciousness as we often meet in the Upanishads, there are also other descriptions of this process, bearing a more markedly mythical hue and keeping in close continuity with the Vedic myth. Within man there are two *puruṣas*, a male and a female (sometimes it is said they may be seen in the right and in the left eye). *He* is styled *Indha,* the "enkindler" – "though they call him Indra for the sake of mystery, as the gods love what is mysterious and hate what is obvious" – ; for in his true nature he is Prāṇa, the enkindler of life[5], but also of the yogic fire-body

[5] See Śat. Br. VI, 1, 1, 2; etc

He is not only the power building up the concrete shape of the individual, but also the faculty of *perceiving* forms (perception, as a form of consciousness, is "realization": from the utterly psychological point of view of these texts the essential distinction we make between facts of "experience" and facts of "reality" does not occur at all: experience is reality and reality nothing but experience).

At the moment preceding death the "puruṣa in the eye", prāṇa, departs, and therewith "one ceases to perceive forms" (*athārūpajño bhavati*, BĀU IV, 4, 1); the dying man "becomes single", for the vijñāna alone, after having absorbed all the

(*yogāgnimayaṃ śarīraṃ* Śvet.U I, 12d) : the fundamental vital power, which, according to the form – or rather the direction – of its activity, determines the lot of the individual : the downward direction leads to individuation, the upward one to salvation. Whereas *she* is styled Virāj, with a very ancient epithet of the all-goddess Vāc (see already ṚV. X, 189, 3 *triṃśad dhāmā vi-rājati vāk* ..., and later on ChU I, 13, 2 : *yā vāg virāṭ*. "Prāṇa is the male, the mate of Vāc", Śat. Br. VII, 5, 1, 7). Her character is that of consciousness, *prajñā* or *prajñātman*, only partially actual in the individual self-consciousness distinguishing the I from the Not-I, the inner world from the outer one. In common self-conscious existence the potential all-consciousness lies asleep in the depths of human being, but it may be awakened in yoga. – The place where both "puruṣas" unite is the heart; they have a path in common : it is the vein *suṣumnā* leading upwards from the heart to the top of the skull (BĀU IV 2, 3; ChU VIII, 6, 6). When their union takes place, self-consciousness disappears – there is no longer any distinction between the outer and the inner world (*ayaṃ puruṣaḥ prajñenātmanā sampariṣvakto na bāhyaṃ kiṃcana veda nāntaraṃ* BĀU IV, 3, 21) – , and is superseded by all-consciousness (*aham evedaṃ sarvo 'smīti manyate*, 20); thus man has reached the highest sphere of reality (*so 'sya paramo lokaḥ, ibid.*), the Form free from ill, fear and grief, free from desire, for the aim of all desire is reached

consciousness-functions (*ibid.*), will proceed to continue in a new life, in connection with a new prāṇa (cf. 3, 36), the particular existence of the deceased individual. This *ekībhāva* is fundamentally different from the intimate unification of both principles in which any particular existence is overcome. (As concerns the composition of this passage, see *Il Mito Psicologico*, p. 78f.).

(21). This Form is no less than the Form of the universal Androgyne Puruṣa, who is now reconstituted: "his eastern organs are the East (of the universe), his southern ones the South...", and so on for the western, the northern, the upper and the nether regions and for the totality of all world-regions (BĀU IV, 2, 4). This supreme reality of ātman can be only hinted at by denying the possibility of any expression, "*neti neti*" (*ibid.*), for all limited names are merged now in the transcendent universality of the unuttered Vāc.

Thus "*nāmas* and *rūpas*" are the negative, mortal, differentiated condition of the one nāma, all-consciousness, consubstantial with the one rūpa, the Universe as the latter's "own form". – While the *nāma* is the inner power of the individual being or thing, the *rūpa* is its sensuous appearance. [The latter is realised by perception (*dṛṣti*) or imagination (*saṃkalpa*), the former by audition (*śruti*) or thought (*dhī*)]. *rūpa*, the physical organism, is built up by *prāṇa*, who in his own essence remains "shapeless". The Upanishads greatly emphasize the difference of potentiality between that which is "shaped" or "corporeal" (*mūrtam, saśarīram*) and that which is "shapeless" (*amūrtam, aśarīram*) (see BĀU II 3; ChU VIII, 12, 1): the latter can sever its present connection and rise upwards to the highest sphere of "Immortality", of universal being (see above, ChU VIII, 12). The "essence" (*rasa*) of whatever is "shaped" is the eye, (because the eye realizes forms; macrocosmically it is the Sun). The essence of whatever is "shapeless" is the "puruṣa in the right eye", that is to say Prāṇa-Indra[6], the enkindler of the yogic union. In this sense his

[6] Śat Br. X, 5, 2, 9f.; Kauṣ.U III, 2; KenaU 25ff.; BĀU I, 5, 12.

(*amūrtaṃ*) *rūpam* is further on visualized in the classical series of colours, constantly attributed in the Upanishads to the ardent liquid in the space of the heart, the entity Virāj-Vāc-Prajñā. It is evidently the frameless body of yogic fire. The union and common sublimation of nāma and rūpa having thus been brought about, and therewith the transfiguration of the individual into the transcendent ātman, this culminating point of the process is again hinted at by *neti neti*.

Reduced to its shapeless aspect of prāṇa, *rūpa* is no more actually different from the invisible *nāma*, as their separation depends only upon the sensuous manifestation of *rūpa*. So the contrast between the categories *nāma* and *rūpa* is confined to sensuous reality, and there is always a potential continuity between the two categories, which can be actualized as a unity of both in the yogic process of disembodiment. The text BĀU II, 3, along with a lot of other texts, shows us *prāṇa* as the immortal part of man, whereas according to BĀU III, 2, 12 the part of man that does not leave him at death is *nāma*: "for *nāma* is infinite". Indeed only finite reality is mortal. It thus appears that there is a sphere of reality where *nāma* and *rūpa* are not yet separated, rūpa having not yet taken sensible consistency: this sphere is *ākāśa*. Ancient Indian cosmologies consider the world as a downward succession of layers or spheres (elementary or other; the criterion varies), each having been produced out of the preceding one by progressive grossening. It seems that the highest cosmic sphere, being not as yet accessible to the senses, is not yet *rūpa*, but only *nāma*; at the same time it is the boundary between the upper world of *nāma* and the nether world of *rūpa*. "*Ākāśa* is *nāma*, says the ChU (VIII, 14), and the separator of *nāma* and *rūpa*". The corresponding microcosmic sphere is, as we have seen, *hṛdyākāśa*, the space in the heart, the domain of *nāma*, the consciousness-principle, with which *prāṇa* unites when he retires into this space; whereupon the organic frame, *rūpa*, is stripped off, and the ascension to the highest sphere takes place: the Androgyne Puruṣa-Vāc is reconstituted.

In the postvedic texts the current designation of Vāc as the inner power and essence of things is *brahman*[7]. European exegesis, based on that of the late Vedāntist commentators, uses to consider the Upanishadic *brahman* as a synonym of *ātman* (or as the cosmic aspect of *ātman*), completely losing sight of the fact that the term *ātman* has often in the Upanishads a markedly cosmic purport, while *brahman* is as often explicitly the name of a psychic power. In the conception of the texts things appear to be less simple. *brahman* is = *ātman* only on the highest, transcendent level of existence, that is to say precisely in the reality of *ātman*, of the universal Puruṣa. But on the lower levels, in dynamic existence, *brahman* is only a differentiated part of the original *ātman*; the other part is *prāṇa*. As this male aspect of the universal Androgyne, besides being split up in the particular frames of the individuals, is moreover in each of them divided[8] into the vital functions or prāṇas, similarly also his female aspect, besides being differen-

[7] Vāc is *brahman* (BĀU I, 3, 21; see already ṚV. X, 114, 8d: *yāvad brahma tiṣṭhati tāvatī vāk*); *brahman* is the unity of all that is named (BĀU I, 5, 17).

[8] These two systems of division are never mentioned together in the texts, because the psycho-physical individual is never analysed from the point of view of its being a part of the cosmos, but constantly from the view-point of its analogy and substantial identity with the cosmos as a multifarious whole. It is only for the sake of an exhaustive analysis we

tiated in the particular "names" or essences of the individuals, is subdivided within the single entity into several planes of consciousness, located in a series of psychophysical spheres or centres, to which the structure of the cosmos exactly corresponds. In the oldest texts only three spheres are distinguished: the upper sphere of the brain, the middle sphere of the heart and the nether sphere of sex. Their cosmic *pendant* are the "three worlds" or spheres of the world, which are nothing else than the three *vyāhṛtis*, the "utterances" of the unexpressed pre-cosmical Vāc whose cosmogonic function is the "utterance" of the world (ṚV. X, 125, 5a; cf. MaitriU VI, 6[9], reproducing a very ancient conception: "This world was indeed unuttered; he, *satyam*[10], Prajāpati, having glown in *tapas*, uttered it as *bhūr bhuvaḥ svaḥ*..." Taitt.U I, 5: "*bhūr* is this sphere, *bhuvas* the atmosphere, *suvar* yonder sphere." Cf. Śat. Br. XI, 1, 6, 3). Later on the number of the spheres is increased. Within the individual brahman manifests itself in the different forms of consciousness: as self-consciousness in the waking state[11], as multifarious consciousness in the state of dream; in the

coordinate as separate data the two points of view from which the antithesis between unity and multiplicity is considered: (a) as the opposition between the one Being and the many beings, (b) as the opposition between the transcendent unity and the differentiated organism (in fact, human and cosmic organism are considered on equal terms).

[9] See also Pañcav. Br. XX, 14, 2; etc.

[10] For *satyam*=*brahman*=Vāc see below. *satya* is the sphere of Vāc also according to Mahā-NārāyaṇaU 63, 2.

[11] This co-ordination between the kinds of consciousness located in the "centres" and the states of consciousness in the different conditions of life is the effect of a secondary speculative synthesis of the primitive yoga scheme and the Yājña-

lowest sphere brahman as potential all-consciousness lies asleep in the shape of a radiant serpent. In the manuals of Haṭhayoga this serpent is called Kuṇḍalinī or Vāg devī. The representation itself is very ancient and already familiar to the ṚV. (X, 189) where Vāc-Virāj is represented as Sarparājñī, the Serpent-Queen, and to the AV. (IV, 1), where the radiant serpent (*suruco hvāraḥ*) brahman is called "fatherly queen" (*pitryā rāṣṭrī*, st. 2; cf. the hymn of Vāc ṚV. X, 125, 3a *ahaṃ rāṣṭrī*). The process of yoga consists in rousing the radiant serpent brahman and in lifting it up from the lowest sphere to the heart, where in the union with prāṇa its universal nature is realized, and hence to the top of the skull. Here the brahman finds an issue out of the micro- and macrocosmic frame through the opening called *brahmarandhra*, to which in the cosmic organism corresponds the opening formed by (or in) the sun on the top of the vault of the sky; thus, on returning to its primordial transcendent condition of all-consciousness, the brahman is revealed in "its own Form", as the universal Androgyne Puruṣa-Vāc. This ideological scheme of the yoga-process is traced in the Atharvanic hymn IV, 1 (as I have shown in a detailed analysis of the text[12]). The mover of this process is Prāṇa-Skambha, the leading power of yoga, who in uniting with brahman leads it to freedom and is himself regenerated. As soon as they cross the "threshold of brahma", the state of all-consciousness dawns again, the highest, transcendent sphere of existence is reached. Psychologically it is conceived of as a fourth state of consciousness beside waking, dream

valkyan scheme. Its first trace is found in the Ait.U; later on it is frequent.

[12] *Il Mito Psicologico*, pp. 49-53.

and dreamless sleep, as the *turīya* celebrated in the later Upanishadic yoga texts; cosmologically it is a fourth sphere, beyond *bhūr, bhuvas* and *svar, brahman*[13]: according to the terminology of later Upanishads and of the Bhagavad-Gitā *avyaktam paramam, paramam brahma* or *brahmanirvāṇa;* in Buddhistic terminology it is *nirvāṇadhātu* beyond the three lokas.

The first act of the drama thus brought to an end, the description of the cosmogonic and anthropogonic process of the primordial Being's entrance into the human and cosmic frame, is preserved in a highly corrupt record in Ait.U II, while passages like the above mentioned of ChU and BĀU present us with more or less summary descriptions of the soterical process. In the passage ChU VIII, 3, 4 – exactly paralleled to ChU VIII, 12, 3 but for the equivalent variant *eṣa atmeti...eṣa brahmeti* instead of *sa uttamaḥ puruṣaḥ* – the ātman = brahman is finally also styled *satyam*. This is the fundamental term used (beside the shorter form *sat*[14]) in the doctrine of Uddālaka Āruṇi – ChU VI –, where the psycho-cosmic drama is treated in all its stages, from the cosmogonic descent to the soteric return.

At the outset the topic of the treatise is announced as "the doctrine by which the unknown becomes known",

[13] In AV. IV, 14, 3 the fourth sphere is *svar*, hypercosmic light (*jyotis*) beyond the triad of *pṛthivī, antarikṣa* and *dyaus*.

The ritual teaching of the Brāhmaṇas is concerned only with the third loka, the sphere of the gods. When confronted with the mystic notion of the fourth, transcendent sphere, it adopts an agnostic attitude: *anaddhā vai tad yad imāṃl lokān ati caturtham asti vā na vā*, Śat. Br. I, 2, 1, 12; 4, 21.

[14] The term *sat* is used to denote the primordial Being in its unitary undifferentiated reality, *satyam* denotes the same Being as immanent within differentiation.

as a synthetical knowledge effacing all discrimination of particulars, a knowledge by means of which, as we see further on, one becomes identified with the ātman (*tat satyaṃ sa ātmā tat tvam asi*). The cosmogony adopts the traditional scheme of emanation : *sat* produces out of itself *tejas*, then out of *tejas āpas* are produced and out of *āpas annam*. Secondly, *sat* penetrates as *jīvātman* into these three "deities" and, in mingling them up so as to "make each of them threefold", "differentiates name and form"[15]. Thus, we are said, the red rūpa of fire being the rūpa of *tejas*, its white rūpa the rūpa of *āpas*, its black rūpa the rūpa of *annam*, the specific character of fire (*agnitvam*) disappears, for its differentiation is but the name derived from Vāc (*vācārambhanaṃ vikāro nāmadheyam*), while the three *rūpas* are truth (*satyam*). Thus by knowledge one can reduce the variety of being, reconduct it to the primitive stage ere the rūpas were mingled up, that is to say, before the differentiation of name and form. The fundamental form of everything is that of the three rūpas; M. SENART has shown long ago that they are nothing else than the three cosmic spheres. Now let us observe that on the primitive stage sketched 2, 3-4 (the exemplifying glosses must be expunged), on the stage of transition between transcendency and contingent multiplicity, the three rūpas are not yet separated, but form a continuity : they are the three-world-shape of the cosmic Puruṣa. Their unique essence, first hovering above them and then penetrating into them as *jīvātman*, is the Sat, is Vāc not yet differentiated in

[15] A similar conception underlies the somewhat hybrid version Śat. Br. XI, 2, 3, 3, 1ff. the brahman, having emanated the worlds, enters them again by means of rūpa and nāman, of which everything consists. Cf. also Taitt. Br. II, 2, 7, 1.

particular names, is brahman. The three rūpas still form a unity, so long as Vāc is not differentiated.

Further on however, in the paragraphs analysing various aspects of contingent reality, what is spoken of as *satyam* is no more the threefold rūpa, the cosmic totality in its maximum expansion, but the *aṇiman*, the imperceptible core of all particular beings, the jīvātman: "of this Minimum consists the personality of the Universe, this is *satyam*, this *ātmā*, this thou art." Death leads the particular beings back into Being, where they lose their individual form and self-consciousness (=nāma[16]), which are however fatally produced again. The way of common death is no definitive return.

But in the 14th and 16th paragraphs the refrain about satyam is again applied to yet another fact: this time to the soteriological knowledge imparted by a teacher, a knowledge which shows the living and conscious individual the way back to Being. Just as, according to the closing parable, the satya in the truth-assertion (the *satyavākya*) is the magical power changing the

[16] In the simile of the rivers and the ocean, frequently used in the Upanishads of subsequent periods to illustrate the "throwing off of name-and-form" (cf. Muṇḍ.U III, 2, 8), our text (10, 1) says: all becomes mere ocean, and they (the rivers) are no longer self-conscious. Nāma as the principle of self-consciousness is conditioned by the presence of the individual rūpa.

Let us note by the way that this simile implies far more than a simple comparison. The Ocean is Vāc=brahman (cf. *Il Mito Psicologico*, passim, v. Index s.v. Oceano), which, in its cosmogonic descent, is divided into several rivers (ṚV. I, 164, 42; cf. Śat. Br. VI, 1, 1, 9). As the nāma-rūpa reality is produced by the rivers' issue from the Ocean, it is overcome by the rivers' return into the Ocean.

natural course of things so as to prevent the glowing axe from injuring the innocent, so is the truth of the saving knowledge the power that breaks the fatal course of *saṃsāra* in leading individual consciousness, by means of illumination, definitively back to its universal source. After such a conscious return, realized in life time and fulfilled in death, there is no more falling away from the highest sphere of universal Being. It is not by a chance similarity that the turn of phrase 14, 2 *tasya tāvad eva ciraṃ yāvan na vimokṣye 'tha saṃpatsye* reminds us of the Buddhist statement *na param itthattāya*.

Thus brahman-sat-satya appears in the course of the cosmo-psychic drama in several aspects : (a) as transcendent universal Being, anterior to any concrete reality, (b) as the causal factor of differentiation, (c) as the innermost essence of the beings determining their individual existence (= nāma), (d) as the dynamic essence of soteriological knowledge, reconducting the differentiation to the original unity, freeing the individual from the bonds of ignorance and becoming.

The term *satya* is met with twice in the BĀU in the specific formulation *satyasya satyam*. According to the passage BĀU II, 3, analysed above, *satyasya satyam* is the name of the *amūrta puruṣa* in the sphere where he has got a name (for in the ātman-sphere he has none, therefore being styled only *neti neti*), i.e., in the intermediate sphere between bodily individuation (nāmarūpa) and the transcendent universal unity. This "name" is explained as follows : "the *prāṇas* indeed are *satyam*, and he is the *satyam* of them". A comparison with the closing sentences of the first brāhmana of the same 2nd Adhyāya may shed a good deal of light on the meaning of this concise explanation : *satyasya satyam* is the mystic reality (*upaniṣad*) of the *vijñānamaya puruṣa* while he dwells in the veins of the heart, that is to say in the hṛdyākāśa = vijñāna, in his "own" sphere (cf. *svam apīta* ChU VI, 8, 1 and Śat. Br. X, 5, 2, 14). As we have seen above, this is the sphere where the union of prāṇa (the *amūrta rūpa*) and vijñāna takes place. In this centre, which is particularly his own, the vijñānamaya puruṣa is no more self-consciousness; the all-consciousness is there[17], but it is not yet awake, not yet actual (as it will be in the highest centre). It is there because he has re-absorbed all the particular consciousnesses of the senses (*prāṇān gṛhītva* II, 1, 28, cf. IV, 4, 1 *enam ete prāṇā abhisamāyanti sa etās tejomātrāḥ*[18] *samabhyādadāno hṛdayam evānvavakrāmati*), their consciousness-particles (*savijñānam eva*, BĀU *ibid.* 2) which are particles of light – of the hypercosmic light-ocean brahman – imprisoned in the cosmic and human frames. This light is *satyam*[19], the immanent aspect of *sat*. As he reabsorbs and elates the particles of satyam while abiding in his proper sphere of the heart, this vijñānamaya puruṣa is *satyasya satyam*. And this is also "the name to be imposed" on prāṇa while he is united, i.e. identified, with vijñāna in the sphere of the heart[20].

In this sphere (corresponding to ākāśa where there is yet no rūpa implying sensuous differentiation) the rūpa of prāṇa is vijñāna (the hṛdākāśa) itself: the individual sensuous rūpa is overcome, "one does not distinguish the outward from the inward" (BĀU IV, 3, 21), and there-

[17] Cf. BĀU IV, 4, 22.

[18] *tejas* is *hṛdyākāśa*, cf. ChU VIII, 6, 1 and 3.

[19] See, as an instance, the ancient prayer BĀU V, 15 (= IśāU 15ff.) *hiraṇmayena pātreṇa satyasyāpihitaṃ mukham...*

[20] In this same sense the Kauṣ.U uses the term *satya*: it is the unity of prāṇa and prajñātman and herewith "the All". See below, p. 38.

with the differentiation of the beings ceases (22). We must bear in mind that such current coordinations of microcosmic and macrocosmic processes are not based on vague ideas of analogy, but reflect the conception of a fundamental identity of the facts and events on both the scales, which are considered as only twin projections of one common complex of facts and events. Therefore simultaneously with the cessation of rūpa-individuality (based on the prāṇa's differentiation in various prāṇas), in the psycho-physiologic process of yoga, the cosmic rūpa-differentiation is censed to cease : reality is transposed to a stage where there is no bodily individuation but one cosmic body only (see ChU VI). At the culminating point of the yoga-process this cosmic consciousness-body —all-pervading and omnipresent as ākāśa and containing all the potentialities of differentiation as ākāśa contains the potentiality of all rūpas—is also left behind, and reality is transposed to the transcendent plane of the universal all-consciousness-body. The two modes of differentiation of Vāc and Puruṣa (in the many nāma-rūpas and in the differentiation of nāma and rūpa within each of them) are overcome simultaneously, by one common process which, though psychical in itself, has also a cosmical purport.

In ChU VIII, 1-3, again, *satyam* is mentioned as the name of brahma. Brahma in the yogic *samprasāda* becomes ātman, the Immortal, after leaving the body and reaching the supernal Light. In contingency brahman is the space within the lotus of the heart (*antarhṛdaya ākāśa*) coextensive with universal space and therefore all-embracing. Thus anything one desires can be fashioned (*saṃ-kḷp*) out of this universal essence (as in the cosmos everything is concreted out of ākāśa). But these (objects of the) *satya*-desires are veiled by *anṛta*, therefore one does not find them inspite of one's daily entering this brahmaloka (in dreamless sleep. *anṛta* thus appears to be the waking consciousness). In fine, conformably to the current method of esoteric etymologies, the word *satyam* is decomposed into three parts, *sat-ti-yam*, *sat* being interpreted as "the immortal", *ti* as "the mortal", *yam* as the unity of both in brahman. (Cf. also BĀU V, 5, 1). This explains why out of brahman mortal *lokas*, attainments of mortal desires, can be fashioned (VIII, 2) as well as the reality of ātman, who is also *satyakāma*, the aim of a satya-desire, and *satya-saṃkalpa*, a feature of satya (= *ākāśātmā* ChU III, 14, 2). The mortal attainments proceed downwards from the ākāśa-hṛdyākāśa-sphere, as their sensuous lokas are inferior to the brahma(= satya)-loka, while the immortal attainment proceeds upwards; the former are manifested in the mūrta rūpa, the latter in the amūrta rūpa. Thus the two rūpas, the two aspects of satya = brahman, appear to be nothing else but the two opposed functions or potentialities of the same psychic essence, the ardent luminous manicoloured fluid of the hṛdākāśa, also called *tejas* (VIII, 6, 3) and sometimes—by its Ṛgvedic name—*salila*[21] (BĀU IV, 3, 32).

Therefore the realization of ātman—the upward movement of satya in samprasāda—is the bridge (*setu*) separating and at the same time uniting (*asambhedāya*) the opposite worlds of mortality and immortality (VIII, 4, 1-2; BĀU IV, 4, 22): "For that great, unborn ātman is latent in that which, among the functions, is the one consisting of consciousness, in that which is the ākāśa within the heart" (BĀU, *ibid.*).

This vertical bridge is of course nothing else than

[21] See *Il Mito Psicologico*, pp. 18ff, 21, 34, 72.

the cosmic Skambha, *satyam*. In his cosmogonic quality he is represented as turned upside down (diving headlong into contingency from his hypercosmic sphere), his head being *bhūr*, his arms *bhuvas*, his feet *svar* (BĀU V, 5, 3-4; in his soterical quality he is upright, his head is the fire-region of the sky; see Muṇḍ.U II, 1, 4). He is the puruṣa in the sun and in the eye, and his *upaniṣad* is, in his macrocosmic aspect, *ahar* ("day" as the factor of cosmic contingency, *v. supra*, p. 6), in his microcosmic aspect, *aham* (see BĀU I, 4 on *aham* as fundamental principle productive of multiplicity). This *mahad yakṣaṃ prathamajam* is again called *satyam* at BĀU V, 4.

Elsewhere (I, 6) the meaning of the term is completely inverted, and – owing to the fundamentally immanent character of satya – it becomes a synonym of *nāmarūpa*, denoting the "mortal" side of reality. Besides being nāma and rūpa reality is also *karman*, including both, and represented by the unit of the person (*ātmā*). But beneath the gross personality an unsensuous one is hidden : it is prāṇa, the "immortal" reality, veiled by *nāmarūpa* = *satya*. Prāṇa, the *amūrta-amṛta* aspect of immanent being, is here clearly conceived as another aspect of karman, opposite to nāma-rūpa. In later yoga-texts ample commentaries of this conception can be found : the yogic karma of prāṇa leads to immortality by means of a transfiguration of the organism; it is the only karma leading to release, while any other karma is a bond (Mokṣadharma 217_{11}). This doctrine is already familiar to the 1st Adhyāya of the BĀU (3): by his non-egoistic action[22] Prāṇa wins a victory over Death : he immortalizes the organic functions by reuniting them in himself and transposing them to the plane of universality.

[22] See the analysis of the text in *Il Mito Psicologico*, p. 91f.

The scheme contrasting satya (= nāmarūpa) and amṛta as dependent on, or implied in, two opposite aspects of karma is not confined to that single passage; the conception expounded in the Ānandavallī (6-7) is to a great extent analogous: after the cosmogonic act of emanation brahman-satya has two aspects, two modes of existence: an immanent one as *sat*, a transcendent one as *tyat;* in other terms, these aspects are: the expressed (*nirūkta*) and the unexpressed (*anirūkta*); in other terms still, the based (*nilayana*: cf. ChU VII, 24, 2 *anyo hy anyasmin pratiṣṭhita;* it is the later Buddhist conception of *pratītya-samutpanna* or *paratantra*) and the not-based (cf. ChU *ibid. sve mahimni* [*pratiṣṭhita*]; it is the Vedic conception of *svadhā;* Mahāyānic *anutpanna* = *pariniṣpanna sva-bhāva*); or: the *vijñāna* and the not-vijñāna (= *abhaya* [= amṛta] = *ānanda,* cf. the following anuvāka, 7), or, finally, *satya* and *an-ṛta* as opposed to *ṛta* (which is the cosmic law of multiplicity and becoming produced by means of the primordial dismemberment whence the first *dharmas* originated [cf. ṚV. X, 90, 16b]; Aditi-Vāc as the hypercosmic universal ocean bestows *ṛta,* but guards *an-ṛta,* AV. IX, 15, 23).

"*Satyam* became whatever there is". But the way back to the Immortal is open, for the mystic essence of ānanda, wherein by the universal power of love *sat* was born of *asat* in self-generation (*ātmānaṃ svayam akuruta*), is still potentially present in our intimate ākāśa; through the power of love *ānanda* is actualized within man, who thus "finds a fearless rest in the invisible, impersonal, unexpressed, not-based". The self-same power of love through which manifestation proceeded from the unmanifest, is able to lead it back to the transcendent source. The soterical *rasa* of Ānandavallī is a function analogous to the soterical knowledge of ChU VI. The analogy is corroborated by the introductive paragraph of Ānandavallī, where three aspects of brahman are distinguished, *satya jñāna* and *ānanda*[23]. Jñāna — as mystic *upāsana-jñāna* or *vidyā* (see the following paragraphs) — is the sublimating power leading from satya to ānanda, the latter being located, not in a far-off yonder world (see the "problem" formulated in the first half of § 6), but in the innermost kernel of human personality.

In the doctrines expounded at length in the three vallīs of the Taittirīya U this fundamental triadic formula, based on the nāma-rūpa conception and expressing the three degrees or conditions of the brahman's existence (in this formula *satya* represents the nāmarūpa reality, *jñāna* the reality of the plane of pure nāma, *ānanda* the transcendent reality of the Androgyne Puruṣa-Vāc), is extended by and by; in the more archaic Śikṣāvallī it is connected with the scheme of the vyāhṛtis and thereby extended to a tetrad, *brahman* = *mahas* being the transcendent unity of the three vyāhṛtis or lokas (5; in 6 the theory of the yogic ascension through the vyāhṛtis, the macrocosmic spheres and the microcosmic centres is explicitly connected with the scheme *satya* — *jñāna* — *ānanda*, slightly varied in the formulation: *prāṇārāmaṃ manas* is clearly the brahman's *amūrta jñānarūpa*, the *ākāśaśarīra brahman* as it is called in the same place); this is the earliest instance of a superposition of the trailokya scheme — in which the first three items are opposed to the fourth as their transcendent whole — on the scheme derived from the nāma-rūpa conception and consisting of three items only.

23 DEUSSEN'S emendation of the traditional reading (*ananta*) must be accepted as indisputably correct, in consideration of the sequel.

The tetradic climax is elaborated also in the Māṇḍūkya U, where it is governed by the yogic scheme of the moras and superposed on the Yājñavalkyan scheme of three stages of consciousness, the transcendent stage of yogic ecstatic consciousness being superadded as the fourth one corresponding to the "unexpressed" fourth mora; the cosmic part of the climax is constituted by the *trikāla*, a counterpart of the trailokya (cf. MaitriU VI, 5: Prajāpati's *kālavatī* and *lokavatī tanū*); on the four stages of the climax four stages or *pādas* of the ātman are located: on the waking stage he is represented by *vaiśvānara* (= prāṇa, as productive of the mortal rūpa, distinct from nāma, the consciousness, which is "turned outside"), on the dream-stage by *taijasa* ("derived from *tejas*" which is hṛdākāśa; not yet one with tejas but already liable to such a union, as "the consciousness is turned inside"), on the dreamless sleep stage by *prājña* (prāṇa being unified – *ekībhūta* – with consciousness, his aspect is *cetas* [cetomukha]; he is designed as *antaryāmin*, after BĀU III, 7, 3ff., as he is now the vijñānamaya puruṣa, satyasya satyam); the fourth stage is the ātman *kat' exochen* (*sa ātmā*), transcending both perception and expression.[24]

[24] In the Nṛsiṃha-uttara-tāpinyU the tetradic climax of MāṇḍūkyaU is extended to a heptadic one, based on the seven-world-scheme. The heptad is formed by a superposition of the four dhyāna-stages on the three stages of normal life (see *Il Mito Psicologico*, p. 236) The motive of this extension may be gleaned from the fact that this Upanishad distinguishes seven yogic centres (see III). The seven bodies according to Nṛsiṃhott.U are: (1) *sthūla*, the material rūpa, real in the waking stage, (2) *sūkṣma*, the unsensuous manomaya rūpa produced in dream, (3) *bīja*, the potential ("seminal") but immanifest rūpa of dreamless sleep; these are stated to be "only māyā", namely *nāmarūpa*, but they owe their nāmarūpa existence to the

In the Ānandavallī and in the Bhṛguvallī the climax is extended to a pentad, the items of which form the landmarks of an inward progression according to Ānandavallī, of an upward progression – realized by means of a progressive sublimation of jñāna – according to Bhṛguvallī. The kośa-doctrine of the former is but a parallel and complementary formulation of the kramayoga-doctrine of the latter; they are exact *pendants*. On the axiomatic assumption that brahman-knowledge is always tantamount to identification with brahman, Bhṛgu's progressive ascension to five degrees of brahman-knowledge implies his gradually assuming the five forms of brahman-existence (as explicitly stated in the 10th anuvāka of this vallī (6)). Thus the microcosmic penetration through the concentric kośas, or bodies – as they could, more exactly, be called considering the formulation of the Ānandavallī – is equivalent to the macrocosmical ascension through the successive spheres of the cosmic brahman-reality, and the innermost body, the person of the *ānandamaya* ātman, hidden within the vijñānamaya –

inherence in them of three *turīya*-bodies respectively, namely: (4) *ota*, (5) *anujñātar*, (6) *anujñā* (which are "consciousness only"); *avikalpa* or *sākṣin* is the seventh transcendent body, the "fourth of the fourth". "To the Turīya's *cidrūpa* the world's character of nāmarūpa is due, but in so far as he is *avikalparūpa* the universe is such".

But there are only three cosmic bodies, *mahāsthūla*, *mahāsūkṣma* and *mahākāraṇa*(= °*bīja*); the three contingent turīya-bodies inherent in the first three microcosmic ones are, in their macrocosmical location, obviously assigned to a hypercosmic sphere, not the supreme, but an intermediary one corresponding to the dhyānic state of consciousness which transcends the latter's three normal states, though not yet absolutely exempt from any connection with them, as the supreme stage is now considered to be.

i.e. the ākāśa-hṛdākāśa body—, is identical with the uppermost, hypercosmic sphere of the transcendent brahman.

The pentad has developed out of the fundamental triad: the genetic relation can be easily traced; if we consider that in ChU III, 14, 2 the *antarhṛdaya ātmā*, the *satyasaṃkalpa* reality of brahman, is said to be *manomayaḥ prāṇaśarīra... ākāśātmā* (=*vijñānātmā*)—we can follow up the yogic pentad of TaittirīyaU to its triadic source. The three intermediary bodies of prāṇa, manas and vijñāna are the outcome of an analysis of the "shapeless rūpa".

At the outset of the Ānandavallī a curious attempt is made at coordinating the microcosmic scheme of the five concentrical ātman-bodies with the pentadic elementary scheme constituted independently from this complex of speculation. This attempt is prompted by the habit of representing the soterical process as an inversion of the cosmogonic evolution. Since the scheme of the former was extended to a series of five items, the triadic cosmogonic scheme based on the nāma-rūpa conception had to be put aside as well as the tetradic scheme based on the trailokya-conception: therefore the author of the paragraph tries to adapt for his purpose the pentadic scheme of the elementary layers. But the juxtaposition necessitates the extension of the pentad to a hexad, the hypercosmic reality of ātman being considered as the starting-point of the evolution. The difficulty is tackled by the queer expedient of inserting *oṣadhayaḥ* and *annam* between the elementary series and the kośa series.

The ascension through the vyāhṛtis or lokas towards the transcendent inexpressed Vāc, the brahmaloka, is realized by the soteric power of *satyasya satyam*. In the 2nd chapter of the Aitareya Āraṇyaka, where, as I have stated on another occasion, the same characteristic doctrine as that of TaittirīyaU is expounded, this soterical process is celebrated in a set of five stanzas:

1. "When the fivefold goes back to union in the Static (*akṣara*), towards which the companions (the prāṇas or indriyas) proceed in yogic union (*yujo yuktā*), and when satyasya satyam accedes (the brahman in the heart is united with the unified prāṇa), then all the gods become one.

2. "When the fivefold coming down from akṣara goes in yoga (*yuktam*) towards akṣara... (etc. *ut supra*).

3. "The seers, stripping off that which of Vāc is "yea" and "no" (i.e. her differentiation), that which is concrete and that which is additional, have found (the inexpressed undifferentiated Vāc): (whereas) those who cling to names rejoiced at *śruti*.

4. "This (same entity) in which the names[25] rejoiced at *śruti* (i.e. in Vāk's form revealed in the Vedas) is that in which the gods become united to the universal whole (*sarvayujo bhavanti*); by means of this brahman the knower, casting off evil, goes upward to the heavenly world.

5. "Neither he who by speech designs Him as female, nor he who designs Him as neither-female-nor-male, nor even he who designs Him as male does indeed design Him (truly)".

It is not difficult to guess that the entity alluded to is the Androgyne Vāc-Puruṣa, the transcendent ānandamaya body reconstituted by satyasya satyam in the yogic

[25] See *Il Mito Psicologico*, p. 120 n. 1. Cf. also AV. X, 7, 21a.

process where the fivefold brahman becomes one again and is unified with the unified prāṇa. It is the hypercosmic and innermost rūpa of the brahma freed from all differentiations, from concreteness and manifestation hiding its real nature like the membrane surrounding the embryo (note the term *ulbaniṣṇu*).

Thus the idea that yonder brahman is ever present and immanent, though unmanifest and hidden by its own manifestation, is distinctly implied in the kośa-conception, and the first step is taken towards the assertion of the identity of satya and amṛta, of contingent and transcendent reality – which is tantamount to an acosmistic negation of multiplicity and becoming. There is a foreshadowing of this thesis in the KauṣītakiU, where it is based on the affirmation of the constant unity and identity of prāṇa and prajñātman. According to the conception examined above, this unity is actual in the sphere of the yogic process, where prāṇa-Indra is unified with prajñātman and thereby becomes the soteric factor; in Kauṣ.U III the exponent of this unity is the saviour-god Indra = satyam (III, 1 *satyaṃ hīndraḥ*) initiating Pratardana (in Kauṣ.U II it is the saviour-god Brahmán, the embodiment of the universal unity (*sarvam*) as *sat* + *tyam*). In our text this unity and non-plurality (*na u etan nānā*) is affirmed as a general axiom: this means that the sphere of reality is transposed unto the yogic plane. But whereas the doctrine of Kauṣ.U still admits of a secondary, derivative existence of differentiated nāmarūpa reality, the doctrine represented by KaṭhaU (KU) IV, 2, ĪśāU 9-14 and BĀU IV, 4, 10-20 (the last named passage being an interpolation of later doctrine in the ancient bulk of the BĀU) goes still farther in asserting the absolute identity of this world and transcendent reality (*yad eveha tad amutra, yad amutra tad anv iha; etad vai tad*) and categorically denying the existence of any differentiation whatever. Thereby the whole extent of existence is transposed to the amṛta-sphere of absolute unity. As a consequence the two dynamic aspects of brahma (the cosmogonic and the soteriologic one), are put aside, while its minimum aspect is considered actually – not potentially – identical with transcendent totality. But this extreme position is no more upheld later on: the MuṇḍakaU shows us a conception of *satya* closely related to that of the ChU; all the four aspects of *satya* met with there are represented here. *Satyam* is the doctrine put forth in the Upanishad (II, 1, 1 and I, 2, 1 – where the phrase *tad etat satyam* has been shifted from its natural place after I, 1, 9 for the sake of mechanical analogy –), it is the brahmavidyā by means of which the akṣara-Puruṣa is known as *satyam* (I, 2, 13), i.e. as the *akṣara* (brahma) from which the differentiated beings emanate and into which they return (II, 1, 1), and also as the *macro-anthropos* who is *sarvabhūtāntarātmā* (II, 1, 4). But there is the *amūrtaḥ puruṣaḥ* superior to the akṣara (II, 1, 2): he is the *manomayaḥ prāṇaśarīranetā*, "the psychic guide of the prāṇa-body", by means of whose vijñāna in samādhi (*hṛdayaṃ saṃnidhāya*) the radiant Immortality is realized[26], the Form of which is ānanda (II, 2, 7): he is to be reached by satyam (III, 1,

[26] Possibly the oldest evidence of this conception of the saviour-Puruṣa as a supersensuous "psychic" guide of the soul towards final *mukti* occurs in the description of the *devayāna panthā* (BĀU VI, 2, 15). When the "knowers", who have practised upāsana adopting tapas for their śraddhā, at the furthest cosmic end of their postmortal voyage reach the region of lightning and therewith become "lightning-like", a *puruṣa mānasa* joins them and transports them to the hypercosmic brahmalokas (*tān vaidyutān puruṣo mānasa etya brahmalokān*

5a), but can be reached only by those whom he elects (III, 2, 3c) for his incarnation (III, 1, 5c and III, 2, 3d). Through this union with the intimate god ātman they first obtain universal existence (III, 2, 5), therewith entering brahmaloka; here, at the time of pralaya (*parāntakāle*) the highest mukti is realized (6). The first part of the process is *ekībhāva*, following on the dissolution of the organic frame, whose functions (*karmāṇi*) -- now quintessentiated in Prāṇa as the sixteenth component of the structure (see ChU VI, 7, PraśnaU VI; cf. BĀU I, 6), – are unified with the vijñānamaya ātmā in the *param avyayam*, i.e. in the "higher" brahman (*v. infra*, p. 48ff.) as the saviour-Puruṣa's own nature (7). The second part of the process of mukti goes beyond this sphere of rūpaless unity in the soteric brahma and abuts in the sphere of the transcendent Puruṣa, "higher than the higher (brahman)" (8). While the brahmaloka, the sphere of unity in the *amūrta puruṣa*, is pure nāma-existence, the attainment of the transcendent sphere implies the utter abandonment of both rūpa and nāma.

Thus satyam forms the divine "way" (III, 1, 6b) – or "bridge", as Skambha reaching up to the transcendent sphere of Immortality (II, 2, 5) – leading to the highest abode of satyam (III, 1, 6d).

gamayati). In the ChU version of the passage (V, 10, 2) this lightning-puruṣa is said to be "non-human" (...*candramaso vidyutaṃ, tat puruṣo 'mānavaḥ*), i.e. not embodied. The difference in the formulation is easily accounted for by the equivalence of the meaning: the disembodied psychopompos is *mānasa* or *manomaya*, "of psychic shape" (=*arūpa, amūrta*).

III

We have seen that the conception of the three contingent abodes of the "sounding" or uttered Vāc – the micro- and macrocosmic trailokya – as opposed to the transcendent abode of her unuttered totality, was fundamentally connected with yoga-ideologies; it is on this ground that the yogic process of intimate sublimation was also figured as a meditative ascension through *śabda* to *aśabda*, the "sound" as the exponent of the soteric aspect of Vāc being represented by the syllable OṂ. Like the three vyāhṛtis, the three moras of OṂ are the three spheres of the cosmos and, microcosmically, the three stages of waking, dream, and dreamless sleep (see Māṇḍ.U, above, p. 34), successively dwelt upon during the enacting of the yoga-process; the "fourth", the unuttered stage, the transcendent ātman, is realized in the consummation of yoga-ecstasy. The syllable OṂ, connecting the three lokas in their sound-symbols to a unity of sound, appears hereby as the nāma-aspect of the soteric Skambha, as his "shapeless" totality-form. The soteric aspect of brahman being constantly interpreted as the inversion of the cosmogonic aspect, the character of OṂ is sometimes attributed also to the latter, as in MaitriU VI. According to the doctrine exposed in this chapter, on the plane of sensuous rūpa the *satya* (= *śabdabrahman*) becomes *asatya* (or *anṛta*, VII, 11). The ancient ideology of the descent and division of Vāc is re-connected with the motive of the two forms of brahman, the shaped and the shapeless. The *mūrta rūpa* is asatya, while the *amūrta* is satya : the one is brahman, the other is light, is Āditya (the essence of *mūrta* according to BĀU II, 3). How did it come about that the brahman transformed itself by taking shape? In its condition of ātman it had been OṂ; it differentiated itself in the three moras, wherewith and wherein the universe is woven. Therefore one should re-unite the ātman by meditating "OṂ"[1] (3). The *praṇava*, OṂ, is indeed the leader, *praṇetṛ* : while threefold, he is the cosmic tree turned upside down, and thus the fountainhead of the manifold elementary manifestation constituted by its branches; but by steady meditative concentration (*upa-ās*) upon OṂ the intimate leader (see above: *praṇetāraṃ* .. *jñeyaṃ nihitaṃ guhāyām*) can be rendered "one" again and thereby become the Awakener, the producer of bodhi : *eko 'sya sambodhayitā* (4). Thus *mūrti* is a consequence of the division of the śabdabrahman into the three fundamental śabdas – the "utterance" of *satya* into its three-world shape (6) – further developing into the condition of *pṛthagdharmatva* (22) : another formulation of the Ṛgvedic conception of the descent of Vāc into the three worlds and of the consequent origin of *dharmas* and their manifestation in the differentiated *rūpa*-reality. The complementary notion – of the contrast and reciprocal exclusion between the cosmic *dhāmas*, mainly represented by the sun, and the pre- and hypercosmic light of the universal Ocean Vāc – is extensively developed further on in our 6th prapāṭhaka. Already the AV. (XIX, 53, 1; XIII, 2, 39; 3, 3) and the BĀU (I, 2) identify Āditya and Kāla; the BĀU passage

[1] Read *dhyayān ātmānam*...

moreover figures Kāla-Mṛtyu as the organic archetype of the cosmos, thus introducing him as the cosmogonic anti-Puruṣa. In the Gītā the macrocosmic Puruṣa as creator and destructor reveals himself in the shape of Kāla[2]. He is past, present and future: the three constituents of Kāla (= the three moras according to Māṇḍ.U 1) thus appear to be an equivalent of the three lokas as constituents of the cosmic Skambha: they are, respectively, his *kālavatī* and *lokavatī tanū*, according to MaitriU VI, 5. That is why our Upanishad says (VI, 14) that Kāla is *mūrti;* but it adds that he is also susceptible of *amūrti*, and this faculty is actualized by yogic inversion, as we are shown further on (VI, 18). Two are the forms of brahman, Kāla and Akāla. The latter was there, undivided (*akala*), before the sun, whereas *Kāla sakala* began with the sun which is the cradle and the grave of all particular beings (15). And how can one bring about Kāla's transfiguration into the cosmic saviour? By identifying him in the upāsana-meditation with brahman: "then Kāla is removed far away"; i.e., by the brahma-upāsana of Kāla one brings about the pre-mūrti and pre-kāla reality of the universal brahman. Mythically the leader from Kāla to Akāla is Kāla himself as *amūrtimat;* from the beginning of the prapāṭhaka we learn that Kāla-Āditya is the macrocosmic aspect of Prāṇa and that their co-ordinated paths in the outer and inner cosmos are "inverted" (*vyāvartete*) according as it is day or night. Kāla-Āditya as the sun-fire and Kāla-Prāṇa as the heart-fire "proceed downwards". They are to be made the object of meditation

[2] Such is also the Īśvara as creator-destructor in the Śvet.U (cf. *Il Mito Psicologico*, p. 184f.); *beyond* the trikāla he is the intimate god of yoga (VI, 1-5).

by means of OṂ (1-2). Thus, evidently, they are reverted to their "upward" nocturnal paths, as appears from the following exposition. The "embodied" Kāla is the ocean of the creatures, and he who consists of him is called Savitar, as he generates the luminaries from which there proceeds the whole visible cosmos; thus the (*mūrta*) brahman is personified in Āditya. Therefore Āditya called Kāla is to be made the object of upāsana. Hence also some people assert that Āditya is brahman. But the (*amūrta*) brahman (Akāla akala) was this world at the beginning as the infinite One : infinite to the East and South and West and North and Zenith and Nadir, universally infinite. No regions are distinguished in it. All the forms of micro- and macrocosmic light are only his splendour-shape (16-17). "But two are in truth the forms of the brahman-light : one is quiet and one abundant"; only a particle of the light hidden in the (intimate) ether is that in the sun, in the eye and in the fire; that (light) is brahman, the Immortal. The all-seeing sees the eight-footed pure imperishable *haṃsa* encompassed by the three threads (the microcosmic Skambha encompassed by the three psychic guṇas, buddhi - manas - ahaṃkāra [*adhyavasāya - saṃkalpa - abhimāna*] = the macrocosmic Skambha encompassed by the three cosmic guṇas or worlds[3]), who is blinded by *dharma-duality* (contrasts or *dvandvas* of differentiated reality on the subject-object plane), but by the power of *tejas* (the "hidden light"; *tejas* is the light of the intimate "union", VII, 11, cf. ChU VIII, 6, 3) becomes Indha" (36, 35)[4]. "That higher *tejas* is, in truth, the own Form (cf. ChU VIII, 3, 4; 12, 3) of the light hidden

[3] See *op. cit.*, p. 414ff.

[4] Original sequence of the passages, disjoined and trans-

in the (intimate) ether...that syllable OṂ is, in truth, the own Form of the (light) hidden in the space of the (intimate) ether. By means of it (OṂ) in fact this (light) is awakened, rises and breathes upwards incessantly... In his (Prāṇa's) movement it has its place in the light-irradiating heat – as in the movement of smoke: in the ether having gone forth in a stem it pursues from *skandha* to *skandha*[5] (as the smoke rises and ramificates, the ever thinner column ascending out of the expanding stem appears as if progressively stripped of the enclosing parts stretching diagonally; the sheaths successively discarded are obviously the three guṇas): such is the expansion of the meditator (in width and height at the same time: while becoming more and more extensive, he simultaneously ascends to ever higher regions in progressively sublimated essence). In this connexion they ask: 'why is he called "of the nature of lightning"?' For, inasmuch as he has risen forth, he renders the whole body lightning-like. Therefore the unlimited light should be attained in meditation (*upāsita*) by means of OṂ" (VII, 11). Follows the "rule" of this "practice" (*prayogakalpa*) described as a *ṣadaṅga yoga* (VI, 18)[4], by

posed in the extant – largely revised and interpolated – form of the text. (See *op. cit.*, pp. 210-227).

[5] Possibly the oldest Upanishadic occurrence of the term; the underlying image survives in the Buddhistic comparison of the skandha-reality with the "marrowless" plantain tree (cf. Mahā-Nidd. p. 410; SN III, p. 142). The doctrine of the *skandhas* as such is not unknown to later Upanishadic speculation: it appears, half-suppressed by a clumsy orthodox revision, in a treaty of the Mokṣadharma teaching *anātmatā* (218-219; the term *vikāra* in 219_9 [substituted for the word *jīva* recurring in the parallel verse 240_{13}] corresponds to the Buddhistic *vyavakāra*, a synonym of *skandha* [see below, Ch. VIII]) – a tenet familiar to our Upanishad, in connexion with the guṇa-

which "the prāṇa (as *praṇetṛ*) is to immobilize the prāṇa in that which is called *turīya*, the jīva called *prāṇa* having been born from the Aprāṇa (as Kāla from the Akāla)"; thus also its complementary factor, the citta (=vijñāna), and the substrate-less (*nirāśraya*) *liṅga* it constitutes (the unsensuous yogic consciousness-body), is dissolved in the Acitta, the unthinkable supreme mystery (19). The process is the well-known "egression" through the suṣumnā, the "track of prāṇa": as soon as the "limit" (the brahmarandhra) is crossed, the union with the Unlimited is attained at the extremity of the head (20). Thus "by means of the *śabda* the *aśabda* is realized, – in the ascension through the *śabda* OṂ to the quieting down in the *aśabda*, the Aim, the Immortality, the Union, the *nivṛtatva*." The *śabda* is the ākāśa in the heart: as its differentiations (*pṛthaglakṣaṇa*) are overcome, the meditators are *apṛthagdharmiṇaḥ* and 'set' to rest in the *aśabda* (22). (So *nivṛtatva*=overcoming the differentiation of *dharmas* produced by the primordial utterance.) "By means of thought-concentration (*ekāgra*) they discard the hṛdayākāśa and are identified with the light that rises out of it. The citta along with its *āśraya* (namely the *nirāśraya liṅga* of 19, the hṛdayākāśa) is destroyed". In fact, in its (transcendent) aspect of higher *ālaya* the kośa of the hṛdyākāśa is ānanda; in its immanent aspect (*svam*) it is the sphere of yoga and (in its contingent macrocosmic aspect) it is the light of fire and sun (cf. *supra*, p. 44) (27). Final autonomy is attained by progressively discarding the brahmakośa consisting of four nets (29). This process of simultaneous penetration into the inmost and elevation towards the uppermost is illustrated by the

doctrine (II. 5—V, 2; see *Il Mito Psicologico*, pp. 211ff.) The above simile visualizes the reversion of the cosmic tree.

old myth of the nuptial union of Indra and Virāj and of their common ascension through the suṣumnā. After the egression is completed (*vinirgatam*), the "sound" (*svara*) is again the "maternal essence", the unuttered Vāc (VII, 11).

Also according to Nṛsiṃhott.U the meditation of OṂ as a unit "elevates the three-bodied universe" (*idaṃ sarvaṃ triśarīram aropya*, I) into the sphere of yogic reality: the sphere of the brahma unified as OṂ (*oṃ iti ...brahma...ekīkṛtyā, ibid.*), of the "higher" brahman in its unitary three-world-shape (*triśarīraṃ param brahma, ibid.*). The meditative ascension pursued in this sphere leads up to the highest, undifferentiated (*avikalpa*) condition of the ātman, the "fourth of the fourth" (*turīya-turīya*).

IV

In the metrical Upanishads Muṇḍaka and Śvetāśvatara and also in the older stratum of Upanishadic texts contained in the Epic, the foremost of which is the Gītā, the brahman appears as the female power of the personal All-God Puruṣa. It is a twofold power, creating or saving, according to the double aspect of the psychocosmic Puruṣa, as creator and ruler of the world or as enlightener, saviour and teacher. The brahman's manifestation in one of its aspects, as *aparam brahma,* as *avidyā,* "nescience", or in the other, as *param brahma,* as *vidyā,* "wisdom", depends on the direction of its activity : the downward direction is the psycho-cosmic evolution and differentiation (analogous to the function of the Ṛgvedic Vāc as "expressing" the world), while the upward direction is the yogic involution and sublimation of the differentiated existence, the synthesis of the totality of being in human consciousness and its regeneration in the personal unity of the universal Puruṣa. This function of the brahman consists in awakening the *jivātman,* the psychic Puruṣa, unconscious of his own reality, from individual self-consciousness to all-consciousness, in identifying him with the All-God Puruṣa; it is a psychical activity performed by a psychical factor, this brahman being nothing else than the highest faculty of the soul, "pure consciousness" (*buddhi śubhā, buddhi viśuddhā, sattvaṃ viśuddham*) or "primordial

Wisdom" (*prajñā purāṇī*), imparted to man by the saviour Puruṣa, teacher of yoga ever since the beginning of time. The internal process of salvation is mythically represented in the Gītā as a self-manifestation of the God Puruṣa, who by means of his illuminating doctrine transforms man's consciousness through initiation to the yoga-mystery. Thus the "higher brahma" or vidyā is at the same time the saving doctrine expressed in verbal form by the divine teacher and the latent divine core of man's being, awakened at the contact of this teaching and actualized in the yoga-process. The way of its actualization – the *yoga-pravṛtti* (Śvet.U II, 13) leading to the final *nivṛtti* (I, 10) through the *parivṛtti* produced by acceding to the saviour-teacher's "higher" *plane* (VI, 6b)[1] – is described or rather hinted at by technical terms in Śvet.U I and II. The universal means of this transfiguration is an attitude called *abhidhyāna* (in the Gītā simply *dhyāna*), an intense contemplation of the saviour-god, synonymous with "knowledge" of God (*tasya* [sc. *devasya*, cf. 10b] *abhidhyānāt* I, 10c, 11c = *jñātvā devam* 11a), conducive – through the contemplative union with the object – to identification with his essence (*tasyābhidhyānāt yojanāt tattvabhāvāt*). This contemplation, however, is introspective; it is an intimate upāsana (*devaṃ svacittastham upāsya* IV, 5d) – it is nothing else but the intuition of one's own intimate essence; hereby the contemplator, the embodied jīva, "becomes one" (*tad ātmatattvaṃ prasamīkṣya dehī ekaḥ...bhavate* II, 14), being no more split up in the twin principles effecting nāmarūpa. He is not disembodied, but the five elements composing his body are "elevated" in the evolution

[1] See below, p. 53.

of the yogic quality (*pṛthvyāptejo'nilakhe samutthite pañcātmake yogaguṇe pravṛtte*): this evidently means that they are elevated to the sphere of their subtleness (*sūkṣmatva*); the contemplator has left the sphere of gross *rūpa* and has won an indefectible body (*yogānimayaṃ śarīraṃ*) (II, 12). This new rūpa is "one" with nāma; it is a consciousness-body, *manomaya*, all-pervading (*vibhu*) like that of the God with whom the contemplator has identified himself through the conquest of dhyāna. In this identification the final goal is not yet reached; there is indeed a further goal representing "more" than this: *bhūyaś cānte viśvamāyānivṛttiḥ* (I, 10d; cf. *ābodhiṃ...dhyānāntye* AK.[2] VI, 24ab). This intermediary goal is called *tṛtīyam*, i.e. *tṛtīyaṃ sthānam*, and is a state by attaining which the adept obtains after death *viśveśvarya*, that is to say the condition of the cosmic Puruṣa. The individualizing Māyā or Prakṛti having been conquered now, his is the realm of the "higher", divine Māyā of which the God is born for his soteric purpose. But when the dhyāna-process is carried further on, it finally leads to *kaivalya* (I, 11d), to the total cessation of all māyā. The contemplator soars above the supersensuous sphere of determined, manifested nāma — of the śabdabrahman constituting the saving Doctrine and the essence of the saviour-God — and thus leaves the cosmic structure. This culminating moment of the dhyāna-process is *brahmanirvāṇa*, the brahman's being "ex-spired" (by the power of prāṇa) out of the cosmic body and returning to its hypercosmic sphere; in the wording of the ChU, it "comes forth in its own

[2] AK. = Vasubandhu's Abhidharmakośa (trsl. by L. DE LA VALLEE POUSSIN).

Form", i.e. in the inconceivable Form (*acintya rūpa*)[3] of the universal Androgyne Puruṣa. The complete actualization of brahman as universal knowledge, universal consciousness is again coalescent with the realization of universal Form : the one nāma coincides with the one rūpa.

Besides the terms *brahman* and *satya*, each of them denoting the hypercosmic and cosmic essence of reality in its various aspects as a static unity, as differentiation and as power of unification, one more term appears, or rather reappears, as early at least as the earliest metrical Upanishads : *dharma*. As we have seen, the characteristic feature of this stage of Upanishadic speculation is a radical affirmation of absolute identity between the contingent and the transcendent world (*etad vai tad*). Any experience of the world as differentiated and dynamical is due to our faulty perception of its reality, which in truth is uniform and statical and does not differ from the highest brahmadharma. Mortality is an effect of this erroneous vision, of perceiving the one dharma as a multiplicity of particular dharmas. He who perceives a differentiation of dharmas (*dharmān pṛthak paśyan*) is condemned to the restless flowing he perceives in them[4] (KU IV, 14). As already pointed out above, the later Maitri-U calls *apṛthagdharmiṇaḥ* ("they for whom there is no differentiation of dharmas") the yogins who have overcome individuality by means of the intimate ascension. The one dharma, mentioned in the 1st valli of KU, in the verses forming

[3] The term is used of the transcendent Puruṣa in the Muṇḍ.U (III, 1, 7) and in the Gītā (VIII, 9c).

[4] See also IV, 11:

manasaivedamāptavyaṃ neha nānāsti kiñcana/
mṛtyoḥ sa mṛtyum āpnoti ya iha nāneva paśyati//

the prologue to the initiation of Naciketas, is the reality of Nirvāṇa[5], while the sensuous differentiated reality of the world, opposed to that unitary one and born of the erroneous differentiation of experience, is denoted by the adjective *dharmya*. By means of *adhyātmayoga* the sage discards whatever is *dharmya* and reaches the unsensuous reality, the one *dharma* (cf. *aṇur eṣa dharmaḥ* I, 21 and *pravṛhya dharmyam aṇum etam āpya* II, 13b), the transcendent-immanent Universe, just as according to the doctrine of Uddālaka Āruṇi the sage discards the *nāmas*, being but a differentiation of Vāc, and perceives *satyam* (*ya eṣa aṇiman...tat satyam*), the one-and-total form of the pre-cosmic Being. Thus "tearing off (the veil of) the contingent dharma-experience" Naciketas "opens up" for himself the "residence" (13d), the immortal sphere of the transcendent Dharma, present here and now though "elsewhere" than the dynamic dharma(=nāma)-reality coupled with its opposite (*adharma*=rūpa) (14a). In this way the cosmological distance of the spheres of reality is directly reduced to

[5] As I have shown in my analysis of the KU (*Il Mito Psicologico*, p. 136), the crucial question of Naciketas does not at all refer to the post-mortal state in general. This cannot possibly be a problem for the boy who abides in the house of Death and has already obtained as a former boon the means of ascending to *svargaloka*, to the temporary immortality of the gods, the now despised Vedic ideal of post-mortal existence. His question explicitly refers to the *mahān sāmparāya*, the "great departure" from which there is no return, and which, as stated later on (II, 6), is not realised by the fool who therefore becomes over and over again a prey of death. Moreover let us remark that the question is formulated in the classical terms so often recurring in Buddhist literature in the question about existence in Nirvāṇa: "some say 'he is', others

its prototype, the psychological difference of the forms of experience.

As the "theistic" position of the successive period brings about the revindication of becoming and a synthesis of both its modes in the divine personality which is static in itself, i.e., in its "own", transcendent, sphere, the term *dharma* assumes again the specific meaning it had in the oldest records of this current of thought: in fact, in the ŚvetāśvataraU – whose quotations from the hymn ṚV. I, 164 are rather symptomatic – the *dharma* is the enlightening power of the saviour-God, manifested in the human soul. In his soteric manifestation, as the perennial teacher of the yoga-path, lord of *bhaga* or *bhakti* (cf. VI, 6c, 23a), Śiva is *dharmāvaha,* the bringer of dharma, taking his abode in the psyche as immortal all-*dhāma* (VI, 6cd), i.e. as the *buddhi śubhā* or *viśuddhā* (III, 4; IV, 12), the Prajñā Purāṇī (IV, 18), the higher brahman (VI, 10). As such he is superior to the cosmogonic Puruṣa-Skambha manifested in the nāmarūpa-cosmos and is *arūpa* (III, 9-10), or *viśvarūpa* (VI, 5c, 6a); from his plane onwards the *prapañca* (= nāmarūpa) "returns" (*parivartate*) (6b) to its transcendent source. So his plane is the intermediate plane of the "shapeless" brahman-dharma, in whose unsensuous manifestation all the forms are one. The adept is invested with the dharma in acceding to or "taking refuge" (*śaraṇam prapadye*) in this sphere of the intimate saviour and teacher, in an act of *upāsana* (*devaṃ svacittastham upāsya,* 5 = *devam ātmabuddhiprakāśaṃ śaraṇam aham*

say 'he is not' (20b)". *sāmparāyika* is the nirupadhiśeṣa-nirvāṇa according to the Itivuttaka, 44; similarly Majjhima-Nikāya II, p. 144 opposes the *samparāyika attha* to the *diṭṭhadhammika attha.*

prapadye, 18)[6], and thus attains the "bridge" to Immortality (19c). In his own character however the God thus manifested is "undivided, inactive, quiet...like an extinguished fire" (19a, d). How is it, then, that in his soteric character he "becomes becoming" (5c) – what is it that imparts the saving wisdom in the formless sphere? It is his *śivā tanū* (III, 5a), his enlightening "body" (*ibid.*, d), not identical with his absolute reality of transcendent Puruṣa, but nearest to it, or the approach to it; in the terminology of the Gītā, his "own Māyā" (IV, 6); in early Buddhistic terminology, his *dharmakāya.*

Kṛṣṇa, the saviour Puruṣa of the Gītā, enters the world in order to resuscitate dharma: here the term apparently means no more than "justice" or "righteousness"; such indeed is its meaning from the point of view of the Epic and the Purāṇas, presenting us with a series of incarnations of Viṣṇu as avenger and saviour. But the internal speculative structure of the Gītā transposes these conceptions to the sphere of psychological facts: on the same ground as the personal god Kṛṣṇa, manifested in a human shape, is simultaneously conceived of as the "inner teacher", as a psychic factor, also the dharma brought by him into the world and imparted to his adepts in the form of a secret yoga-doctrine, is conceived as the dharma-brahman, the supersensuous reality he resuscitates in human hearts, thus bringing about the state of consciousness termed *brahmabhāva* (*brahmabhūyāya kalpate, brahmano hy pratiṣṭhāham amṛtasyāvyayasya ca śāśvatasya ca dharmasya* XIV, 27 a-c); as the power of universal love by virtue of which man gradually ascends to all-consciousness in *brahma-nirvāṇa,* "seeing himself in everything and everything in

[6] Cf. *Il Mito Psicologico*, p. 354f.

himself'' (VI, 29) or ''Puruṣa in everything and everything in Puruṣa'' (*ibid.*, 30). Thus the actualization of *dharma*, blotting out all differences, all that is *dharmya*, produces the form of existence of divine universality — the one *dharma* coincides with the one *rūpa*.

In the cycle of Upanishads contained in the XIIth book of the Mahābhārata under the cumulative title Mokṣadharma[7] (''doctrine of salvation'') the two contrary aspects of brahman, evolutional and involutional, are exhaustively discussed under the new term: *pravṛttilakṣana-dharma*, ''dharma bearing the character of evolution'', is the cosmogonic and individualizing power of saṃsāra (= the *bhūtabhāvodbhavakaro visargaḥ karmasaṃjñitaḥ* of the Gītā[8]), whereas the soteric power opposed to it, the involutional function of yoga, annihilating the differentiation of dharmas and transforming the cosmic as well as the human being into the universal reality of the Puruṣa, is styled *nivṛttilakṣaṇa-dharma*, ''dharma bearing the characteristic of involution or cessation''. It is the power leading to nirvāṇa. The identity of these two aspects of dharma with the corresponding two aspects of brahman, the ''higher'' and the ''lower'', vidyā and avidyā, is repeatedly and expressly stated in the texts. In both aspects of the psychic and cosmic power dharma its intimately verbal nature is also kept in view: pravṛttidharma and nivṛtti-dharma are sometimes also represented as two doctrines verbally expounded (see Mdh. 217_{2-4}).

[7] Henceforward quoted as Mdh.
[8] VIII, 3cd.

V

In the Suttas dealing with the fundamental subjects of Buddhistic speculation the compound *nāma-rūpa* occurs frequently, as a designation of differentiated contingent existence, both individual and cosmic (the texts speak also of a *bahiddhā nāmarūpa*[1]). When the contrast of the two constituents of contingency is implied, the binomium reappears on Buddhistic soil in the other formulation introduced as early as the Ṛgveda, namely *dharma-rūpa*.

That an old, "precanonical", form of Buddhism classified the complex of worldly reality under two opposite categories, *rūpa* and *dharma*, is a fact to which already Prof. ST. SCHAYER has called attention in a penetrating and highly interesting article[2] showing that in some texts we are faced with traces of doctrines incompatible with the tenets of Abhidharma-systematization. He quotes the ancient Mahāyānist *dvikāya*-doctrine

[1] *ayaṃ c'eva kāyo bahiddhā ca nāmarūpam*, Saṃyutta-Nikāya (SN.) II, p. 24. The comparatively much lesser frequency of its occurrence in the latter sense is merely proportionate to the uneven distribution of interest between the two unit-aspects of concrete existence, the individual and the extra-individual as shown in these texts.

[2] *Precanonical Buddhism* (PCB), in Archiv Orientálni, vol. 7 (1935), p. 121ff.

as a piece of evidence in support of this classification, whose criterion is illustrated by the theory of the three spheres of the cosmos, conceiving, in contrast with the character of the *kāma-* and *rūpa-dhātus,* the elements of the *ārūpya-dhātu* as all-pervading and omnipresent. Moreover, Prof. SCHAYER points out that by combining the antithesis *dharma-rūpa* with the climax of the Ṣaḍdhātusūtra (and taking into account the ancient Indian notion of the evolutional unity of this series) we find that the antithesis does not necessarily imply an original and fundamental diversity between the *dharma-* and *rūpa*-elements, but rather a diversification due to the transformation (through progressive coarsening) of a unique basic element, *vijñāna*[3]. In a more recent communication Prof. SCHAYER has observed that *nāma,* as equivalent to the citta-(*arūpa*)-element in the series of *skandhas,* is synonymous with *dharma* in the precanonical signification of the term[4]. Now, as the classification *nāma-rūpa* is obviously also very ancient (as ancient at least as the Causal Formula, according to which "*nāma-rūpa* comes-to-be on the ground of vijñāna"), the question arises, whether the two forms of the binomium are simply equivalent, or different in meaning and purport — and if the latter is the case, what does the difference consist in? The solution that will result from the following considerations will be found to be in a line with our initial statement that the two forms of the binomium express respectively the coexistence and the contrast of its components.

[3] Pp. 126-8, 130.

[4] *Ueber den Somatismus der indischen Psychologie,* in Bulletin de l'Académie Polonaise des Sciences et des Lettres, Cracow 1936, p. 161.

Prof. SCHAYER draws attention to the fact that in the list of Pāli Abhidhamma the four *saṃskṛta-lakṣaṇas* are ascribed only to *rūpa*-elements, and compares this evidence with the record that some old heterodox schools classified the four realms of the *ārūpya-dhātu* with the category of *asaṃskṛta*-elements. Hence, he draws the conclusion that "the *dharma-dhātu* as opposed to the *rūpa-dhātu,* denoted a permanent, eternal reality...In this sense, the *dharma-dhātu* is also the Highest Truth... penetrated and fully realised by the *dharmacakṣuḥ* of the Omniscient Buddha. The *dharma-dhātu* as a name for the monist Absolute of the Mahāyānists lies possibly on this very line of evolution" (p. 129). Further on (p. 130f.) the author connects the above evidence of an exemption of the dharma-element from the laws of the *saṃskṛta* with the traces, abundantly found in Pāli texts, of a doctrine "in which *vijñāna* is treated as a relatively stable element which transmigrates", and thus puts up an equation of the precanonical *dharmadhātu* = *vijñāna-dhātu* with the *prabhāsvara citta* of the Mahāsaṃghikas, also encountered in an old Nikāya-record (AN. I, p. 10), and with the infinite radiant consciousness, representing Nirvāṇa in DN. I, p. 223 and MN. I, p. 329.

It might however be objected that, even if considered as originally pure, the *upakliṣṭa citta* as such is at best only potentially identical with the infinite radiant vijñāna (= Nirvāṇa), but, in any case, not actually. On the other hand, *asaṃskṛta* is not necessarily synonymous with *absolute* and *transcendent*. It may be noted that the same heretics who considered the ārūpyas as asaṃskṛtas are also recorded to have classified with the asaṃskṛta-category the pratītya-samutpāda, the very principle of impermanence—and the relative point of their doctrine

(41)[5] immediately precedes the point on *ādiśuddha upakliṣṭa citta* (42)[6] – ; and much in the same sense some unspecified heretics of the Kathāvatthu (XIX, 5) asserted that the fundamental character of all the dharmas – their *idampratyayatā,* which they called the *dharma-tathatā* – was asaṃskṛta. Such a view, which must appear utterly contradictory and incomprehensible from an ontological standpoint, is quite congruous from the soteriological standpoint, the proper standpoint of Buddhism. Evidently, the principle of impermanence is not considered here "as it is in itself", but inasmuch as it is realized – the realization of the idampratyayatā of Saṃsāra discloses and constitutes the way[7] to Nirvāṇa. In this sense the Fourth Truth is often represented in the Nikāya-records as an inverted Pratītyasamutpāda, a sequence of "non-origination". The fundamental doctrine of the Prajñāpāramitās is only the furthermost consequence of this standpoint, arrived at by the extreme formulation of the exclusivistic view implying the ideological elimination of the "way" : the *pratītyasamutpāda* is an *anutpāda,* and therefore the *tathatā* or *śūnyatā* of contingency, when realized, coincides with transcendent reality. On the earlier stage of thought the insight into the principle of Saṃsāra, by which its impulse and effectiveness are overcome, is not taken to coincide with, but to

[5] As rendered from Hiuan Tsang's version by J. MASUDA, *Origin and Doctrines of Early Indian Buddhist Schools,* in Asia Major II, 1925; p. 29.

[6] The Tibetan version even directly includes this citta in the list of the asaṃskṛtas.

[7] The analytic Mahāsaṃghika list of the asaṃskṛta items counts separately each entity and its soteric realization: such is the case with regard to Nirvāṇa (a and b), ākāśa (c and d), and pratītyasamutpāda, realized in the *mārga* (h and i).

lead to Nirvāṇa. Thus it is *asaṃskṛta*, this qualification being understood much in the same sense as *anāsrava*. *anāsrava* is not only Nirvāṇa, but also the way to it, not only the plane of *nirodhasatya*, but also that of *mārga-satya*. In this sense also the arūpadhyānas, as stages of the ascensional progress to Nirvāṇa (v. *infra*, Ch. VII.), could be classified as asaṃskṛtas. Two at least of these spheres visibly coincide with the two unsensuous "elements" of the ṣaḍdhātu-list: the *ākāśānantyāyatana* with the infinite sphere of ākāśa, and the *vijñānānantyāyatana* with the infinite sphere of vijñāna. The ārūpyadhātu = dharmadhātu which they constitute is thus not identical with the Nirvāṇadhātu, but intermediate between it and the lower sensuous sphere of contingency, and forms the third dhātu in the classical dhātu-scheme, which is tetradic.

We can now answer the question as to the relative purport of the two forms of the binomium *nāma-rūpa* and *dharma-rūpa*. The first was applied exclusively to denote existence on the sensuous plane, while the juxtaposition of the terms composing the second intimates the opposition between the sensuous and the unsensuous reality. To the unsensuous essence of being the terms *dharma* and *nāma* were applied according as it was conceived in its own higher sphere, apart from rūpa[8], or in its individuation, as a constituent part of the nāma-rūpa conglomerate[9].

[8] The realm of derivative reality extending beneath the sphere of dharma is denoted by the general term *rūpa*, as its foremost characteristic is sensuousness, but its peculiar nature is that of nāmarūpa, as it includes also differentiated consciousness, which is the core and seminal power of every phenomenon.

[9] Consciousness of the dharma-plane is not necessarily

On the other hand there is no doubt that the term *dharma* was also applied in early Buddhism to the transcendent reality of Nirvāṇa; not only the Abhidharma-interpretation (see AK. I, 2b[10]), but also Nikāya-texts (Udāna, p. 55; AN. IV, p. 22) bear out this fact. Their references to the "Great Ocean" as hypostasis of Dharma = Nirvāṇa are connected with the traditional image which is likewise outstanding in the current illustration of the "immeasurableness" of those delivered, and principally of the Tathāgata, through a reference to the Great Ocean, e.g. MN. I, p. 487; SN. IV, p. 376, 388; it is the supernal Ocean "in which the manifold streams of name and form cease to exist" (SN. I, p. 15), "the imperceptible infinite *viññāna*, universally radiant" (DN. I, p. 223). *Dharma* in this acceptance was distinguished from, and put above the entity of the Doctrine personified in the Buddha as Teacher, as may be seen from passages like SN. I, p. 138ff., AN. II, p. 20f., III, p. 122, introducing the Dhamma as an entity superior to the Buddha[11].

We thus see that ever since the most ancient stage of Buddhist speculation there are two dharmadhātus

undifferentiated, although it is not fully individual; let us for the present note only the evidence of the representation of the inhabitants of the highest cosmic sphere as individual beings framed of mere consciousness and of the conception of the *pratisandhi-vijñāna* as existing apart from rūpa with an uncorporeal consciousness-framed body. (See also Mīmāṃsāślokavārttika p. 704, 3 (quoted by La Vallee Poussin in JA 1902_2, p. 299): *tasmin [ativāhike śarire] jñānasyāmūrtasya tatra saṃcaras.*).

[10] La Vallee Poussin, vol. I, p. 4.

[11] See *Il Mito Psicologico*, *passim*, Index s. vv. *Dharma* I, Oceano (= Dharma, Nirvāṇa).

(ārūpya- and nirvāṇadhātu), structurally located one above the other, both consisting of vijñāna-essence. But while one of them is identical with the radiant, universally pure vijñāna, the śuddha prabhāsvara citta, the other is, on the one hand, identical with the kliṣṭa citta, as the starting point of the cosmic evolution of the dhātus and of the microcosmic evolution of the individual (as avidyā)[12] – eventually reappearing in connection with sensuous shape on the plane of *nāmarūpa* –, its essence as principle of impermanence being manifested in the pratītyasamutpāda; on the other hand it is identical with the *samyak-praṇihita citta* (the term appears in the AN. [I, p. 10] in connection with the doctrine of the prabhāsvara citta, its defilement and its purification), realizing and thus overcoming the idampratyayatā of contingency, the citta actuating the Doctrine and ascending through bhāvanā towards Nirvāṇa: the anāsrava citta manifested in the fourth Truth, in the mārgasatya or the pratītyasamutpāda of cessation.

If thus the *anāsrava-dharmasaṃtāna* is the way to the reality or sphere of Nirvāṇa, it is structurally evident, though no more admitted in the oldest available form of the dogma, that *dharma* as contingent *vijñāna*, as the āsrava-saṃtāna, the reality of pratītyasamutpāda, must have descended from the highest Dharmadhātu. (Descent in this sense does not necessarily imply direct evolution through alteration of the basic substance: if conceived not "substantially", but psychically, i.e. functionally, it can as well be represented as derivation through opposition or negation[13]). Such a relation is

[12] See *op. cit.*, p. 329f.

[13] See *Il Mito Psicologico*, p. 373f., and *passim*, Index s.v. dualismo per esclusione.

however still implicitly admitted in the semi-heretical doctrine of the prabhāsvara upakliṣṭa citta; but only the Mahāsaṃghikas, decidedly branded as heretics from the crystallized dogmatical standpoint of the Hīnayāna, venture the assertion that this citta is ādiśuddha, namely in origin the radiant nirvāṇa-vijñāna – in other terms, that the *dharma* = *nāma* essence derives from the transcendent Dharma. The composite whole of the cosmos, represented under the scheme of the six dhātus[14], as well as every single nāmarūpa would thus appear to be differentiations of the highest Dharma, of the absolute radiant all-consciousness.

The above results seem to suggest that the term *dharmāḥ* as a designation of the multiple elements of contingency (unlike the corresponding plural term in the Ṛgvedic and Upanishadic signification simply equivalent to *nāmāni*) was introduced at the time when the interpretation of the nāmarūpa as a compound, ever changing bulk of separate elements had arisen as a consequence of the denial of personality, but the original psychological outlook of Buddhism had not yet been given up in favour of the later objective ontology: the *dharmas* were the elements of the manifold experience constituting contingent existence, as opposed to the unique extatic universal experience constituting the transcendent reality. In its original use the p l u r a l term *dhammā* meant, in fact, nothing else but the changeful elements of experience, the contents of the function of *manas* (see e.g. Dhammapada 1), and in this acceptance covered the whole range of the notion of contingent reality, both in its sensuous and

[14] It seems that according to older conceptions the sphere of the "uncorporeal" (*aśarīra* = *amūrta* = *arūpa*) extended further down, comprising also *vāyu* and *tejas* (cf. ChU VIII,

in its unsensuous aspects. This outlook, in which reality is, first and last, merely the content of experience—and thus of psychic essence throughout—, is in conformity with the point of view underlying the ṣaḍdhātu climax, in which sensuous existence appears as only a secondary derived aspect of reality, whose primary aspect is unsensuous, psychic. In time, as the objective ontological outlook superseded that original viewpoint, the transvaluation of the meaning of the plural term *dharmāḥ* struck a twofold path. On the one hand, the existential contrast denoted by the binomium *dharma-rūpa* was valued as an essential one, the nature of the dharmas as psychic elements of being was considered substantially different from that of the non-psychic, "external" elements, the dyad of the interconnected aspects of contingency (structurally superposed as dharma and rūpa, coexistent as nāma and rūpa) was broken up into a duality of disconnected essences; a trace of this doctrinal configuration is to be seen in the Abhidhamma-classification of the twelve āyatanas and the eighteen dhātus pointed out by Prof. SCHAYER, PCB, p. 126, according to which the dharma-āyatana and the dharma-dhātu contain the non-rūpa elements of the apparent individual unit[15]. On the other hand, the term *dharma* was altogether deprived of its original psychological meaning and applied to the abstract atomical "elements",

12, 2), while the hṛdyākāśa corresponding to the cosmic ākāśa was the essence of vijñāna (*yo 'yaṃ vijñānamayaḥ prāṇeṣu ya eṣo 'ntarhṛdaya ākāśas* BĀU IV, 4, 22).

[15] Here *dharma* is obviously a mere synonym of *nāma*, unlike the *"asaṃskṛta" dharma* of the ārūpya-dhātu, the psychic skandhas being viewed in their connection with the rūpa-skandha. The Abhidharma-classification as codified by Vasubandhu has rendered this category quite hybrid by introducing

"moments" or "constituents" of existence invented by scholastic speculation. Prof. SCHAYER'S opinion (PCB., p. 129) that "the term *dharma* as a general designation of all the elements of Being is a scholarly, artificial innovation" holds good only with regard to these later developments; but as he considers the dharmas only "in the technical acceptance of monads each of which is bearing its own essence" -- i.e. in their scholastic acceptance —, one can entirely adhere to his view. The plural term *dharmāḥ* in its oldest acceptance, discernible in the Nikāyas, of manifold and impermanent elements of experience, cannot, however, be severed from the oldest available stratum of Buddhistic doctrine and cannot, in fact, be severed ideologically from *dharma* (singular number) denoting the transcendent reality of the nirvāṇa-dhātu[16]. The choice of the term *dharma* for these elements must have been due to the awareness of the contrast between their multiplicity and the unique Dharma (*dharmatā*) from which they derive (although the genetic relation is not always admitted). In the Preface to his *Ausgewählte Kapitel aus der Prasannapadā* (Kraków 1931) Prof. SCHAYER has made it clear that the

additionally under the common heading the asaṃskṛtas — one of which, ākāśa (obviously understood as the ākāśa-dhātu beyond the sensuous world) belongs to the dharma = ārūpya sphere, while the other, Nirvāṇa, belongs to the transcendent Dharma-sphere —, and *avijñapti,* the moral value of psychic factors, which is nothing else but their "orientation", the criterion according to which they are duḥkhasatya or mārgasatya.

[16] Nor, of course, from *dharma*(*dhātu*), the intermediate purely psychic sphere, with its twofold functionality (*rūpa,* as we have seen, being only a transformation of this *dharma* in its evolutional character, both dharmas and rūpas, as elements of experience, can be called *dhammas*); this *dharma* is never

Mahāyānist tenet of *dharmanairātmya* is based on the monistic universalism of this current of thought : only the totality is real (p. xvii)[17]; therefore all multiplicity, all difference, is illusory, deprived of actual existence. – The term *nairātmya* (and the synonymous term *anātmatā*) originally signifies, according to the oldest evidence extant in the Suttas, not a vague "essencelessness", but quite specifically the "absence of ātman" stated by Buddhism (and by analogous Upanishadic doctrines) with regard to contingency[18], in opposition to the ancient metaphysical views about the transcendent ātman as immanent in all the beings[19]. Only from the acosmistic point of view introduced by the Prajñāpāramitās and elaborated in the Madhyamaka, the non-ātmic character (i.e. the dynamic character of contingency, produced by causes) is tantamount to the absence of any character of (true) reality, as Reality can be only static, non-causal ("absolute"). Thus the *dharmanairātmya*[20] as conceived from the "higher" – or the adequate – point of view[21] of the Madhya-

conceived as an absolute unity, but always as a process; and it is the locus of the dharmas, in the specific sense of elements of unsensuous experience (pertaining to the ārūpya sphere).

[17] See also STCHERBATSKY, *The Conception of Buddhist Nirvāṇa*, p. 41.

[18] See *Il Mito Psicologico*, pp. 282f., 305, 313, 380f., *et passim* (Index s.v. *anātman*). *Nairātmya and Karman*, IHQ., XVI, pp. 459ff.

[19] The second meaning of *nairātmya*, when the term is used as key-word of the "non-unit" theory, is that of the theory of *dharmas*. *V. supra*, p. 63ff.

[20] As to *pudgalanairātmya* in the Suttas, in the Abhidhamma-Abhidharma and in Mahāyāna, cf. *Il Mito Psicologico*, p. 380 n. 1. *Nairātmya and Karman*, n. 25

[21] *V. infra*, Ch. IX, the analysis of the double or triple

maka is the complementary aspect of the exclusive universal existence of the one Dharma = the ancient Ātman.

We see that the acosmistic position of Mahāyāna Buddhism with its doctrine of absolute identity (Saṃsāra = Nirvāṇa) stands on the same ground as the acosmistic doctrine of absolute identity (*yad eveha tad amutra yad amutra tad anv iha, etad vai tad* and so on), proclaimed in the KaṭhaU and BĀU IV, 4, 10-21.

point of view (= perception of reality) as distinguished in Buddhistic doctrines.

VI

We have noted that the transcendent Dharma = Nirvāṇa was conceived in precanonical Buddhism as radiant all-consciousness. The highly significant stanzas DN. I, p. 223 corroborate our statement that in this ancient Buddhist vijñānavāda the quality and position of the radiant vijñāna was not that of a permanent element within the impermanent structure of things, i.e. within nāmarūpa, or even that of the pure nāma = dharma, but that of the transcendent infinite vijñāna where contingent nāma as well as rūpa have ceased to exist. It should be borne in mind that the last line of the reply stanza runs as follows: *viññānassa nirodhena etth'etam uparujjhati*[1]; *viññānassa nirodha,* "the immobilization of viññāna", is the transformation of the consciousness-stream into the transcendent, radiant, universal viññāna. The bhikkhu's question is slightly modified by the Buddha. One should not ask: where do the four elements completely cease? But: where (in what sphere) do they find no foothold? These four elements, as constituting rūpa (MN. I, p. 185, 223, etc.), have their foothold, their stay in the individual nāma, their root in nāma = dharma, the unsensuous sphere from which they derive; they have no foothold whatsoever in

[1] Cf. also Sutta-Nipāta 1037ef.

the undifferentiated transcendent vijñāna. — Finally let us notice that we have got another variant of the stanza, namely Udāna I, 10 (p. 9), which on the other hand is also a variant of the famous Upanishadic stanza, recurring thrice in the metrical Upanishads (KU V, 15, Muṇḍ.U II, 2, 10, Śvet.U VI, 14)[2] and describing the transcendent abode of the universally luminous ātman-brahman (see also the successive st. in Muṇḍ.U [II, 2, 11], where the motive of BĀU IV, 2 and ChU VII, 25 is taken up again : the supreme brahman-ātman is the true unitary Universe). Now a most noteworthy fact is that this Udāna-stanza constitutes one of the rare passages in the Pāli-Canon where the ātman in the specifically Upanishadic sense is spoken of : "when the holy man, brāhmaṇa by holiness, is aware of the *attan*, then (in the abode transcending all elements and cosmic lights described in the first three lines) he is freed from form (*rūpa*) and non-form *arūpa*), from joy and sorrow". This abode is Nirvāṇa, the state (*abhisamparāyo*: cf. *mahān sāmparāyo* KU I, 29) to which the freshly initiated Bāhiya has passed, having won the highest insight by applying the meditation-rule he had been given by the Buddha : *viz.*, to ascertain that in the reality of worldly experience there is no ātman, and that in so far as there is the transcendent reality (*tathatta*)[3] there is neither this world nor yonder world nor the middle one.[4]

[2] See above, p. 8.

[3] The wording is recorded in several partly corrupt versions (see the variants in STEINTHAL's ed., p. 8 n. 1). By comparing them, we may restore the original reading as follows: ...*tato tvam Bāhiya na te attā, yato tvam Bāhiya tathattaṃ, tato tvam Bāhiya nev'idha* ..

[4] This exclusivistic position is the original standpoint of Buddhism, perceiving in the nairātmya of contingency the

Thus understood, the early vijñānavāda is not at all in contrast with the famous Sati-episode of the Mahātaṇhāsaṅkhāyasutta, in which the Buddha blames Sati for understanding vijñāna to be an immutable element, transmigrating in saṃsāra. It should be noted that the Buddha first asks: "what viññāna do you mean?" (MN. I, p. 258). The infinite static vijñāna as reality of Nirvāṇa ought not to be mistaken for the vijñāna-skandha.

Such evidence renders the deep affinity between the Buddhist conception of the transcendent Dharma and the ancient Vedic and Upanishadic conception of

warrant of the realization of ātman on the transcendent plane, whose reality is contradictorily opposed to that of the world and is therefore its Naught, its *śūnyatā* (the later hypostasis of *śūnyatā* derives directly from statements like SN. IV, p. 54: *suñño loko ti vuccati...yasmā suññam attena,* through simply intimating the complementary conclusion that the *śūnya* of the world is *ātman*); it is still very clearly put forth in two stanzas of the Mahayāna-Sūtrālaṃkāra, IX, 23-24:

śūnyatāyāṃ viśuddhāyāṃ nairātmyān mārgalābhataḥ/
buddhāḥ śuddhātmalābhitvāt gatā ātmamahātmatāṃ//
na bhāvo nāpi cābhāvo buddhatvaṃ tena kathyate/
tasmād buddhatathāpraśne avyākṛtanayo mataḥ//

This traditional position, largely represented in the earlier Mahāyāna (Prajñāpāramitās and some glimpses in their systematization by Nāgārjuna, see *Il Mito Psicologico* pp. 380ff.), is naturally abandoned in the immanentism of Vijñānavāda. The above quoted stanzas are visibly a piece of older doctrine, not all too organically inserted in a context describing the higher immanent Doctrine-body of the Tathāgatas; they are introduced only for the sake of completing the series of excluded opposites (22: *na śuddhā nāśuddhā buddhatā,* 26 *naikatā na bahutā*) by adding the traditional tenet *na bhāvo nābhāvaḥ*.

The term *ātman* is mostly (not always, as we have seen) avoided in older Buddhism because of its primitive immanentistic implication; it reappears, quite consequentially, on the

the transcendent brahman sufficiently obvious. The equivalence of the two terms, attested both in Upanishadic and in Buddhistic literature[5] (we shall yet have opportunities to find its justification with regard to the other aspects of the entity they designate, to value the purport of the early equation *dharmakāya* = *brahmakāya*, of the twin denominations: *dharmacakra* and *brahmacakra*, applied to the Wheel of the Doctrine, *dharmayāna* and *brahmayāna*, applied to the "upward" career of salvation), is only an external corollary of the internal evidence, whose extension increases with the later developments of Buddhist speculation. In the oldest conception of the transcendent *brahman* = *dharma* which we have been able to trace as far back as the Ṛ̣V., it appears as the pre-cosmic and hyper-cosmic silent Vāc, unuttered and unutterable in her real essence of ecstatic all-consciousness, though uttered as the enlightening and sublimating *dharma* for the human mind, which is henceforth bent on the upward course. Ever since the beginnings of the Mahāyāna movement the notion emerges that the Buddha, in his own transcendent nature, does not enunciate the Doctrine. The Mahāsaṃghikas hold that

Prajñāpāramitā-stage of the doctrine of absolute identity; cf. *op. cit.*, p. 380f.

[5] One of the principal results of the long and detailed inquiry made by Mrs. M. GEIGER and Prof. W. GEIGER into the use of the term *dhamma* in the Pāli-Canon (*Pāli Dhamma, vornehmlich in der kanonischen Literatur*, Abh. d. Bayer. Ak. d. Wiss., Philos.-philol. u. hist. Kl., XXXI, 1. Munich 1921) is the conclusion that "the concept *dhamma* takes in Buddhism the place of the *brahman* of older Vedānta" (p. 77). We have shown above that in Upanishadic thought, even since its Vedic beginnings, the equivalence of both terms reflects the sameness of the entity they designate.

he unites all the *dharmas* of the Teaching in one sound[6] —which, however, does not undergo the differentiation of utterance: in fact he never pronounces any *nāmas*, as he is constantly in the state of ecstasy[7], realizing in one *citta* the totality of dharmas in one instant[8]; but the sentient beings perceive the Doctrine in the form of nāmas[9]. Later texts explain: from his enlightenment to his nirvāṇa the Buddha did not pronounce even a single word[10]. Similarly Nāgārjuna's Nirupamastava praises the Bud-

[6] See Vasumitra's treatise (WALLESER, *Die Sekten des alten Buddhismus*, from the Tibetan version; MASUDA, *Origin and Doctrines of Early Indian Buddhist Schools*, from the Chinese version), I, 4.

[7] *Ibid.*, I, 13, Chin. vers. I, 12. Cf. Laṅkāvatāra-Sūtra (L-S) p. 6ff.: the Tathāgatas are silent, for they realize only the plane of *samādhisukha*, which they do not differentiate.

[8] *Ibid.*, 15-16, Chin. vers. 13-14. (Cf. the *ekacittakkhaṇikam appanā-jhānam* described by Buddhaghosa). The two tenets I, 4 and I, 15-16 (Chin. v. 13-14) are strictly complementary formulations of a common notion, as the integral undifferentiated Vāc represents the *nunc stans* of universal consciousness.

[9] *Ibid.*, I, 14. The chinese version (I, 12) specifies more distinctly that the nāmas are only in the perception of the audience.

[10] See, a.o. texts, L-S, p. 143, 194, 240. The Yogācāra conception attributes the function of conveying the soteric teaching to the worldly beings either to *nirmāṇakāyas* or to mere "voice-productions" (*vāg-nirmāṇa*), independent from any corporeal substratum and only apparently connected with casual objects perceived as sources of its enunciation by the listeners. The classical Mādhyamika point of view has naturally no place for any nirmāṇas as attributable to the Buddha; their function however being largely attributable to the recipients of the teaching, the limit of coherent doctrinal adoption of this tenet cannot be sharply drawn, so much the

dha who did not utter anything, even a single syllable, there being no differentiation in the Dharmadhātu[11].

The unuttered hypercosmic sound of the Mahāsaṃghika-theory is evidently the Dharmadhātu or Dharmatā of Nāgārjuna. Significantly, the Madhyamakavṛtti avails itself of the old Mahāsaṃghika-formulation of the tenet – namely that the Buddha's teaching is one instant-sound – while quoting it from a Sūtra which states that the Buddha is silent[12]. This singular way of interpretation clearly shows the doctrinal purport of the tenet: the assertion of the Tathāgata's mystic silence does not imply that the essence of the soteric Dharma is extraneous to his nature, but that its true essence, not being differentiated in *dharmas* or *nāmas*, is identical with the transcendent Dharma. There is no "real" transition from the true Doctrine's spaceless and timeless oneness to its differentiated perception in space and time. The shower of *dharma* drunk by the faithful (Nirupamastava, st. 7, cf. ṚV. I, 164, 26ff.) does not descend from its transcendent source: it is a contingent perception of the Dharma's universal indivisible essence on a psychical plane which is not its own, and which is not ultimately real.

less as the distinction of modes of reality – varying with the schools –, on which it is based, by no means coincides with the Western criteria of "subjectivity" and "objectivity".

The kāyanirmāṇa and the vāgnirmāṇa are closely coordinated from the point of view of the *kāya*-doctrine (*infra*, Ch. IX), both being only the pseudo-phenomenic reflection of a purely noumenic entity, a citta- or manomayakāya, also figured as a light-essence or -emanation (cf. *i.a.* Śatasāhasrikā Prajñāpāramitā, p. 7ff., 9f., 11ff.).

[11] See st. 6 and 7.

[12] Madhyamakavṛtti, p. 366; see LA VALLEE, *Vijñapti-*

In the light of this conception of absolute reality as utter silence of any discursive process the characteristic doctrinal standpoint of the Madhyamaka, consisting in the renouncement of any "logical" thesis, the *ārya-tūṣnīmbhāva,* reveals itself in its essentially practical purport, as an aspect of the mystic endeavour of "assimilation" to the Bodhi-reality; and its characteristic *prasaṃga*-method, bent on dissolving any conceivable or predicable intellectual notions, on silencing discursive processes (*nāmasaṃjñāvyavahāra*), reveals itself as an essentially soteriological method, intended to lead, through the elimination of *prapañca* which is "speech"[13], to the realization of the undifferentiated inexpressible Dharmatā, the Naught (*śūnyatā*) of contingency, the fullness of transcendent static all-consciousness (*tathatā*).

From the Yogācāra-Vijñānavāda point of view the unuttered supreme Dharma is the Dharmakāya, the personal unity of the pre- and hyper-cosmic Universe, and at the same time the transcendent archetype and source of the uttered Doctrine. This position marks the return to a point of quasi-coincidence with the Vedic view, according to which the hypercosmic entity of the un-

mātratāsiddhi, La Siddhi de Hiuan-Tsang; Buddhica, I, T. V (henceforth quoted as *Siddhi*), *App.*, p. 796. The Nikāyas afford a significantly different version of the ultimately identical notion: the all has been cognized in the Tathāgata's Awakening; therefore all that he utters between the night of bodhi and the night of nirvāṇa is true (see e.g. AN. II, p. 24). The Tathāgata's utterances are the contingent reflections of the truth of his all-cognizance, which in itself, in its transcendent all-unity, is unutterable.

[13] Madhyamakavṛtti, p. 373.

uttered Vāc is the personal unity of the archetypal Universe as well as the fountainhead of the soteric *dharma*. But in its former quality it is also the fountainhead of Becoming, as the static unity of its pure all-consciousness-essence is dissimilated, through the psycho-cosmogonic process, in the individuation of the dynamic consciousness-units. Such a connection *a parte ante* between the transcendent static all-consciousness (=Nirvāṇa) and contingent dynamic consciousness (=Saṃsāra), theoretically inadmissible from the standpoint of the earlier Buddhist exclusivism, although not extraneous to its ideological substrata (*supra*, p. 30f.), re-emerges in the monistic position of the Vijñānavāda.

According to the Vijñānavāda the *ālayavijñāna*, the fundamental, "eighth", consciousness-principle[14], undifferentiated in itself, but containing the potentialities of differentiation (therefore also called "*the bīja*" [MSA. XI, 44 bh.[15]], as receptacle of all the bījas, *sarvabījakam ālayavijñānam* [Triṃśikā 2cd[16]]), is split up or transformed (*pariṇāma*) into a series of pravṛtti-vijñānas[17], processes

[14] Beyond the sense-consciousnesses, manovijñāna and manas.

[15] MSA.=Mahāyāna-Sūtrālaṃkāra, ed. SYLVAIN LEVI, 1907, BEHE fasc. 159. Cf. also XI, 32 bh. (see the emendation of the ms. reading in S. LEVI's translation, p. 114 n. 1); Mahāyāna-saṃgraha (E. LAMOTTE, *La Somme du Grand Véhicule d'Asaṅga*, T. II, Louvain 1938) I, 30; 57, and the Upanibandhana of Hiuan-Tsang *ad* I, 14. 1 (*op. cit.*, p. 32) and *ad* I, 27 (p. 47).

[16] Vasubandhu's Triṃśikā, and Sthiramati's bhāṣya (ed. SYLVAIN LEVI, 1925, BEHE fasc. 245), p. 18; cf. *Siddhi*, p. 97ff.; Saṃdhinirmocana-sūtra ed. LAMOTTE, Louvain, 1938), V, 7; M.-saṃgr. I, 2; 8; 14, 1; 21.

[17] See, e.g., Triṃś. 1cd and bhāṣya (p. 18).

of individual consciousness consisting in *vikalpas*. This pariṇāma results in nāmarūpa, the individual psycho-physical organism. The saving intuition of truth, by revealing the inconsistency of vikalpas, brings these processes to a progressive cessation (*nivṛtti*)[18] and thus finally realizes the pure *tathatā*, the intimate, inexpressible *svarūpa* of reality[19], the psychical but transcendent *dharmatā*[20]. This process of purification and return (represented as an ascension from kāma- and rūpadhātu, where the personality is still upādāna of nāma and rūpa, through ārūpyadhātu, where only nāmopādāna is left[21], to the dharmatā or bodhi) is achieved in two stages named *āśrayaparāvṛtti*, "return of the *āśraya*"; on the first stage it reaches the plane of Sambhogakāya, on the second that of the transcendent Dharmakāya. On the sensuous plane the āśraya is nāmarūpa, the individual organism (cf. Triṃśikā, bh., p. 19 *āśraya ātmabhāvaḥ sādhiṣṭhānam indriyarūpaṃ nāma ca*); on the unsensuous (ārūpya) plane (which, if realized as a stage of the ascensional nivṛtti-process, is anāsravadhātu, *v. supra*, p. 60, and *infra*, p. 77, cf. Ch. IX) it is pure citta, the ālaya by

[18] To explain the possibility of this reversion the Vijñānavāda assumes that the potentiality of *nivṛtti* is ever inherent in the ālayavijñāna in the form of congenital bījas of indifferentiation or of the Way (cf. *Siddhi*, p. 218. "*The* bīja" in this sense is the Tathāgatagarbha [according to the Uttaratantra, v. H. JACOBI, SPAW, 1930, p. 328f.]). This view reiterates the old notion of the *sammāpaṇihita* citta's inherence in the *micchāpaṇihita* citta, of the Upanishadic satya-desires covered up by anṛta (*v. infra*, p. 83f.).

[19] See Trimś.bh. p. 17, and L-S II, p. 87.

[20] Trimś. 28 bh. (p. 43) *svacittadharmatāyāṃ cittam eva sthitam bhavati*.

[21] Cf. Trimś.bh. p. 19.

itself[22], and its mind-shaped frame is omnipresent – no more limited by the laws of individuation (cf. MSA. XI, 44 *padārthadehanirbhāsaparāvṛttir anāsravaḥ dhātur bīja-parāvṛtteḥ sa ca sarvatragāśrayaḥ* "the Return of the manifestation of the appearance of the material body is [realized as] the anāsravadhātu, owing to the Return of the Germ [hence onwards, the ālaya is no more bīja or sarvabījaka, as the possibility of a repeated development of new individual sensuous organisms is henceforth eliminated]; and this is an omnipresent āśraya[23]"). The second parāvṛtti, the ālayaparāvṛtti proper[24], is the passage thence to Nirvāṇa (L-S p. 62 1-2, cf. p. 98); here it is no more *vijñapti* (*vijñaptir ālayam* L-S p. 272, st. 59; cf. p. 322), but the *para ālayavijñāna,* the tathatā (*ibid.*). The relation between the ālayavijñāna and the pravṛtti-vijñānas, the former's differentiated manifestation, is

[22] Hiuan-Tsang, who misses the point of Vasubandhu's thesis on the twofold āśrayaparāvṛtti (Triṃś. 29-30; *v. infra*, Ch. IX) and displays fluctuating views of the matter, at times holds that the *āśraya* envisaged in the notion of āśrayaparāvṛtti is the eighth vijñāna alone – without even the pravṛtti-vijñānas – (cf. *Siddhi*, p. 665), but on other occasions (cf. p. 684) contradicts this statement. The *āśraya* is obviously the whole personality, whose constitution varies according to the planes of existence. It is the "subject" of the process of pravṛtti or nivṛtti.

[23] The bh. interprets this *sarvatraga* in a restricted sense, as "āśraya common also to the Śrāvakas and Pratyekabuddhas"; we shall see in fact that this school identifies the ultimate attainment of the Hīnayāna-saint with the first parāvṛtti as elimination of the sole *kleśāvaraṇa*, reserving the second part of the ascension to the Bodhisattva's career, by a proceeding of superposition already attempted in the Saddharma-Puṇḍarika.

[24] The parāvṛtti of the cittāśraya, L-S p. 152.

that of the whole to the parts, the division giving rise to the karmalakṣaṇa (L-S p. 37-38, cf. p. 225) and thereby to complete otherness; in a similar way the relation between Vāk and vāgvikalpas is described (p. 85-87); such definitions reflect the ancient conception of the relation between the one Dharma and the many dharmas.

The passage from pravṛtti to nivṛtti is styled *vyāvṛtti*, the "turning round", the "reversal" of the mind process, the inversion of the current[25] of the transformed ālayavijñāna.

Originally the vyāvṛtti is, of course, located at the very outset of the Way. The AK. records this view as maintained in Hīnayāna dogmatics: the entrance on the *samyaktva niyama* is the *vyāvartana* of the character of pṛthagjana; henceforth the disciple is an ārya (VI, 26a[26]). A similar view is still maintained in some, evidently older, portions of the L-S, where it is applied to the career of the Bodhisattva: the vyāvṛtti is located at the point of the attainment of *pramuditā-bhūmi*, the initial stage of the career (p. 226). In the AK. the vyāvṛtti point is characterized by the disposition admitting of the knowledge of *dharma* (*dharmajñānakṣanti*); it is similarly described in the L-S, namely as the juncture whereat the adept becomes *lokottaradharmagatisamavasṛta*. Up to this point the

[25] *vartate srotasaughavat* (the srotas being the saṃtāna), Triṃś. 4d. and bh. preceding and following; *ogho yathā vartati sarvabījo*, Madhyamakāvatāra, Muséon 1911, p. 250; Saṃdhinirm. V, 7; Triṃś.bh. p. 34.

[26] LA VALLEE, p. 180ff. In a general sense, *vyāvṛt-* is expressive of deflection of a productive energy towards the alternative effect; thus e.g. the caus. *vyāvartay-* is used of the "turning" of *bhogavipāka* into *āyurvipāka* or viceversa in AK. bh. II, 10a (LA VALLEE, p. 120f.).

psychical process, determining the character of *pṛthagjana*, is "turned hither" (*āvṛtta*, L-S p. 225) or "upside down" (*paryasta*, cf. MSA. XI, 58cd), – the process of saṃkleśa (cf. *saṃrajyante* L-S *ibid.*) being very characteristically styled *viparyāsa*[27] –, whereas to the contrary process the "upright", ascensional, direction is accordingly attributed (*aparyasta* MSA. *ibid.*, etc.). In the Sutta-texts this conception was expressed by the terms *samyak* and *asamyak*, already current in the younger strata of Upanishadic literature[28]; in both categories of texts they are especially applied to the directions of the citta (cf. e.g. AN. I, p. 8, contrasting sammā paṇihita citta and micchā paṇihita citta). The latter terminology is maintained in the Hīnayānic Śāstras (*samyaktva* and *mithyatva*), but also in the Mahāyāna Sūtras, e.g. in the Laṅkāvatāra, according to which *samyagjñāna* is the vikalpa or citta-caitta as turned away from the plane of nāma-rūpa (*nāma-nimitta*) and turned towards the Tathatā (p. 225f.). Thus the vyāvṛtti or revulsion of the vikalpaka manovijñāna (as the exponent of the ālaya's pravṛtti; or of citta, manas, manovijñāna, p. 185) is potential nirvāṇa (L-S p. 126), as it opens up the way to the Tathatā (by the realization of the intimate *dharma*, p. 185; the vyāvṛtti is called *dharma* at p. 180); the samyagjñāna is therefore already counted as *pariniṣpanna* (p. 227), though in itself it is only pure *paratantra*: the adept has already a foot-

[27] See Sthiramati's quotation *ad* Triṃś. 6 (bh., p. 23).

[28] A noteworthy feature of this terminological correspondence is the regular connection with the verbal stem *vṛt*, from which derives the specific yoga-terminology of psychic dynamism; *asamyag vartate* is synonymous with *pravartate*, *nivartate* with *samyag vartate* (Mdh. 219_{39}, etc.).

hold in the Tathatā (*tathatāvasthitaśca... nirābhāsagocara-pratilabhitvād*, p. 226).

Vyāvṛtti being the point at which the plane of nāma-rūpa is overcome, it evidently coincides with the first āśrayaparāvṛtti, the latter having been originally conceived of as the starting point of the "Way" proper. (The Bodhisattvabhūmi refers to this āśrayaparāvṛtti in connexion with the attainment of *śuddhādhyāśayabhūmi* =*pramudita vihāra* [p. 368; cf. Triṃś. bh. *ad* 10cd-11ab], while the above mentioned passage of the L-S mentions in this connexion vyāvṛtti.) The terminology of Hīnayāna dogmatics preserves the designation *parivṛttajanman*, which the AK. bh. (*ad* VI, 41c) applies to a particular type of *anāgāmin* (the quality referred to is essentially concomitant with that of *avinipātadhamma*, see below, p. 102ff.). What *parāvṛtta* (or *parivṛtta*) originally implied can be gleaned from Yaśomitra's definition of the attainment of *anāsrava-dharmasaṃtāna* as *āśrayaparivṛtti* (AK. VII, p. 81 n. 1). It is the attainment of the pure, upward-bound, personality of the mārga (cf. *āśrayaviśeṣalābha* VI, 41c). The passage beyond the limits of the old āśraya, effected by *vyāvartana* as the Way is entered upon, is also referred to in the AK. (*āśrayasyātyantam*, IV, 104cd, p. 217). In time however, as Mahāyāna-thought more categorically contrasted the bodhi-career with the Śrāvaka-career leading only to nirodha, and eventually superposed the former to the latter, the vyāvṛtti of the psychical dynamism – as the outset of the definite progress towards bodhi – was located on the 8th bhūmi, on the stage of the Śrāvaka's and Pratyekabuddha's nirvāna; for the Bodhisattva, whom his determination to win bodhi holds back from immersion in the *nirodhasamāpattisukha* (L-S, p. 212f.), this stage is not final, but only intermediate, and initial with regard to his peculiar and "higher" course. Engrossed in the bliss of this condition the Śrāvakas and Pratyekabuddhas realize directly *vikalpanirvāṇa,* without realizing "*dharma* alone" (p. 213f.)[29], Thus the Bodhisattva's vyāvṛtti, the real vyāvṛtti of the ālayavijñāna towards bodhi, is secondarily located on the stage of arhatship (*tasya vyāvṛttir arhattve,* Triṃś. 5a). It is, in a sense, nirvāṇa, since henceforward there is no more pravṛtti of the vikalpa (L-S, p. 213), though in itself the plane attained is only the *animitta* (=arūpa) (cf. p. 200)[30]. It is possible to say that from the eighth bhūmi onwards there is no more ālayavijñāna, as the latter is no more conceived as an ego (*Siddhi,* p. 164), the individuality having disappeared. Henceforward the Bodhisattvas proceed (*pravartante*) without effort in the swift current of *dharma,* since they are *avaivartikas* (*ibid.*)[31] : the danger of any "turning away" again is eliminated.

In pravṛtti and nivṛtti, in vyāvṛtti and parāvṛtti, as also in the ideology founded on the opposition of the one Dharma and the many dharmas, the recurrence of terms and conceptions already met with in Vedic, Upanishadic

29 *na viviktadharmamatibuddhayaḥ;* cf. p. 200: *aviviktadarśanād vikalpasya vyāvṛttir eva na syāt.* See also Saddharma-Puṇḍarīka (S-P), p. 90ff.

30 This is the plane of the Sambhogakāya, which, according to the M.-Saṃgr. and the *Siddhi* (p. 708), is attained by the vyāvṛtti of the seven pravṛttivijñānas.

31 According to Nanda – a doctor more conservative in this regard – the Bodhisattva is *avaivartika* ever since the first bhūmi, i.e ever since his entrance on the Way. The term seems to have been originally applied to the Dharma-dynamism: *avaivartya* is the *dharmacakra,* Saddharma-Puṇḍarīka, p. 2. According to the Mahāyānasaṃgraha

and Epic thought is now easily discernible. Yet this evidence does not justify the conclusion that on such points of Buddhist speculation direct Brāhmaṇical influence had been at work. These points, congenitally inherent to the structure of Buddhist thought and traceable as far back as its oldest extant texts, have been worked out on the same ground as their Brāhmaṇical parallels : this common ground is the native soil of yoga. The early pluralistic developments in Hīnayāna dogmatics obliterated the fundamental relation between the one Dharma and the many dharmas, implicit in the notions of the oldest vijñānavāda, without quite effacing it. The conception of the unitary transcendent Dharma = Nirvāṇa is no late Mahāyānic innovation : it would even appear incomprehensible, were this the case, why for the absolute universal unity just the term currently denoting the irreducible plurality of the elements of being should have been chosen. Between the one Dharma and the many dharmas there is originally the same relation of genetic dependence and existential contrast as that which we have observed at the very outset of ancient Upanishadic speculation between the one transcendent Vāc-brahman and the many names or essences of particular beings. In each of the many the transcendent unity is potentially latent and by purification, i.e. inversion of functionality, it is actualized as all-consciousness in which the particular consciousness is annihilated; thus also the dharmadhātu (the *tathāgatagarbha*) potentially abides in the inmost depth of every

(II, 33 [6] the Doctrine of the Bodhisattvas is *apratyudāvartya*, their activity – which is essentially promulgation and actualization of the Doctrine – is *avivartanīya karma* (II, 34 [9b], also defined as *aviparyāsakarma* [2b]; cf. above, p. 79).

particular being[32] and by purification, i.e. inversion of the consciousness-stream, it is actualized as *sarva-jñatva*[33] in which the vikalpas are annihilated. The differentiation or *pariṇāma* can either be regarded as relatively real, as in the Yogācāra branch of Mahāyāna, or as only illusory, as in the Mādhyamika branch. Both positions – not so divergent as it may seem at first sight – are also represented in Upanishadic speculation, as has been shown above.

Neither is the conception of the ālayavijñāna as a receptacle of all the latent possibilities of existence a new invention of the Mahāyānic Vijñānavāda; this conception is already familiar to the early Upanishadic vijñānavāda, where that entity is called *hṛdyākāśa*. According to the ChU (VIII, 1) "in it is stored up everything that there is and that there is not in this world"[34]. And when the concretely manifested things are overcome by decay and death, their 'types' are not destroyed along with them, for the desires out of which they arise are stored in the hṛdākāśa. Out of these kāmas and the "formative tendencies" or "imaginations" (*saṃkalpa*) they constitute, the desired "spheres" are fashioned (*saṃkalpād eva...samuttiṣthanti*) (VIII, 2); but the potential satya-desires are covered up with anṛta, therefore one does not find them, even as a treasure hidden in the soil, inspite of one's entering daily this brahmaloka (in dreamless sleep)[35]. The potentiality of ātman-realization

[32] L-S, *passim;* Dharmadhātustotra; etc.

[33] Triṃśikā-bh. p. 15.

[34] Cf. Triṃś.bh. p. 18f., p. 37; *Siddhi*, pp. 96, 167; Saṃgraha I, 22.

[35] As we shall see further on, satya and anṛta are not a couple of coexistent factors, but two alternative manifestations

is thus contained in this heart-space and can be actualized in "the perfect Quiet (*saṃprasāda*) rising out of the body and ascending unto the supreme Light"[36], so as to "come forth in its own Form" (VIII, 3).

The same entity is known to the Atharva-Veda (X, 8, 43; X, 2, 31-32) as *kośa* or *puṇḍarīka* filled with the three *guṇas* (the three colours of hṛdākāśa, the three states of consciousness), and potentially containing the ātman[37].

The late MaitriU already refers to this entity the terms *āśraya* and *ālaya,* used in a technical sense: when disembodied in the yogic process, the kośa of the hṛd-ākāśa is the *nirāśraya liṅga* consubstantial with the citta, its own āśraya; when that process culminates in the ānanda state, it is the higher ālaya (VI, 19, 27; see above, p. 46). This notion is an exact counterpart of that formulated in the L-S (st. 59, p. 272, see above, p. 77), distinguishing two aspects of the ālaya, namely the lower, which is *vijñapti,* and the higher, *param ālayavijñānam,* which is the *tathatā.* It also corresponds to the notion outlined in the Triṃś.bh., that in the sphere attained by

of a common factor, of the hṛdākāśa or vijñāna itself; they are its two orientations, the "upward" and the "downward", rendered in later Upanishadic literature by the qualifications *samyak* and *asamyak.* So the "dissimulation" of satya by anṛta is its *dissimilation* from its original nature of the supernal Light, ātman; its revelation is in fact the process of its re-assimilation to that original nature of its own (*svarūpa*), as appears from the sequel of the passage.

36 The disembodied saṃprasāda is an unsensuous, omnipresent cosmic body: cf. Mdh. 246_{33} *yaḥ saṃprasādo jagataḥ śarīraṃ sarvān sa lokān adhigacchatiha.*

37 For particulars see *Il Mito Psicologico,* pp. 414ff.

the first āśrayaparāvṛtti the ālaya is consubstantial with the matter-less āśraya, the pure citta or nāma (p. 19; cf. MSA. XI, 44; see above, p. 76f.). The MaitriU equates this āśraya with the śabdabrahman, whose pravṛtti and concomitant differentiation produce *pṛthagdharmatva*, but whose "purification" (VI, 34, st. 3) or unification leads to the aśabda as that utter *śūnya* (VI, 23) in which *ātman* is realized in his autonomy (*svatantra*) and universality (*sve mahimni*, cf. II, 4, and ChU VII, 24, 1).

In primitive Buddhist vijñānavāda the notion of the ālayavijñāna is foreshadowed in the conception of *citta* = *mano* = *viññāṇa*[38] (synonyms in Pāli literature) as origin, source and essence of all the dhammas (Dhp. 1); already at this early stage the idea of its fundamental radiance and purity is met with. In its saṃkleśa it is the *bīja* from which the *aṅkura* of the individual nāmarūpa grows forth at every birth (AN. III, 61, 9; SN. II, p. 66)[39]. Its purification is brought about by the inversion of its direction (from *micchā* to *sammā*), concomitant with its expansion to cosmic omnipresence in the exercise of *dhyāna* = *brahmavihāra*[40]. Its complete *visuddhi*, the *viññāṇassa nirodha*, actualizes the transcendent universally radiant viññāna.

In some Upanishads of the Mdh. the corresponding

[38] The denomination *kośa* is again used by the Pudgalavādins, as we shall see further on (Ch. VIII).

[39] Cf. Bodhicaryāvatāra-ṭīkā quoted by LA VALLEE POUSSIN, JA 1902/2 p. 310f.: *vijñānabījam.. nāmarūpāṅkuram abhinirvartayati*. The notion is implied in the well-known passage DN. II, p. 63 (cf. Madhyamakavṛtti, p. 552).

[40] See note 30.

entity is designated by the term *sattva* (declaredly a synonym of *buddhi* in the terminology of these texts), and represented as the innermost of three concentric receptacles – the outer ones being *rajas* and *tamas*, identified with *manas* and *ahamkāra*, its emanations – ; it is "similar to an ātmanlike principle" and is the *bīja* of the living individual inasmuch as it contains the bījas of karman, developing at every birth into a sense-organism whose character is duḥkha (213_{12-15}). This sattva or bīja, the "eighth" consciousness-principle (above the senses, ahaṃkāra and manas), is called *jīva* (*ibid.*); in the texts maintaining the immanence of an ātman-principle the "eighth" is the kṣetrajña (248_{17}); whereas the texts maintaining that the whole living complex is of non-ātmic character assert the tenet *buddhir ātmā manuṣyasua* (249_{3}). Its *samyag vṛtti*, its "purification", brought about by the inversion of its orientation from common waking consciousness to dhyānic consciousness, is its *nivṛtti* – enacted in the progressive exercise of the dhyānas (*catuṣṭaya* $217_{1,13}$ = *dhyānayoga caturvidha* 195_{1}) and producing final nirodha (cf. 213_{19}), which in its turn realizes the transfiguration of the *sattva* into the highest brahman.

It is finally denoted, both in Epic-Upanishadic and in Mahāyānic texts, by another couple of terms: *adhyātma* – the "psychical" fountainhead of reality – and *svabhāva*. Epic speculation has partly elaborated a pluralistic conception -- in its evolutional climaxes it currently puts ahaṃkāra as the first item on the list of the tattvas, often identifyng it with the apratibuddha kṣetrajña or sattva – ; the evolution of its adhyātma is therefore an individual series (as however the fundamental position of the coincidence of microcosmos and macrocosmos is still upheld, the difference with regard to the preceding stages is hardly noticeable[41]: the fact that this series represents the individuum comes into evidence only where its inversion and consequent transfiguration into the universal entity is considered – precisely as we become aware of the individuum nature of the ālayavijñāna and of its pariṇāma-series only where its vyāvṛtti and consequent parāvṛtti is spoken of). Nevertheless, the whole complex of subjective-objective reality is deduced from it and assumed to be latent in it: *manasy antarhitaṃ dvāraṃ deham āsthāya mānuṣam/yad yat sad asad avyaktaṃ svapity asmin nidarśanaṃ/sarvabhūtātmabhūtasthaṃ tam adhyātmaguṇaṃ viduḥ//*(216_{11})[42]; similarly in Buddhist Vijñānavāda the whole complex of reality is deduced from the ālayavijñāna (= *adhyātma* MSA. XVI, 25a and bh., L-S p. 10, etc.). According to Mdh. 194_{1-6} the adhyātma is the ocean, from which the evolutional differentiations arise like waves (an exact *pendant* to the current *dṛṣṭānta* of the ālayavijñāna-doctrine); it is the bhūtātman = bhūtakṛt = ksetrajña "witnessing" his own differentiations (*sākṣivat sthitaḥ* $_{12-13}$, 248_{17-18}):

[41] Even the Sāṃkhya-Kārikā, in spite of its dogmatic assertion of the plurality of puruṣas and hence of the evolutional series formed by their connection with prakṛti, still reads (as H. OLDENBERG has rightly observed) like a text concerned with the one Puruṣa.

[42] Unless the manas is destroyed (*manasas tv apralīnatvāt*), all these potentialities will enter existence in the countless saṃsāras ($216_{6,8}$); all, in fact, is stored in the manas (*manasy antarhitaṃ sarvam*) – an echo of the doctrine of ChU VIII, 1. also expressed in the statement MaitriU VI. 34 *cittam eva hi saṃsāras*. Cf. the definition of the ālayavijñāna in the Mahāyāna-Abhidharmasūtra (quot. Triṃś.bh. p. 37): *anādikāliko dhātuḥ sarvadharmasamāśrayaḥ/tasmin sati gatiḥ sarvā nirvāṇādhigamo 'pi ca//*

this definition corresponds exactly to the Yogācāra doctrine of the *svasākṣitva* of the citta; in the sequel of the passage a dhyānic *abhijñā*[43] is mentioned as a landmark of the involutional process towards *śama uttama*: in fact—as the text immediately explains—the whole world consists of the essence of buddhi, it arises from buddhi and dissolves in it. When this awareness is attained, the buddhi "dwells" (*adhi-sthā*) no longer in the senses and in their "objective" perceptions, but on the manas-stage of purely noumenic experience ($_{19-25}$, the rūpas having been dissolved in the manas, cf. 204_{19}), in its "own" essence (*svabhāvaṃ svabuddhyā viharet*, 194_{18}): therewith the individual attains omnipresence (*sarvabhūtātmabhū*,$_{46}$)—the way to the highest aim is entered upon (*ibid.*). It is the way of the fourfold dhyānayoga (=*svabhāve sthāna* 195, cf. 205_{9}); the buddhi having now realized its brahman-nature (204_{17}), it proceeds to *pralaya*, thereby ultimately issuing in the unsensuous, inconceivable "highest sattva" ($_{18}$), i.e. in the adhyātma in its purity, the paramātman, termed *buddha* in several chapters (305-309).

The same entity is represented as the pravṛttilakṣaṇadharma, which contains the whole trailokya ($217_{2cd-3ab}$),[44], but, if turned into the nivṛttilakṣaṇadharma, becomes the eternal unmanifest brahman ($_{3cd}$). No doubt is left as to pravṛttilakṣaṇadharma and nivṛttilakṣaṇadharma being the two alternative aspects of vijñāna (*etāvad idaṃ vijñānam* 217_{31}—sequel of the exposition of pravṛttilakṣaṇadharma and nivṛttilakṣaṇadharma); in

[43] See *Il Mito Psicologico*, p. 252.

[44] Cf. also 240 $_{27ab}$ *sarve 'ntasthā ime lokā bāhyam eva na kiñcana*.

its alternative functionings it "is and is not"[45] (*asti ca nāsti ca*) the supreme reality; cf. $203_{1,7}$: when in the involutional process it reaches the stage of buddhi (in its *manasi sthāna*, see above, p. 88), the parama svabhāva is not yet manifest, but it cannot be said that it is not (*na ca nāsti*): it "is" already in the potentiality of its realization. In this very sense the short Buddhistic treatise on the three *svabhāvas*[46] states that the *pariniṣpanna-svabhāva* "is and is not" in the ālaya's condition of *paratantra*, when this stage is reached in the progress towards enlightenment (*tathā hy asāv eva tadā asti nāstīti cocyate*, st. 25cd[47]). On the score of such data the author of our chapter Mdh. 217 states ($_{6ab,7\text{-}10}$) that the difference between pravṛttilakṣaṇa and nivṛttilakṣaṇa is the same as the difference between avyakta and puruṣa: they are distinguished only by the svalakṣaṇa ($_{9cd}$), the dharma of prakṛti being *sarga* and *triguṇa*, that of the "contemplator" puruṣa its absence ($_{9ab,10ab}$). In other words, in this yoga-doctrine the relation between avyakta and puruṣa, unlike that conceived by the Sāṃkhyas (and later codified in the Sāṃkhya-system), amounting to the coexistence of two essentially different principles – one essentially active, the other essentially inactive –, is an alternative of two aspects of the same essence, consciousness: both are realized by activities, but these activities are of opposite orders ($_{11}$), the one karma being

45 For the technical purport inherent (since KaṭhaU) in the terms *tad* and *etad*, *asti* and *nāsti* see *Il Mito Psicologico*, pp. 145-149, 151, 219, 254, 259, 272f., 296, 316, 343ff.

46 La Vallee, *Le petit traité de Vasubandhu-Nāgārjuna*, *Mélanges Chinois et Bouddhiques* II, pp. 147-161.

47 P. 155. This stage is the *nāmni sthāna* or *cittasya citte sthāna*, see below, pp. 180ff.

saṃyogalakṣaṇotpatti, the pravṛtti of contingency, while the other, the (yogic) karma which brings about the cessation of karma (*ibid.*), is conducive to the "other", "greater", reality of the static, karmaless ātman beyond avyakta and puruṣa($_{6cd}$); those two aspects are also termed "two puruṣas" ($_{10cd}$).

Pravṛttilakṣaṇadharma and nivṛttilakṣaṇadharma, the two alternative modes of the psyche, are at the same time interpreted as verbal entities (217$_{2cd,4ab}$; above, p. 55) — as the two aspects of the immanent Vāc, which can be expounded in two kinds of doctrine, the one worldly, the other leading to deliverance (exactly the same conception is expressed by Āryadeva, Catuḥśataka, st. 183); the one is *punarāvṛtti*, the other *paramā gati* ($_{4cd}$). The latter is obviously identical with the śabdabrahman, into which the organism and its nāmarūpa-experience are absorbed in dhyāna (*dehavañ chabdavac caret* 217$_{21}$; cf. 234 $_{17ab}$ *ākāśasya tadā ghoṣaṃ taṃ vidvān kurute 'tmani*[48]), to be finally elevated in the consummation of *dhyāna* to the transcendent silent realm of the aśabda[49]. Quite analogously the MSA. describes the mental progress towards the attainment of Tathatā (XI, 5 bh.) as beginning with a reduction of the subject-object experience of the nāmarūpa-plane to *manojalpa* (*ibid.*, 6, 7 and bh.; 23ff.; XIV, 7ab), i.e. to nāma only — a stage correspondent to the lower (parāvṛtty)āśraya (XI, 9; XIV, 29) —, and culminating in *nirjalpa* (XIV, 7c) or *ajalpa*[50],

[48] The śabdabrahman or "higher brahman" is the direct manifestation of the hṛdākāśa in its upward function leading to the aśabda, to the unuttered transcendent Vāc.

[49] This is the *ekāyana dharma*: 217$_{30}$.

[50] This or *apajalpa* is inferable from the Tib. rendering (inst. of *alpajalpa* as in Skt. Ms.): see *Trad.*, p. 103, n.

the superior or fully realized (parāvṛtty)āśraya (XI, 9), — the whole process taking place in dhyāna (cf. bh. *ad* XIV, 7, and XI, 7 with XVI, 26).

The doctrine nivṛttilakṣaṇa is obviously identical with the *Dharma kat'exochen*, the Doctrine of salvation expounded by the divine Teacher of yoga. The dharma = vijñāna in its ascending function essentially coincides with it (see above, p. 53f.) as its psychic actualization; analogously, on the ground of Buddhist ideology, the Hīnayānic citta or viññāna, the Mahāyānic ālayavijñāna, in its process of nivṛtti, of purification (as samyakpraṇihita citta, bodhicitta), essentially coincides with the *Dharma*, in the third meaning of the term, denoting the saving doctrine of the Buddhas, which illuminates human consciousness and thus frees it from the bonds of saṃsāra due to *avidyā*[51], by awakening wisdom (*vidyā*) institutes the "way" (*mārga*) of salvation leading to Nirvāṇa. With this aspect of dharma we have also met already in the ṚV., and, in our survey of the Upanishadic conceptions of dharma and of brahman, as early as the ChU, according to which brahma = satyam as the saving doctrine revealed by a teacher shows human consciousness, hitherto blinded, the "way" back to the transcendent universal Being. (It is the "upward" path [*pathi*] of the divine manas according to ṚV. I, 164; in the Upanishads the realization of this way [*panthan*] is the yogic mukti-ascension through the suṣumnā to the hypercosmic sphere above *svargaloka*: BĀU IV, 4, 8-9; cf. ChU VIII, 6, 5). In the Śvet.U and in the Gītā this *dharma* is already conceived in a sense equivalent to that of the proto-Buddhistic ideology. It is the gift brought

[51] The *avijjadhātu* is the sphere of the manifold dhammā: SN. III, p. 10.

to mankind by the universal Puruṣa incarnate as Yoga-Teacher. His saving doctrine, imparted to man blinded by self-consciousness and bringing about the inner metamorphosis from avidyā to vidyā, is the "higher" brahman, the psychic current of ascension to brahma-nirvāṇa. This progress (see above, p. 54f.) is cultivated on the yogic path of self-extension in universal love, whose counterpart is the dhyānic path of Buddhistic *maitrī*. The saving doctrine, the nivṛttilakṣaṇadharma, is actualized in the yogic orientation of the individual vijñāna and is epitomized during the process of yoga in the *tāraka* OṂ, in the śabdabrahman forming the "way" (*adhvan*) or the "bridge" (*setu*) of the cosmical ascension. The *dharma* as Doctrine instituting the "way" of salvation is in its actualization the "way" itself; the same feature is manifest in the Buddhistic conception of *dharma* as soteric Doctrine actualized in the *anāsrava-dharmasaṃtāna* constituting the Way.

This third meaning of the term *dharma* underlies the oldest conception of *dharmakāya* as it appears in two famous passages of the Pāli Suttas and is still maintained in the Prajñāpāramitās and in the teaching of Nāgārjuna.

In the DN. this *dhamma*, constituting the Tathāgata's body, is synonymous with *brahman* (*dhammakāyo ti pi brahmakāyo ti pi dhammabhūto ti pi brahmabhūto ti piti* DN. III, p. 84). The Buddha's disciples are "born in it, fashioned of it" (*dhammaja, dhammanimmita*): this evidently means that by the reception of the doctrine they are assimilated to the Buddha as the Doctrine personified. Now, what is the Buddha's brahmakāya? The Suttas often mention the *manomayakāya* with which he ascends to the brahmaloka "unless he chooses to go there with his elemental body" (the latter clause is obviously a pious addition meant to stress the miraculous power of the Buddha, able even to overcome the natural order of things; for the 'regular' means of ascending to the brahmaloka is evidently the possession of the manomayakāya). In his previous existence as Mahāgovinda the Buddha won the brahmaloka by means of the practice of the *brahmavihāras* (DN. II, pp. 238-250). As is clearly borne out by the covering formula, this practice consists in extending oneself to universal existence by radiating the four psychic states of love, joy, compassion and equanimity. This is the only way to brahmaloka or "coexistence with Brahmā", taught by the Buddha to his disciples (DN. I, p. 249). According to the primitive Buddhist notion (cf. e.g. MN. II, p. 193ff.; SN IV, p. 410), concordant with that of the Upanishads of the middle period (cf. esp. Kauṣ.U I), the brahmaloka is the uppermost sphere of the cosmos, in which no individual existence obtains, but personality (whose body and consciousness are no longer distinct) is all-embracing[52]. This sphere is obviously identical with the immanent *dharmadhātu* (above, p. 62)[53]. It clearly ensues therefrom that the Buddha's

[52] See *Il Mito Psicologico*, p. 302f. Hence the winner of the sphere of Brahmā literally "coexists" with Brahmā, becomes himself Brahmā.

In the complex dogmatic classification of the cosmos this peculiar sphere – now the summit of the rūpaloka – is the fourth *vijñānasthiti;* it is characterized by the unity, both in body and consciousness, of all its beings – in each of whom body and consciousness coincide. Cf. AK. III, 4d, 5a-6a.

[53] According to the texts referred to above, this sphere of the holy career is won by the performance of brahmavihāra; further analysis of old sources will show (*infra*, Ch. VII) that the access to it was held to be the attainment of dhyāna. Its upper limit, or the attainment of the nirvāṇa-

dharmakāya, his Doctrine-body, his personality as teacher and saviour, is a cosmic manomayakāya. Its structural function is that of unifying the individuated nāma-rūpa units in its essence of pure nāma = dharma and thereby orientating them towards the hypercosmic absolute unity of Dharma = Nirvāṇa.

The Upanishadic brahman in its aspect as soteri-

sphere, is arrived at, according to some texts, by the effect of the fourth dhyāna (MN. I, pp. 357; 181-4; 276-280; 347f., 412f., etc.). Elsewhere I have assembled ample evidence in support of the conclusion that the dhyānas and the brahmavihāras were originally the same set of psychic attainments, and were formally disjoined in dogmatics by mechanical classification (*Il Mito Psicologico,* pp. 288-294). The respective formulas are complementary, the one set (brahmavihāras) supplying the *quid,* the other the *quomodo.* In the light of such data the paramount importance of these exercises in the original conception of the "Way" becomes fully evident. In the classical Hīnayāna conception of the holy career, which is largely that of the *sukkhavipassaka*—a career of salvation by mere observance of ascetic rules and adoption of dogmatic viewpoints—the brahmavihāras, as well as the dhyānas, are reduced to background factors. In the Mahāyānic revival of the yogic career they are restored to their primitive importance, and the fact of their coalescence (never entirely obliterated, *v. loc. cit.*) is again expressly stated (cf. MSA. XVI, 26). The brahmavihāras are said to be the evidence of the Bodhisattva's intimate qualities (M.-Saṃgr., Upanib. *ad* II, 34, 15), to constitute his transcendental activity (*niṣpannakarma*), in close connexion with *prabhāvaprāpti,* i.e. the attainment of the *abhijñās* (*ibid.*), and the *adhigamaguṇa,* the power of realization (II, 15b, cf. 15a). The supreme perfection, realized in the fourth dhyāna, is experienced in the fourth brahmavihāra (MSA. VII, 2-3). Thus the features of the oldest ideal of the holy career, connecting the brahmavihāras, as immediate condition, with the attainment of the abhijñās and the power of realization of Nirvāṇa, are fully reasserted.

cal doctrine, as "way", is intermediate between its saṃsāra-aspect, as differentiated in nāmas and rūpas, and its nirvāṇa-aspect as undifferentiated universal unity. In the yogic realization of the way, structurally represented in the Upanishads as a gradual ascension through the microcosmic and the corresponding macrocosmic spheres to the transcendent sphere of the hypercosmic brahman, first bodily existence (the *mūrta rūpa* opposed in BĀU II, 3 to the *amūrta rūpa; the śarīra* opposed to the *aśarīra* [*rūpa*] in ChU VIII, 12,2) had to be transcended (i.e., the sphere of *ākāśa-hṛdyākāśa* had to be reached): only on this ground the fusion of the frame-free prāṇa-body with vijñāna was censed to take place (*athāyam aśarīro 'mṛtaḥ prāṇo brahmaiva teja eva* BĀU IV, 4, 7), the individual *nāma*, transformed into brahma, finally giving way to all-consciousness, to the "supreme Identity" (*parama sāmya* Muṇḍ.U III, 1, 3) of the universal brahman = ātman, of the transcendent Androgyne Puruṣa.

In the later Upanishads and in the Gītā that intermediate aspect of brahman is mythically projected on the figure of Puruṣa as saviour and teacher, bent on his mission from time immemorial; his human incarnation is only a limited and imperfect manifestation. His real form (*rūpam aiśvaram* Gītā XI, 3; 9 – cf. *yogeśvara* 4, *viśvarūpa* 16) – a mass of light (*tejorāśi*) visible only to the "divine eye" of supernatural intuition (XI, 8) – is not individual but cosmic and contains all the gods, the whole complex of rūpas, the whole world, in its one shape (XI, 7; 13) – which however is not of the rūpa-plane, but of a plane comparable with ākāśa (IX, 6). His specific essence is "the highest *akṣara* to be known" (i.e. the 'uttered' OṂ as *sambodhayitṛ, v. supra,* p. 42), the "higher" brahman-dharma, the Doctrine, of which he is the eternal keeper or bearer (XI, 18; XIV, 27), the power by which he lifts human beings from the realm of saṃsāra (XII, 7)--represented by the same cosmic Puruṣa as Kāla, creator and destructor, lord of the "lower" brahman – up to the sphere of brahmanirvāṇa, the highest mode of existence represented by the Puruṣa as transcendent unmanifest unity. The same relation between the different aspects of the Puruṣa is set forth in the Śvet.U, where the cosmic arūpa-Puruṣa conceived as saviour, bearer of the higher brahman (III, 7; 10; he is the inner upright Skambha [cf. Muṇḍ.U II, 1, 4] contrasted with the cosmogonic Skambha turned upside down [III, 9cd], – the yogic promoter [*pravartaka*] of sattva [III, 12], of the *buddhi śubhā*, of the *nirmalā prāpti* [*ibid.*], of the only "way" [*panthan*, 8]), opposed to the cosmic Puruṣa = Kāla as creator-destructor, is represented as leader to the transcendent Puruṣa[54].

[54] For details see *Il Mito Psicologico*, chapter VI.

In the yoga-doctrines of the Mokṣadharma the intermediate position is assigned to the 25th principle called *budhyamāna*: he is the *mahān ātmā* (the ancient Skambha) and is *amūrta* (303_{39}); his *pravṛtti* is effected by *jñāna*($_{19}$); in his original reality he is *buddha*, but has fallen into the condition of *abuddhatā* (305_{1-10}); when however he effects the inversion of his immanent functionality, he is called *budhyamāna* (306_{30-31}), and is the guṇaless Īśvara who no longer creates the *guṇas* ($_{32}$; see also 309_{1-10}). When the process of purification is completed, he again becomes *buddha*, the 26th ($_{10cd-11}$, $_{13-16}$, etc).

VII

We have already come across the ancient Buddhist conception of a sphere of unsensuous, purely psychical being as intermediate between the nether sphere of differentiated nāma-rūpa, comprising all psycho-physiological existence, and the transcendent non-differentiated *dharmadhātu*. This sphere is the *arūpadhātu*, comprising the two upper strata of the *ṣaḍdhātu*-structure, the realms of unmixed *ākāśa* and *vijñāna*, of the subtle and "boundless" elements whose share in the nether conglomerate of *nāma-rūpa* represents the component *nāma*. The dhyānic—i.e. yogic—path, effectuating the ascension from nāma-rūpa-existence to Nirvāṇa, consequently belongs to this arūpa-sphere. Now, as it need hardly be recalled, in the dogmatic construction introduced in a number of Suttas the series of dhyāna-planes, ranging from the upper limit of the *kāmaloka* to the *bhavāgra*, consists of two sets, assigned respectively to the rūpadhātu (°*loka*, °*avacāra*) and to the *ārūpyadhātu*. Both this composite arrangement of the dhyāna-series—whose secondary character is even externally obvious in the different formulations of the two sets—and the corresponding construction of three cosmic spheres under a tetradic schema of reality appear to be the result of a doctrinal revision of originally simpler data. Several ancient Pāli texts (Itiv. 51, 73; Suttanip. 755-6; DN.,

Saṃgīti-Suttanta, 10. XIV) bear witness to the existence of a primitive scheme in which *two* contingent dhātus, *rūpadhātu* and *arūpadhātu*, were opposed to the third, transcendent, *nirodha-dhātu*. Prof. PRZYLUSKI is therefore right in stating that *kāmadhātu* has been added later on to the originally triadic scheme *rūpadhātu* – *arūpadhātu* – *nirodhadhātu*, to make up a series of four[1]. But I think he is less right in supposing that this reform of the cosmological conceptions was brought about by an adaptation of the dhātu-arrangement to the four degrees of dhyāna. In fact, the four dhyānas are never brought together with the four dhātus; quite on the contrary, all the four dhyānas are located in one dhātu (in the *rūpadhātu* according to the canonical doctrine, while in the primitive doctrine with its three-dhātu scheme they must have pertained to the arūpa-dhātu), and so is the second superadded tetrad of the *samāpattis*. That original triadic classification of reality is therefore not amenable to the ancient *trailokya*-scheme[2], but must have been based on another criterion, which appears to have been the ideology of nāma-rūpa. *Rūpadhātu* was thus originally the sphere of psycho-physiological existence in nāma and rūpa, *arūpadhātu* the sphere of merely psychical existence as nāma alone (= *dharma*), the non-physiological body (the *amūrta rūpa* in the wording of the BĀU) being constituted by the unsensuous mind-element, while from the *nirodha*(= *nirvāṇa*)-*dhātu* both rūpa and nāma, as differentiated reality, are absent. The later

[1] *Bouddhisme et Upanishad*, BEFEO, 1932, p. 159.

[2] Ever since the oldest specimens of the cosmogonic speculations based on the three-world scheme, the brahman's "own" transcendent existence is clearly separated from the *trailokya* and distinguished from the ancient *svargaloka*.

extension of the dhātu-set saddled dogmatic exegesis with the difficult task of explaining the difference between kāmaloka and rūpaloka. This was done by assuming that in the rūpadhātu only the three inferior senses are absent; whereas in the ārūpya only mind (manas = vijñāna) is left[3]. The Abhidharmakośa (VIII, 9) nevertheless admits that in the *rūpadhyānas* there is no function of the senses. The Kathāvatthu (KV.: VIII, 7) records the opinion of several schools (according to the comy.: the Andhakas and the Saṃmitīyas) "that in the *rūpa*-sphere the individual has all the six senses". The same Andhakas and Saṃmitīyas held that there is even desire in the rūpa-sphere (XIV, 7). They evidently still held on to the primitive conception of the rūpa-loka as the nether sphere of sensuous life. To these "heretics", who simply had not accepted the later dogmatic revision, the KV. even attributes the downright assertion that rūpadhātu is the material sphere, while arūpadhātu is the immaterial one (VIII, 5, 6). In the fact that the second of the three original dhātus was essentially conceived as the sphere of dhyāna we find an obvious explanation of the choice of the term denoting the lowest dhātu in the tetradic list. The formula describing the attainment of the first dhyāna — and *eo ipso* the elevation to the dhyānic sphere — mentions, to begin with, the separation from *kāmas* (*vivicc'eva kāmehi*). This suggested the designation of the lowest worldly sphere thereby relinquished as *kāmaloka* or °*dhātu*, its older name (see above, pp. 60, 97f.) being now referred to the immediately superior dhyāna-sphere.

[3] The Vijñaptimātratāsiddhi (see *Siddhi*, p. 192) shares this view of Pāli dogmatics (e.g. Visuddhimagga, p. 198f.).

When the two sets of dhyānas were superposed, one was assigned to the rūpaloka, the other to the ārūpya. This brings about the erroneous appearance that the dhyāna-way to Nirvāṇa must needs lead through the ārūpya-dhyānas. Traces of ancient data bear witness to the contrary. If we refer to the Mahāparinibbāna-sutta, we see that the Buddha's last dhyānic ascension, that of his passing to Nirvāṇa, comprises only the four dhyānas[4]. In the basic narrative of the Bodhi, recording the first realization of Nirvāṇa, the four dhyānas play the leading part, while the ārūpyas do not occur at all.[5]

If the original climax of the spheres of existence was rūpadhātu, arūpadhātu, nirvāṇadhātu, it is clear that the "way" as realized in the four dhyānas must have belonged to the original arūpa-sphere, whose secondary qualification as *rūpaloka* was due to the later dogmatical collocation of the *samāpatti-series* above the four-dhyāna-series.[6]

[4] The new dogmatic arrangements have been at work on this text too, but they were hindered by the tradition concerning Gotama's last instants, which seems to have been too definitely fixed to be liable to such radical adaptations. The actual moment of the Parinirvāṇa being inseparable from the culmination of the fourth dhyāna, the new 'complete' dhyāna-series was inserted as the last phase but one (DN. II, 155ff.).

[5] Cf. MN. I, pp. 21ff.; 117; 247ff.; II, 93. The famous episode of the Bodhisattva's apprenticeship (I, pp. 163ff.; 240) even shows that *ākiñcaññāyatana* and *nevasaññānāsaññāyatana*, which in the scheme of the ārūpyas are counted as the two higher samāpattis, were, at the period to which the legend belongs, definitely considered as *not* conducive to bodhi.

[6] Consequently, difficulties and disputes arose as to which dhyānic stage held the key of the *nirodhasamāpatti*, located at the summit of the cosmic edifice (*bhavāgra*). The

According to a theory recorded already in the DN. (III, p. 131f.), the four stages of deliverance are the "fruits" of the four dhyānas. This looks very much like an artificial construction for the purpose of enforcing by an old and current notion the dogmatic thesis of the four degrees of the holy career. (Had the dhyānic path not been considered of old as the very Way of emancipation – in fact it was the Founder's way to bodhi –, such an attempt could not have had any *raison d'être*.) But the terms designating the four *phalas* do not form a homogeneous series: only the two middle terms are lexically connected. The dogma of the four degrees as subsequent stages does not seem to have been firmly established at any early date; it is not even

Mahāsaṃghikas assigned it to the fourth ("rūpa"-)dhyāna; Vasubandhu adheres to the dogmatic opinion assigning it to the fourth ārūpya, on the ground that the sūtras describing the nine samāpattis represent them as successive attainments – which implies that one cannot reach the bhavāgra without first passing through the ārūpyas (AK. II, 44d, p. 210). As the opponents of this thesis probably could quote canonic texts to prove their opinion as well, the difficulty was disposed of by assuming *two* nirodhas of the cittacaittas, one of which is realized on the basis of the fourth dhyāna (*asaṃjñisamāpatti*) – but practised only by the *pṛthagjanas*, not by the *āryas* –, while the other (*nirodhasamāpatti*) – practised by the *āryas* only – is realized on the basis of the *naivasaṃjñānāsaṃjñāyatana*, the fourth ārūpya (AK. II, 41-43, pp. 200-204). Still, another serious difficulty is caused by the tradition concerning Gotama's Enlightenment, in which the higher samāpattis have no part. This difficulty is obviated by the assertion that in the case of the Buddha deliverance is produced quite as if he had realized beforehand the *nirodhasamāpatti*, for he has the power of realizing it whenever he likes (44ab, p. 205) The factitiousness of such compromising solutions is obvious.

so in the AK., which plainly admits that besides the *anupūrvaka*-way of winning the fruits there is also the possibility of directly attaining the higher degrees (cf. AK. II, 16cd, LA VALLEE, p. 134ff.). The Mahāsaṃghikas seem to have admitted only two stages, as the relevant point of their doctrine recorded in Vasumitra's treatise (35) mentions only the *anāgāmin* and the *arhat*. Moreover, some traces in the extant terminology suggest that the condition of anāgāmin (=*anāvattidhamma*) was originally considered as the only intermediate stage, extending from the entrance upon the Way to its consummation in arhatship, and that the progression realized in this condition was represented by the dhyānic ascension. The AK.-bhāṣya mentions the fact that the quality of the anāgāmin was developed in the *anāgamya* (*ibid.*, p. 136), i.e. in the state of psychic concentration introductory to the first dhyāna. Now the *srotaāpanna*, the disciple having reached only the first of the four fruits according to the canonical classification, is also given the very ancient title of *avinipātadhamma*, "he whose quality it is not to fall away any more" (evidently from the degree attained[7]). This is scarcely in accordance with the dogmatic tenet that he is liable to be reborn up to seven times as *pṛthagjana*. In the structural representation, which, as we are constantly

[7] Dogmatic exegesis explains *avinipātadhamma* as "not liable to be reborn in hell", for the possibility of "falling off again" to the pṛthagjana stage is now considered inherent to the quality of the srotaāpanna, thus distinguishing him from the *anāvattidhamma* or anāgāmin. But originally the two terms seem to have been equivalent, denoting the same quality as viewed (a) from the stage attained ("not to fall away any more"), (b) from he plane thereby abandoned ("not to return any more to this loka").

led to state, is inseparably connected with the soteriological schemes of Buddhist thought, it is even less conceivable how the *avinipātadhamma,* unwaveringly bent on the upward way, should return downwards, to a lower condition, over and over again. This discordant notion is evidently brought about by the attempt at establishing a gradation of inferior values or attainments with regard to the quality of *anāgāmin* ranked as third degree. The queer notion of the *sakṛdāgāmin* seems also to be an effect of this artificial construction. It has probably been substituted to the simpler notion of the *āgāmin,* "one who is still liable to return", applied to the disciple who has not yet definitely entered upon "the way of no return", into the upward "current of the Dhamma". This *āgāmin* must thus have been primitively inferior to the *srotaāpanna.* The Nikāyas still record such an initial degree previous to the *srotaāpatti* : it is the condition of one who has gone for *śaraṇa* in Buddha, Dharma and Saṃgha on solemnly proclaiming that "the Teacher has revealed the Dharma as if by turning upwards that which had been turned upside down, unveiling what had been veiled, showing the way to one who was astray, bringing a light into darkness". As I have elsewhere tried to show in detail[8], also by a comparison with the analogous Upanishadic records, this *śaraṇāgati* (*saraṇagamana*) — not quite adequately rendered by the phrase "taking refuge" — means a "making for" the domain or sphere represented by Buddha, Dharma and Saṃgha, and this act was primitively conceived as an act of *upāsana,* i.e. a process of psychic concentration on the object with which one wants to get ultimately

[8] See *Il Mito Psicologico,* pp. 354ff.

identified[9]: the accomplishment of this process is the attainment of that sphere, i.e. the entrance into the Stream, the starting on the Way proper[10]. According to the intrinsical logic of this structure, the Stream-winner does not turn away any more, he is an *anāgāmin*. One is liable to fall away only as long as one has not yet accomplished that decisive step of the "entrance". The original scheme of the holy career seems thus to have been: 1. *śaraṇaṃ gata* (=*upāsaka*=*āgāmin*), 2. *srotaāpanna* (=*avinipātadhamma*=*anāgāmin*), 3. *arhat* (=*buddha*, as the *srotaāpanna* is *sambodhi-parāyaṇa*). The initial or lower *upāsana*[9] directed to the essence of the saving Doctrine, to its personification in the immanent personality of the Buddha as Teacher and to its manifestation in the cumulative body of the Saṃgha, is developed in the psychic process called *anāgamya* and fulfilled in the attainment of the first *dhyāna* by which the Stream or Way is entered upon[11]; while the higher *upāsana*, focussed on Nirvāṇa as the transcendent reality of Dharma, is realized in the eliminative progression of the *dhyānas* culminating in Nirvāṇa[12]. (Several ancient texts bear witness to the conception that in and with the *upekkhāsatipārisuddhi* of the fourth dhyāna the "annihilation of the *āsavas*" and the *anāsava cetovimutti paññavimutti* is fulfilled, cf. e.g. MN. I, p. 357).

[9] On *upāsana* see *Il Mito Psicologico*, *passim*, Index *s.v.* and the article *Upāsana and Upaniṣad* in RO. XIII, 1937.

[10] *Soto*=*maggo*, cf. SN. V, p. 347, etc.

[11] Cf. the tenet of the Ekavyāvahārikas (20) and of the Mahāśāsakas (10) (WALLESER, *op. cit.*, pp. 83, 86): "the srotaāpanna has attained dhyāna."

[12] See *Il Mito Psicologico*, pp. 285, 288f

The amplification of the *phala*-series was brought about by cumulating two dyads of originally equivalent terms (such expedients are facilitated by the habit, often to be observed in the Sutta-texts on dogmatics, of classifying different terms as different data). The introductory degree of the first dyad (*śraddhānusārin* = *śaraṇaṃ gata*) was left at its natural place, whereas its counterpart in the second dyad came to be placed above the *srota-āpanna* though below the counterpart of the latter; some logic was brought into the new tetradic scheme by interpreting the *āgāmin* as a *sakṛdāgāmin* and the *srota-āpanna* as an *āgāmin* up to seven times.

The fundamental characteristics of the *anāgāmin* are styled as follows in the coined phrase recurrent in the Pāli Suttas: *opapātiko tattha-parinibbāyī anāvattidhammo tasmā lokā*: "his is spontaneous birth and even there (i.e. in the sphere in which he is thus born) he obtains full nirvāṇa, his character is, never to return any more to this world"[13]. The *opapātika* (*aupapāduka*) beings have no physical bodies; they have only 'mind-framed' (*manomaya*) bodies. This implies that they belong to an intermediate sphere. But to which of the two? The late dogmatic classification of the category of the anāgāmins ranges some of them in the rūpadhātu, others in the ārūpya. But in the Pāli Canon there are still traces of the fact that the *manomaya*-existence of the anāgāmin had been once located in the *ārūpya*-sphere. This opinion is held by Udāyin, the contradictor of Śāriputra, who is of course severely rebuked for his error. The story, which has no intrinsic connection with the Sutta

[13] The notion conveyed by the term *anāvattidhamma* (cf. also n.$_7$) is rendered by the later epithet *parivṛttajanman*.

in which it occurs (AN. III, p. 192), has obviously been inserted to furnish a canonical proof against the asserters of the older, pre-dogmatic tenet. There seems to have been a good deal of disagreement between the schools as regards the sphere to which belong 'mind-framed' beings. The Sarvāstivādins range them in the rūpa-dhātu, the Sautrāntikas in the rūpadhātu and the ārūpyadhātu, the opinion represented by Udāyin in the ārūpyadhātu[14]. These difficulties are a consequence of the canonical arrangement discussed above; it is fairly clear that they are due to the assumption of *two* intermediate spheres. The faculty of "producing" or "deriving" the *manomaya*-body is an *iddhi* mastered in dhyāna. Like the dhyānic process itself, with which it is closely connected, and in which – as we shall see further on – it is realized, the *manomayakāya* has been nominally shifted from the original *arūpa-dhātu* to the canonical *rūpadhātu*.

As it is exempt from the elementary rūpa, the *manomaya* personality of the anāgāmin evidently consists of the four psychic skandhas only[15]. Nāma and rūpa can no more be distinguished in it. It is pure nāma, i.e. *dharma*.

[14] Cf. AK. II, *loc. cit.*, p. 209 and n. 3

[15] These skandhas however, as we shall see later on, have a functional value different from that which they have when they are liable, or when they tend, to connection with rūpa.

VIII

Even the AK. (III, 28b, 30a) still brings together the ancient Buddhist notion of *nāma-rūpa* and the five-skandha-series, thus taking up an equation familiar to the Nikāyas, especially to the SN., where however the binomium appears in the synonymous formulation *saviññānako kāyo* (III, p. 72, 80f., 136, etc.)[1]. On the other hand, according to the Abhidharma-classification pointed out by Prof. SCHAYER, in which, as we have seen above, the term *dharma* is used as a synonym of *nāma*, "the *dharma-āyatana* and the *dharma-dhātu* contain..., according to Vasubandhu's definition, the *vedanā*, the *saṃjñā*, the *saṃskāras*, the *avijñapti* and the *asaṃskṛtas*, and according to the Dhammasangani the same items without the *avijñapti* and the *asaṃskṛtas*" (PCB., p. 126-7). The classification of the Pāli-treatise is obviously the older of the two: *avijñapti* and *asaṃs-*

[1] In the Sammādiṭṭhisutta (MN. I, p. 53) the binomium—in its usual formulation *nāmarūpam*—is explained from both the microcosmic and the macrocosmic points of view simultaneously: *rūpa* is described as "the four elements and the body (which arises) in dependence on them" (*cattāri ca mahābhūtāni catuññañ ca mahābhūtānam upādāya rūpam, idam vuccat' āvuso rūpam*), whereas under the heading *nāma* five items of psychic activity are classified: *vedanā, saññā, cetanā, phasso, manasikāro. cetanā* is the synonym with which the *saṅkhāra-*

kṛtas have been added later on[2]. Upon the score of the above evidence that *dharma* = *nāma* is originally synonymous with *vijñāna*, we are faced with the conclusion that, in the underlying conception, the dyad *nāma-rūpa* and the five-skandha-series were not independent from each other, as the first part of the binomium, vijñāna, contains the other three skandhas, which thus appear to have been originally only three aspects of the vijñāna-element. Are we justified in assuming that the four psychic skandhas developed out of a single nāma- or vijñāna-skandha? We have been able to observe an analogous evolution in the history of Upanishadic thought: out of the vijñāna-ātman (the *arūpa* or *amūrta* aspect of brahman), the unsensous part of human personality, characterized in the ChU (III, 14) as *manomayaḥ prāṇaśarīra*...*ākāśa*(= *vijñāna*)*ātmā*, the Taittirīya-doctrine evolves three kośas or concentric bodies of the inner ātman: the *prāṇamaya*, the *manomaya* and the *vijñānamaya* body. There are still traces in the Pāli Canon of such a primitive binomial stage of the skandha-theory, as e.g. the subdivision of the nāmarūpa into a *nāmakāya* and a *rūpakāya* in the Mahā-Nidāna-Suttanta (DN. II, p. 62)[3], and the ancient conception of the

kkhandha is currently explained, and *manasikāro* is doubtless a synonymous designation of the *viññānakkhandha*. The item *phasso*, which occurs in the paticcasamuppāda-formula as designation of the moment of contact between the individual process and the outer world, is obviously inserted to set forth the simultaneous classification of the *ajjhattam* and the *bahiddhā* nāma.

[2] See above, Ch. V, n 15.

[3] Cf. Nettip. p. 41: *rūpakāyo rūpakkhandho nāmakāyo cattāro arūpino khandhā.*

manomayakāya as evidenced in texts concerning *iddhi*: the manomayakāya is a subtle body hidden within the gross rūpa "like a blade of grass in its sheath or a sword in its scabbard or a snake in its slough" and can be extracted from it by means of dhyānic training. There is no doubt that this *manomayakāya* is the *nāmakāya* of the Mahā-Nidāna-Suttanta.

The ancient conception of the two contingent *kāyas*, *rūpakāya* and *nāma(=manomaya=arūpa)kāya*, is connected with the ancient three-dhātu-scheme. The rūpakāya belongs to the ancient rūpadhātu, the world of sense. The dhyānic production (*abhi-nir-mā*) of the unsensous mind-body or its extraction from the sensuous one is at the same time an elevation to the intermediary arūpa-sphere, to the sphere of the Doctrine, which is then "bodily" perceived (*dhammaṃ kāyena passati*, Dhp. 259). Those who do not linger in this sphere but proceed upwards to the transcendent nirodha-dhātu, thereby relinquishing mortality, must needs give up also the second body. Now two of the texts relating to the three-dhātu-scheme (Itiv., st. 51, p. 45f.; st. 73, p. 62)[4] mention yet another body, in connection with the transcendent *amṛta-dhātu*. This is the body with which the Truly Awakened One has experienced (lit.: touched) the Immortal Sphere, the Nirvāṇa free from upadhis, which is the object of his preaching (p. 46) and to which he shows the Way. The disciple who follows him on this Way becomes a *kāyasakkhī* as soon as he crosses the threshold of nirodha; in fact he "touches the supreme sambodhi" (Itiv. 79, 47,

[4] These stanzas occurring twice in the Itiv. look very ancient, and probably belonged to the primitive stock of Sayings.

34). The Nikāya-evidence concerning the *kāyasakkhī* is rather scanty, but, inspite of the effort employed in fitting it into the frame of the later system (also by means of co-ordinations with other two [AN. I, p. 118ff.], six [MN. I, p. 477ff., etc.], or nine [AN. V, p. 23] kinds of *puggalas* : but the differentiation of these types is far from being fixed or neatly defined), the original conception is still quite evident : the kāyasakkhī, characterized by the dominant faculty of *samādhi* (AN. I, p. 119), "abides" in the successive *vimokkha*-stages by "touching them bodily" (MN. I, p. 478; cf. p. 33), i.e. he experiences them by means of successive bodies conformable to their spheres. The fundamental text, AN. IV, p. 451f., specifies the technical meaning of the term by maintaining that throughout the stages of the dhyānas the term *kāyasakkhī* is applied only *pariyāyena*, whereas the bhikkhu is called *nippariyāyena* a kāyasakkhī only upon reaching the limitary stage of *saññāvedayitanirodha*. This agrees with the explicit information that can be drawn from the AK. : the condition of *kāyasākṣin* is attained by realizing the *nirodha-samāpatti* (VI, 63 a-c, 43c, pp. 274, 223f.)[5]. The formulation is very explicit : *nirodhalābhy anāgāmī kāyasākṣī*.

As reaching the nirodha was originally tantamount to arhatship, the AN. (IV, p. 452) congruously presents the perfect *kāyasakkhī* as an arhat (*paññāya c'assa disvā*

[5] Such a view is also in accordance with the Puggala-paññatti, p. 14—where however, by a secondary and highly artificial limitation (*paññāya c'assa disvā* e k a c c e *āsavā parikkhinā honti; id.* MN. I, p. 478), he is distinguished from the arhat.

āsavā parikkhinā honti). On the ground of the above evidence on "bodily experiencing" the *nirodha-* or *amṛta-dhātu*, the origin of the conception of the kāyasākṣin appears fairly clear : a *kāyasākṣin* was a saint who had realized and witnessed the Nirvāṇa bodily, i.e. by means of a body conformable to the transcendent *nirodha-dhātu*. Even so late a work as the AK.-Vyākhyā (*ad* VI, 43cd) in accordance with the Bhāṣya still records the tenet that there is "acquisition of a body conformable to nirodha" (*tadanukūlāśrayaprāpti*[6]; *kāyena sākṣātkaraṇam...kāyāśrayotpatteḥ*[7]). As, according to the notion of those ancient texts, the nirodha- or amṛta-dhātu is reached by transcending the second or arūpa-sphere, the body of the kāyasākṣin must have been originally conceived as a third body, different from the *rūpa-* and *nāma*(=*arūpa*)-bodies and consubstantial with the Buddha's *amṛta*-body. This conclusion is anything but surprising if we consider that in the ancient texts the title *buddha* and even *sammāsambuddha* was frequently bestowed upon the Buddha's followers having reached perfection, as the primitive career of the disciple was a career of Imitation : a yogic, dhyānic career like that of Gotama[8]. As the Hīnayānic development of Buddhism went the "negativistic" way, reducing the ideal of perfection to a goal of mere elimination of contingency, it is obvious why no direct mention of the saint's *amṛta-kāya* is left in the Canon and why in the exegetic scriptures the kāyasākṣin is artificially distinguished from the arhat.

[6] Yaśomitra, ed. WOGIHARA, p. 566.

[7] *Ibid.*, cf. AK., LA VALLEE, VI, p. 224, n. 1.

[8] For details see *Il Mito Psicologico nell'India Antica*, pp. 353f.

That the modality of the attainment of Nirvāṇa was once represented as the realization of a nirvāṇic body, can still be read between the lines of the controversy reported AK. II, 55d, where the Sautrāntika opposes the Sarvāstivādin's view of Nirvāṇa. The Nirvāṇa being no "thing", but mere cessation, it cannot be *attained*. But how, then, are the Sūtra-passages about winning Nirvāṇa-in-life to be explained? According to the Sautrāntika's explanation, they only mean that "by the possession of the Way the bhikṣu has won a new *āśraya* contrary to the *kleśas* and to rebirth". That is to say: he has not won any actual Nirvāṇa, but only the condition and potentiality of utter cessation at death – this potentiality consisting in the *mārga*-body. Such a way of arguing (which may be an old piece of the Sautrāntikas' traditional Sūtra-interpretation) implicitly presupposes the opponent's assertion that the attainment of Nirvāṇa as concrete reality means winning a body conformable to it (analogous to the kāyasākṣin's body alluded to in the Bhāṣya *ad* VI, 43c-d). Why else should one expressly state that only the mārga-body can be won, there being no "real" Nirvāṇa (and consequently no Nirvāṇa-body)?

Another piece of evidence concerning this archaic notion is provided by Saṃghabhadra's polemics against the Dārṣṭāntikas[9]. According to the latters' teaching, the body produced by avidyā perishes in the attainment of arhatship, and a vidyā-body, constituted by the *bodhyaṅgas*, takes its place. This body is not *bhava* and transcends the trailokya.

[9] See La Vallee, *Mélanges Chinois et Bouddhiques*, I, 1931-32, pp. 120f. (Saṃghabhadra's Nyāyānusāra, p. 331, col. 2-3).

Can the Nirvāṇa-body be "extracted" from the arūpa(=manomaya)-body in the same way as the latter is "extracted" from the *rūpa-kāya* — in other terms: is it already somehow inherent in the contingent consciousness-body? A statement to this effect would contrast with the fundamental tenet of anātman, of the non-immanence of amṛta-reality in contingency. Still, the doctrine of the *prabhāsvara citta* (cf. AN. I, p. 10) — which seems to be a remnant from the archaic period and sounds almost heretical in view of the established dogma — in a way points to this issue. But only the Mahāsaṃghikas' version renders it decidedly heretical, by considering the *prabhāsvara citta* as *ādiśuddha*. As expounded in the AN., this doctrine does not necessarily imply the actual presence of the radiant Nirvāṇa-consciousness in the contingent defiled one, but implies only its potential inherence in the *sammā paṇihita citta* bent on the realization of Nirvāṇa. Likewise the manomaya-kāya, though inherent as nāmakāya in contingent personality, must be "produced" in dhyāna in order to step forth in its proper nature: it is coessential with the *sammā paṇihita citta*, with the consciousness reversed by dhyāna-attainment from its contingent "downward" direction (as *micchā paṇihita citta*) and bent on the upward course. This manomayakāya is doubtless the "body" with which the meditator experiences *sukha* in the first three dhyānas (explicitly mentioned in the formula relating to the third dhyāna). In the fourth dhyāna this *sukha* ceases along with all the other possible functions of manas: the manomayakāya is transcended. In this dhyāna, according to the primitive conception evidenced by the archaic account of the Buddha's passing away (above, p. 100) as well as by ancient texts relating to the typical career (cf. MN. I, p. 357; AN. IV,

p. 454), the transition to Nirvāṇa is realized. The manomayakāya is stripped off and, on crossing the threshold of nirodha, the *amata-kāya* is obtained. According to the dominant orthodox point of view there is no entity crossing this threshold; according to the point of view conveyed by the ancient gāthās, in that instant the dynamic viññāna "ceases" and is thereby transsubstantiated into the radiant amata-viññāna. Thus the manomayakāya, the personality consubstantial with the intermediary psychic (arūpa) sphere, is actualized at the outset of the dhyānic path by transcending the rūpakaya, and at the culminating point of this path, at the limit of contingent reality, it gives way to the transcendent kāya.

To these three kāyas there correspond three *cakkhus* (cf. Itiv. 61) by which they are respectively "seen". While the rūpa-personality is seen by the *maṃsacakkhu*, the *manomayakāya*, invisible to the latter, is perceived only by the *dibbacakkhu*, which is produced by dhyānic *iddhi*. (This is why the *divyacakṣus* is also able to perceive the *antarabhāva*, which is manomaya—see AK. III, 14ab and 40c-41a— ; it is evidently "produced" along with the manomayakāya. It is also called *dhammacakkhu*, the eye seeing the Doctrine[10]). Above the *dibbacakkhu* our Itivuttaka-text places the "highest" (*anuttara*) *paññacakkhu*: while the maṃsacakkhu is consubstantial with (the sphere of the Truth of) the Origin (of duḥkha) (i.e. with the contingent avijjā-taṅhā-sphere), the sphere of the *dibbacakkhu* is the Way; but when the *paññacakkhu* is obtained, all dukkhas are left behind—i.e.,

[10] The *dhammacakkhupatilābha* is closely connected with the *dhammābhisamaya* (SN. II, pp. 134, 138), as has been noted by GEIGER, *Pāli Dhamma*, p. 71f.

Nibbāna is reached. This "eye" conformable to the perception of Nirvāṇa is represented in dogmatics by *ajñātāvīndriya* (see AK. II, 4)[11], coincident with arhatship[12] and realizing the "fruition" of Nirvāṇa (II, 6).

The three stages of the upward Way to Nirvāṇa, originally identical with the Way to Enlightenment, were thus marked by the three kāyas and the three cakkhus, of which the first corresponded to the contingent nāmarūpa-sphere, the second corresponded to the intermediate sphere of sheer nāma and was an exponent of samādhi, the third corresponded to the transcendent amṛta-sphere and was an exponent of prajñā. These three stages of the ascension realized by means of the Dharma were also represented as three *dhammakkhandhas* (or *ariyakkhandhas*): *sīla, samādhi* and *paññā* (DN. I, p. 206ff.), by virtue of which the bhikkhu transcends the realm of Māra (Itiv. 59). This ancient arrangement of the *āryaskandhas* in a climax of three successive attainments appears to be a counterpart formulation of the ancient triadic climax representing the ārya's career: *śraddhānusārin, anāgāmin, arhat.* The *prajñā*-stage, like the *prajñā-cakṣus* and the *nirodhakāya,* is realized in the transcendent amṛta-sphere[13], while the stage of *samādhi* along with the *divyacakṣus* corresponds to the intermediate sphere where the upward way is effectuated by the anāgāmin, the srotaāpanna, by means of dhyāna, i.e. samādhi (the samādhi-

[11] *Loc. cit.*, vol. I, p. 109.

[12] *Ibid.*, p. 112.

[13] *Prajñākāya* seems to have been an older name of the transcendent Dharmakāya: cf. Aṣṭasāhasrikā Prajñāpāramitā, 94, 11. It is the prajñāskandha or vimuktikāya, see below, p. 126.

kkhandha consists in the four dhyānas, cf. DN. I, p. 207f.). *sīla* pertains to the nether nāmarūpa-sphere and is regularly considered as preparatory to *samādhi*. From the treatise expounding the subsequent stages of the bhikkhu's career, a text of frequent occurrence in the Nikāyas (especially in the DN.)[14], it clearly appears that śīla, consisting in preliminary discipline of body-and-mind, is the introductory stage, forming the basis whereon the dhyānic exercise is undertaken. We often meet with the statement (cf. DN. III, p. 227; SN. II, p. 68f.; V, p. 362f.; AN. III, p. 12; IV, p. 405) that the possession of all the sīlas is required for sotāpatti. This is a trace of the fact that originally srotaāpatti was the passage to the second stage, from the preliminary stage of śīla to the stage of dhyānic sublimation properly constituting the Way, whose actual condition however is the realization of samādhi in *pīti – pamujja – passaddhi* (cf. DN. I, p. 73). Buddhaghosa, who deals with a scheme of four phalas, is obliged to make of sīla the characteristic of the first two degrees, *sotāpattiphala* and *sakadāgāmiphala*, in plain disagreement with the Suttas, according to which these stages imply attainments much higher than that of sīla. The rest of his classification meets with no difficulty, being in agreement with the ancient scheme, where samādhi is the characteristic of the anāgāmī-stage and paññā that of arhatship.

When the third cosmic *dhātu* was added to the original two, an additional class of bodies was required to represent the form of existence in the new ārūpyadhātu: it was designed as *arūpi saññamayo atta-paṭilābho* and opposed to the first two, *oḷāriko atta-paṭilābho* and *manomayo atta-paṭilābho*. In consequence, the mano-

[14] See I, p. 61ff., etc.; also MN. I, p. 187.

mayakāya was now characterized as *rūpi,* not however in the sense of its being built up of gross elements—as opposed to the *audārika,* it is evidently *sūkṣma*—but in the sense of its pertinence to the *rūpa-loka.* Now *saṃjñā* is the name of the third skandha[15]. The comparison of the Poṭṭhapāda-Sutta (DN. I, p. 48-49) shows that the relation of this third body to the manomaya body was conceived as quite analogous to the relation between the latter and the oḷārika body; namely as inherence *in posse* and exclusion *in esse*[16]. The actualization of this third kāya takes place in the highest cosmic sphere. Thus we may observe in Buddhist thought the same typical correlation between inward progression and upward progression which we already observed in Upanishadic thought.

The *saṃjñā-kāya* is obtained by passing on from the rūpa-sphere to the ārūpya-sphere in the third *vimokṣa,* which in dogmatics is held to correspond to the fourth dhyāna. In the formula of this vimokṣa we meet again with the phrase *kāyena sākṣātkṛtvā.* As an explanation of this phrase the AKBh. remarks that these two vimokṣas (3 and 2) are "settled" on the end-planes of two dhātus[17]. This implies a definite statement of the notion that the passage from one dhātu to another imme-

[15] It may be noted by the way that at SN. III, p. 144 *attabhāvapaṭilābha* is obviously treated as a synonym of *khandha.*

[16] The Sutta insists on the notion that only one of the three atta-paṭilābhas can be actual at a time. They are like milk, curds and butter. *Vide* this current simile as applied in Śvet.U I, 16: butter is "contained" in milk, but becomes actual only by churning.

[17] AK. VIII, La Vallee, p. 210f.

diately superior coincides with the acquisition of another kāya. In fact the second vimokṣa is described as a condition in which the perception of rūpa is coupled with the absence of rūpa in the perceiver: this immaterial essence perceiving sensuous impressions is undoubtedly the essence of *vedanā* or sensation. The body of the second vimokṣa is the vedanākāya corresponding to the new *rūpadhātu;* it is identified with the manomayakāya of the old arūpadhātu (the sphere of the dhyānas), transformed, with the required modifications, into the new rūpadhatu, second of the four. The passage from the manomayakāya = vedanākāya to the saṃjñākāya is evidently conceived as an elimination even of the sensation-vestige of rūpa. The nirodha-body, as we have already seen, is attained by the kāyasakkhī in saññavedayitanirodha, that is to say in the eighth vimokṣa, by the elimination of saṃjñā also (or more exactly of that saṃjñā which is connected with the effects of sensations). The criterion which determines the conception of this final sublimation being the same as in the previous cases, it is clear that the relation between the third and the fourth kāya was conceived as analogous to that existing between each consecutive two of the three contingent kāyas. The nirodha-body, uppermost in actualization, is innermost in potentiality.

The experience "bodily witnessed" by the saṃjñākāya in the third vimokṣa is shortly featured as *subhaṃ ti.* This phrase can be explained by comparing the scheme of the vimokkhas with that of the *satipaṭṭhānas,* "stages of awareness", which begins with the contemplation of *asubha.* The aim of this initial contemplation on the body as "foul", guided by its juxtaposition with a corpse, is evidently to sever the attachment of the mind to the sensuous body, in which the contemplator still abides. Next comes in the series of satipaṭṭhānas the analysis of vedanā: its aim is evidently analogous, namely to sever off the next concentric skandha, the vedāna—which, after the severance of rūpa, is now the body of the contemplator. The following satipaṭṭhāna concerns citta: if this is to be referred analogically to the third skandha, we must conclude that in the conception underlying the vimokṣa-scheme citta is equated with saṃjñā and that on the third "stage of awareness" (*satipaṭṭhāna*) saññā, sati or citta is turned on itself. The "body" of the contemplator now consists of saṃjñā—and so does the analysing mind. The kāya of this stage coincides with the nāma[18]. The fourth satipaṭṭhāna concerns *dhammā*. Under this head are counted the heterogeneous items enumerated in the current dhamma-lists: the āvaraṇas, the skandhas, the āyatanas, the bodhyaṅgas and the Truths. But as classified with the fourth satipaṭṭhāna most of these items betray themselves as mechanical additions by the simple fact that they are implicit in the previous items. The category of the skandhas is quite obviously redundant in this context, as the entire scheme is based on a progressive contemplative elimination of the skandhas. The elimination of the āyatanas is implicit in that of vedanā, and logically already in the third satipaṭṭhāna the āyatanas are stripped off. The concentration is now so far progressed that the āvaraṇas are left far behind, and, besides, their absence is implicit in the realization of the *bojjhaṅgas*, which can be easily recognized as the abstracted elements of the four rūpadhyānas

[18] This feature, too, reveals its original identity with the dhyānic body which is mano-(citta-, viññana-)maya.

(the entrance into these dhyānas presupposes the abandonment of the āvaraṇas or nīvaraṇas, cf. the dhyāna-formula). The *dhammā* originally forming the object of the fourth satipaṭṭhāna are thus represented by the last two items, the bojjhaṅgas and the Truths, the latter being attained, according to the oldest records, upon the consummation of the dhyānas. In other words, these *dhammā* were originally only the pure or anāsrava-dharmas constituting prajñā, the essence of arhatship, and also the Buddha-body as contrasted with the skandhas (see below, p. 126f.). That this was the content of the fourth satipaṭṭhāna is a fact attested by the old record of the Sampasadanīya-Suttanta (DN. III, p. 104; here the satipaṭṭhānas are called *dassana-sampattis*), according to which the object of this realization is "man's consciousness as not established either in this world or in the higher world" (i.e. the consciousness of arhatship), in contrast with the third satipaṭṭhāna in which consciousness is considered as "established" in contingency (=the contingent *citta* of the third satipaṭṭhāna in the classical formulation). The first vimokkha quite clearly corresponds to the first satipaṭṭhāna: it is the contemplation of sensuous, bodily form by him who still abides in this first skandha. The second vimokkha, the stage of the vedanākāya, corresponds to the content of the second satipaṭṭhāna, namely vedanā (see above, p. 119). At the third vimokkha-stage, characterized by the exclamation "*subhaṃ ti*", the sphere of *asubha,* namely of the sensuous body and of the sensation arising from being in contact with it, is eliminated: this stage corresponds to the third satipaṭṭhāna, in which the person or body of the contemplator, as well as the subject contemplating it, is the citta-kāya or °-skandha. The fourth satipaṭṭhāna is originally a contemplative realization of the dharma- or prajñākāya; after the third item of the vimokkhas follow the four arūpadhyānas, and the last vimokkha is the nirodhasamāpatti of the kāyasākṣin, "bodily" realization of Nirvāṇa, i.e. of the transcendent dharma- or prajñākāya. Vimokkhas 1, 2, 3, 8 coincide with the four satipaṭṭhānas[19] in their primitive purport. The ārūpyas as vimokṣas 4-7 appear to have been inserted into a list to which they did not originally belong. The insertion, due to the secondary introduction of the ārūpyas into the schemes of the soteric path, is likely to have been simultaneous with the superimposition of the ārūpyas upon the dhyānas, and to have been a corollary of the fact that the correspondence between vimokṣas and dhyānas was, at the time, already established. But the form of this correspondence was partly divergent from that assumed in Canonical dogmatics, and much simpler: the third vimokkha corresponded to the third dhyāna; in fact the region of the *śubhas* is located on the plane of the third dhyāna. The fourth, and last, vimokkha was undoubtedly meant to correspond to the fourth dhyāna, its prajñā- or nirodhakāya being coalescent with the upekkhāsatipārisuddhi, the anāsava cetovimutti paññavimutti (cf. MN. I, pp. 357f.). Only the later view of the nirodhasamāpatti as of an attainment subsequent to, and dependent upon, the consummation of the arūpadhyānas may have justified the severance of this last item of the tetrad from the original sequence.

[19] Vasubandhu's notion that vimokṣas 3 and 8 are achieved at the end of two dhātus still contains a trace of the fact that they were originally two subsequent stages: vimokkhas 1, 2, 3 in fact visibly correspond to the three contingent dhātus (see above, p. 117f.).

The criterion of the early co-ordination of the four vimokkhas and of the four satipaṭṭhānas with the four dhyānas is fairly apparent: the progress of psychological elimination in the latter (cf. above, p. 104) was considered as an ideal pattern for the progressive elimination of the contingent skandhas by contemplative analysis. Thus the pre-Canonical scheme of the vimokkhas, as well as that of the satipaṭṭhānas, take us back to a period when three contingent skandhas or concentric bodies were assumed[20]: rūpakāya, vedanākāya and saṃjñākāya — as encompassing the prajñā- or dharmakāya.

We have already noted that the old tetrad of dhyānas is in itself not unconnected with the kāya-ideology. But in the classical description of the dhyānas only one kāya is mentioned, in the formula of the third dhyāna: this kāya experiences the most impalpable form of sukha, after vitakka, vicāra and pīti have quieted down (all that remains of the *savitakka savicāra pītisukha* of dhyāna I, and of the *avitakka avicāra pītisukha* of dhyāna II). As observed above, it is the same kāya throughout the three dhyānas[21], namely the manomaya-

[20] In fact we have seen (above, pp. 118ff.) that the idea underlying the scheme of the satipaṭṭhānas was that of a progressive elimination of three concentric layers of the personality (kāya [=rūpakāya], vedanākāya and citta- or saṃjñākāya), giving way to a fourth, obviously conceived as the innermost one (the dharma- or prajñākāya).

[21] An expanded description of the dhyānas (see DN. I, pp. 73ff., 214f.) mentions in addition to the formula of each stage the compenetration, amounting to a full consubstantiation, of "the body" with the relative mental state (respectively *vivekajena sukhena*, *samādhijena pītisukhena*, *nippītikena sukhena* and *parisuddhena cetasā pariyodātena*). In the case of the third dhyāna, the "body" being already

kāya, about which the other Sutta-texts record that it is

mentioned in the basic formula as the subject of the sukha-experience, the secondary character of the additional formula is particularly obvious.

This express differentiation of peculiar kāya-aspects as corresponding to the successive dhyānas is visibly the result of a later literary elaboration attempting to translate the tetradic construction of the dhyāna-process into a cosmologic scheme. The subdivision of the dhyānic sphere into four planes or strata requires, in the outlook of the period in question, a succession of four corresponding bodies. The attempt is however not carried through to the point of positing the successive dhyānic kāya-aspects as successive kāyas: the notion that throughout the dhyāna-process the kāya is *one* was obviously too strongly rooted in the tradition to admit of such innovations; so the reviser shields himself by reiterating *imam eva kāyam*. Moreover, the literary elaboration appears to have been carried out in two periods, as can be seen from the fact that, contrary to the standing custom of uniformity, the phrasing of the sentence appended to the formula of the fourth dhyāna differs from that of the preceding ones. The cause of this anomaly lies in the double genesis of the set of additional formulas: the first elaborator must have been still aware of the fact that the phrase *imam eva kāyam* could not apply to the fourth dhyāna, forming, in accordance with the original notion, the limit-point at which the nirodha-kāya succeeds to the samādhisukha-kāya. The phraseological nucleus of the first three additional formulas is drawn from the basic formulas to which they are appended. Not so that of the fourth. It is a matter of pure conjecture whether in the case of the fourth dhyāna the additional formula was originally omitted altogether or it contained a reference to the transcendent kāya. This much only is evident from the extant version: that for the purpose of supplementing the fourth additional formula the reviser has had recourse to a phraseological nucleus lying outside the range of the dhyānic formulas and belonging to the formulas of *iddhi* and *abhiññā*, usually fashioned or revealed by the iddhi attained in dhyāna[22]. In the consummation of the fourth dhyāna it gives way to the nirvāṇakāya.

The fundamental structure underlying the schemes of the satipaṭṭhānas and vimokkhas is thus the product of a period subsequent to that in which the dhyānic scheme was established in accordance with a primitive conception of two contingent kāyas, rūpakāya and manomayakāya (nāmakāya), encompassing the transcendent kāya as potentially inherent in the second of the two.

Was there an even earlier stage of the structure, comprising only three satipaṭṭhānas, in conformity with this primary scheme? (In later texts [cf. Abhisamayālaṃk. VIII, 5; AK. VII, 32d] the *threefold* smṛtyupasthāna is attributed to the Buddha only and interpreted as an independent set of attitudes). In the above mentioned text of the DN. the composition of the pre-existing triad can still be discerned. Here, in fact, the first two *dassana-sampattis* are represented respectively by the contemplation on the body as alive and as a corpse

consecutive to the central item of the dhyānas in the extensive descriptions of the holy career. Formally, the reason of the expedient is obvious: no such nucleus could be derived from the basic formula of the fourth dhyāna, the latter's psychic condition being, *par excellence*, devoid of any definable content.

[22] In the Aggañña-Suttanta the manomayakāyas of the primeval beings are characterized as *subhaṭṭhāyino* (DN. III, p. 84). *śubha* appears thus to have been originally a characteristic inherent to the manomayakāya, the matterless dhyānic body. Dogmatic cosmology reserves the *śubha*-characteristic to the saṃjñākāya, which represents the original dhyānic body in the tetradic dhātu-kāya scheme (cf. pp. 120 and 125).

—while in the classical scheme both these *satis*, along with other varieties of the contemplation on the body, belong to the first satipaṭṭhāna; vedanā is not yet introduced as intermediary item between kāya and citta, but the scheme is already planned as a tetrad, and an effort is made to fill it in with data belonging to the original triad: kāya(=rūpa), citta, vimukti.

The evolution of the kāya-series, and of the connected systems of yogic practices, from the triadic to the tetradic scheme was brought about by the extension of the dhātu-climax. This conclusion is verified by the fact that the newly introduced kāya was devised in conformity with the newly introduced dhātu. The nirodhakāya occupies its old position, and so does the sensuous body; the saṃjñākāya is the older citta- or manomayakāya, the consciousness-body mentioned in the formula of the third dhyāna, now appearing in the third satipaṭṭhāna and in the third vimokkha[23] (which however the final vimokkha-scheme equates with the fourth dhyāna, so as to leave room for the ārūpyas). It is the second body, the vedanākāya, that has been newly added, and whose hybrid nature, half-sensuous half-unsensuous, corresponds to that of the new, half-sensuous, *rūpadhātu*[24].

[23] The juxtaposition of the secondary tetrads of vimokkhas and satipaṭṭhānas with the original tetrad of the dhyānas did not bring in its wake any similar juxtaposition of the latter with the tetrad of the kāyas, owing to the preponderance of the kāya-dhātu connexion. In fact the definite location of the dhyāna-sphere within the dhātu-structure, remaining essentially unmodified even when this structure was enlarged, gave no scope for speculative elaborations in that direction.

[24] The essence of this dhātu is variously explained as containing only the subtler portion of the sense-activity (cf. above, p. 99). The mechanical device by which the specifi-

Along with this extension of the series of kāyas to a tetrad we may observe, in the early dogmatic systematization evidenced in the Nikāyas, the extension of the triadic climax *sīla-samādhi-paññā* to a tetradic one by the superaddition of a fourth item, *vimutti*. The method of this extension is the same that we have already observed in a former example of such proceedings: it is merely verbal and formal, *vimukti* being actually and essentially inherent in *prajñā*. Finally this climax of originally three items, which came to be interpreted as the series of *skandhas* constituting the personality of the arhat or of the Tathāgata, was amplified to a pentad by the superaddition of *vimuktijñānadarśana*. This second amplification is due to the tendency of opposing the personality of the holy man to the contingent personality, now conceived as consisting of five skandhas. The proceeding by which the third and final stage of the holy career was differentiated into three separate items can be easily detected by comparing the latter with the classical formula of deliverance recurrent in the Nikāyas: the *paññā* consisting in the realization of the Truths (being a result of the dhyānic ascension), immediately implies, rather than brings about, the *cittavimutti=paññavimutti*, stated in the *vimuttiññāna* (*tassa evaṃ janato evam passato......cittaṃ vimuccittha, vimuttasmin vimuttam iti*[25] *ñānam ahosi*). The pentadic

cation of the new body assigned to the rūpadhyānas was drawn from the connotations of the original dhyāna-body is quite transparent: its characteristic of vedanā is taken from the formula *sukhaṃ ca kāyena patisaṃvedeti;* but this unsensuous dhyānic vedanā is confounded with the ordinary vedanā arising from sense-impressions.

[25] The *iti* is a later insertion; see *Il Mito Psicologico*, p. 306, n. 1.

scheme formally disjoins three strictly connected items.

Originally prajñā was tantamount to vimukti or bodhi, and so to the transcendent buddha-personality; the above mentioned tendency, early manifesting itself, of opposing this personality to the contingent one, led to a subdivision of the former, i.e. of prajñā, into three items or elements of wisdom, *kṣayajñāna, anutpādajñāna* and *samyagdṛṣṭi* (also arranged in a sequence, see AK. VII, 4-5, and VI, 50), which could thus be contrasted with the three contingent skandhas. In fact, even in later dogmatics those three pure (anāsrava) dharmas are considered as constituting the dharmakāya of the Buddha (AK. IV, 32 and VII, 34). When the series of five pure skandhas was devised by an amplification of the three items constituting the Way, to be contrasted with the later series of five contingent skandhas, it was not simply substituted to the former triadic series of tathāgatadharmas, but formally connected with it: the entity of a Buddha is now said to consist of these three dharmas plus the five dharmas defined as their *parivāra*. But the elaboration of this new theory does not succeed in eliminating all the traces of the common nucleus from which both the triad and the pentad evolved: suffice it to point out that the identity of the *prajñāskandha* (contained in the second climax) and the *saṃyagdṛṣti* (contained in the first) is admitted by the AK. (*ad* II, 25)[26], which elsewhere (IV, 32) ranges both climaxes together.[27]

[26] La Vallee Poussin, II, p. 158f.; cf. also p. 159, n 1. This is in conformity with the old Sutta-view: sammādiṭṭhi = paññakkhandha MN. I, p. 301.

[27] There has been also a separate evolution of the three jñānas or tathāgataskandhas to the four jñānas currently

The concentric *kāyas* were ideologically correlated with the *dhātus*—and so were the skandhas. Dogmatic speculation tried to co-ordinate the five skandhas with the three cosmic dhātus (see AK. I, 22d; Vyākhyā, p. 52). The task was anything but easy and obvious, and could be tackled only by subdividing the dhātus. In its first three items the co-ordination of the dhātus with the skandhas is analogous to their co-ordination with the kāyas: rūpa corresponds to kāmadhātu, vedanā to rūpadhātu, saṃjñā to ārūpyadhātu; but the fourth storey of the ārūpyadhātu is reserved for the saṃskāraskandha, and vijñāna is assigned to the whole cosmic dhātu-system[28].

assumed in Mahāyānic Vijñānavada (see *Siddhi* and Bodhisattvabhūmi); the terminal point of this line of development is met with in the theory of the five Jīnas, who are conceived as the five bodies of the prajñākāya.

[28] Probably in consequence of such co-ordinations the skandhas came to be sometimes designated as *dhātus*, and thus directly identified with the cosmic layers. Cf. e.g. SN. III, p. 9. The viññāna bound to contingency by passion relative to the first four skandhas "inhabits" respectively the rūpadhātu, vedanādhātu, saññādhātū, saṅkhāradhātu. The viññāna freed by uprooting these passions is called "homeless" and is identified with the Tathāgata. (See *id.* Mahāniddesa, pp. 197f.). The spheres of contingency enumerated in this connexion are five, viññānadhātu appearing as the fifth. This very significant divergency in the construction of the second part of the passage must not be explained away as a lapsus of the compiler: indeed the Tathāgata-viññāna, the *viññānam anidassanam anantaṃ sabbato pabham* of DN. I, p. 23, is actualized, as the latter passage teaches, by *viññānassa nirodha;* the deliverance of the viññāna from the "dwellings" to which it is fettered is at the same time a total transfiguration of this vijñānaskandha into the transcendent vijñāna: henceforth it does not belong to the viññānadhātu any more than to the other four. (See above, pp. 68f.).

The co-ordination is evidently secondary in its present form, but its criterion rests on ancient notions (cf. above, p. 116f.). The correlation on the one hand of the kāyas and on the other of the skandhas with the dhātus sets off the homogeny of those two series, and suggests that the speculative origin of the skandhas, arranged into a climax in the order of decreasing coarseness (see AK. I, 22b), is to be looked for in the same ideologies which gave rise to the kāya-scheme. Further evidence points to this fact: according to the AK. (I, 20 ab), *skandha* is a synonym of *rāśi*.[29] Now Nāgārjuna[30] uses the term *rāśi* in the sense of *kāya* – and so does Cāraka in opposing this "conglomerate" to the cetanā = puruṣa counted as a sixth dhātu[31] – and so does the Gītā (XI, 17).

And the fact that the skandha-climax implies an inward-upward progression makes it appear more than probable that the background, if not the admitted basis, of the Buddhist skandha-doctrine was the ancient Indian theory of progressive derivation of contingency from the transcendent amṛta-sphere, the upward progression being understood in all Indian soteriologies as a "return". The term *vokāra*, currently used in the Abhidhamma as a designation of the skandhas[32], shows that down to a comparatively late date they were felt to be "diversified

[29] See also Vyākhyā, Bibl. Buddh. XXI, p. 44, l. 6ff. For the parallel datum in Pāli terminology cf. Atthasālinī, p. 141.

[30] Or the pseudo-Nāgārjuna quoted in the Nāmasaṃgītiṭīkā; cf. La Vallee Poussin, JRAS 1906/2, p. 954, n. 3.

[31] Cf. S. N. Dasgupta, *History of Indian Philosophy*, I, p. 214f.

[32] KV. III, 11; Vibh., p. 137; Vism., p. 572. Cf. PTS Dy., s. v. *vokāra*.

derivations" rather than outright different entities; and, significantly enough, the AK.-Vyākhyā and the Vibhāṣā[33] relate that *vyavakāra* was the term used by the ancient Tathāgatas.

The original two skandhas, rūpa and citta, appear to have been nothing else than the two contingent kāyas, rūpakāya and nāmakāya (=manomaya°, =citta°, =vijñānakāya), attested to in the archaic Pāli-doctrine. The series of the kāyas and of the skandhas underwent initially a common development: the dhātu-series having been increased by the expansion of the original *arūpa*, one aspect of the original nāma-kāya or citta-skandha was adapted to the new-fangled *rūpa-dhātu*. But the classical skandha-series arises out of a separate development. We may now venture a hypothesis as to the reason why the skandha-series was extended to five items, while the number of the contingent kāyas never went beyond the three, implicitly opposed to the fourth, transcendent, kāya—in other words, why the original relation of the skandha-system to the dhātu-system was given up, so that a new one had to be devised later on with a considerable amount of artifice. The reason of this diverging of the two series is to be found in the fact that the *skandhavāda*, doctrinally interpreted as a *skandhamātravāda*, became the basic argument for the anātman-dogma in its later canonic purport. The sense of the arrangement of the kāyas and of the ancient skandhas = *vyavakāras* was inseparable from the conception of the transcendent amṛta(=ātmā)-dhātu and °-kāya, from which they descend—not by essential derivation (as such a direct continuity seems not to have been admitted even by pre-Canonic Buddhism, which in its own way was also an

[33] La Vallee, AK. II, p. 207 n. 4.

anātmavāda), but by existential supervention (the idea of mutual exclusion and of the necessary alternative providing an effective link[34]) – and to which, when successively transcended, they finally give way (in the wording of the Udāna, when Tathatta = attā is realized there is neither this world nor yonder world nor the middle one). The Canonic anātmavāda on the contrary is bent on the construction of an autonomous scheme of contingency, quite independent from implications concerning transcendent reality. For this purpose a system based on the four-dhātu scheme was unsuited. But there was another scheme of dhātus, not directly connected with the conception of the amṛta-dhātu, on which the new skandha-system could be based: it was the ancient elementary system of five dhātus, with the upward sequence of which the inward sequence of the skandhas or concentric bodies could be placed in a parallel. Thus the skandhas were extended to five; by using an ancient method of computation, vijñāna as the "whole" of the psychic skandhas was added to their number; it was evidently meant, in accordance with the ancient conception, to correspond to ākāśa, the uppermost sphere of "totality". The blank left between this innermost vijñāna-body and the first two psychic skandhas, whose origin was a distinction of two aspects of psychic activity, sensation and consciousness – now counted apart from the whole –, was filled in by a further subdivision of psychic activity, namely by the insertion of the *saṃskāra*-skandha representing the psychic pre-conscious activity building up the organism by the force of karman, and represented in conscious life by impulse (*cetanā*). In the Abhidharma, the *caittas* being still far more

[34] See *Il Mito Psicologico*, pp. 322-327; cf. above, p. 62.

differentiated, the saṃskāraskandha is defined as containing all the caittas apart from vedanā and saṃjñā (AK. I, 20cd, cf. 15ab).

On the ground of this (purely schematic and speculative) co-ordination of the skandhas with the five elementary spheres we obtain a simple solution of the problem how the anomaly constituted by the Buddhistic ṣaḍdhātu-list, if compared with the contemporaneous 'Brāhmaṇical' doctrines, could have come about. When the notion of the consubstantiality of ākāśa and vijñāna (based on the ancient conception of the hṛdākāśa as co-extensive with universal space) was lost, the evidence was lacking for the correspondence between the centrifugal progression (implying evolution through progressive coarsening) of the skandhas from the innermost one, vijñāna, and the downward progression of the cosmic layers: therefore vijñāna was superadded as a topmost and subtlest layer.

It thus appears that the genesis of the Buddhist doctrine of the skandhas was up to a certain point analogous to that of the Upanishadic doctrine of the kośas. The kośa-climax was formed by the extension of the original three items to five – kośas 2-4 having been developed out of the qualities inherent to the rūpa-less brahman-body of the ancient Upanishads –, and was only indirectly and not very successfully brought together with the element-series; whereas the development of the skandha-series, at first proceeding along similar lines, finally deviated owing to a change of outlook and produced the canonic pentad through a co-ordination with the ancient elementary series.

In fact the four Upanishadic kośas contain the ātman and unveil him or give way to him when gradually stripped off or transcended in the process of yogic superlation; whereas the five Buddhistic skandhas, when gradually stripped off or transcended in the process of dhyānic superlation, do not unveil anything at all[35], and only give way to utter nirodha, thus betraying the *nairātmya* of the apparent personality. This view however was not even at the Canonic age shared by all the schools: some Pudgalavādins seem to have maintained —according to the Mādhyamikaśāstra polemizing against them[36]—that "the *pudgala* is *arūpin*, and consists in the fifth, inexpressible (*avācya*) *kośa*", i.e. evidently in the fifth skandha, vijñāna. But in what sense can the latter be considered as inexpressible? A comparison with Upanishadic ideologies, whose affinity with the last mentioned doctrines is sufficiently obvious, may help us on in the interpretation of the passage: the vijñānamaya śarīra is the rūpa-less body of the contingent, "uttered" and utterable brahman. But through the inversion of its activity and the "cessation" ensuing thereon it is turned into the infinite luminous consciousness, the unuttered and unutterable brahman, the personality of the ānandamaya ātman. This potential presence of the highest brahman in its lower forms is what is meant by its "concealment" in, and revelation out of, the latter (cf. the simile of milk, curds and butter Śvet.U I, 15-16: *v. supra*, p. 117, n.16). In this sense the BĀU says that the unborn ātman lies within the vijñānamaya, the antarhṛdaya ākāśa. In this same sense the Pudgala-

[35] The notion of the dhyānic path of deliverance from contingent existence is preserved in canonical dogmatics, while that of the potential amṛta-nucleus is suppressed.

[36] X, 16, comy., see WALLESER, *Mittlere Lehre Chinesisch*, p. 72. Cf. Taishō, 1564, p. 15c2, where the equivalent of *ātman* is used.

vādins appear to have maintained that the *pudgala* consists in the fifth kośa which has become unspeakable, i.e. in the vijñāna's translation into the unutterable radiant vijñāna. As I have tried to show elsewhere, the heterodox current of the *pudgalavāda* represented the first reaction of the yogic awareness of continuity between the opposite planes of Saṃsāra and Nirvāṇa, as against the unconditional dogmatization of the exclusivistic tenet from the standpoint of contingency, which became the leading feature of orthodox Hīnayāna. From this point of view the Pudgalavādins were the pioneers of the Mahāyānic revival of the yoga-current in Buddhism: their undefinable *pudgala*, common to both modes of existence, Saṃsāra and Nirvāṇa, and yet not to be grasped as such on either plane, is a timid precursor of the Vijñānavādins' *ālayavijñāna*: his existence is inferred from the act of the yogic reversal from Saṃsāra towards Nirvāṇa, as in Upanishadic thought the potential presence of ātman was inferred from the inversion of the function of Indha, turning away from his contingent activity as prāṇa-vaiśvānara, builder of the mortal body, to his soteric "upward" activity as builder of the yogic fire-body leading to the ex-spiration (*nirvāṇa*) of brahman. He thus connects in his contrary dynamic aspects the opposite planes of existence. We know from Vasumitra's treatise that the ancient Sautrāntikas, also in several aspects forerunners of Mahāyāna-views, postulated an *ekarasaskandha*[37], a "subtle consciousness"[38], as root-essence of the contingent skandhas. Dr. MASUDA was right in concluding that this "subtle consciousness" is the same as the *mūlavijñāna* of the Mahā-

[37] *Loc. cit.*, XII, 3 (Chin. vers.).
[38] *Shu-Chi*, quoted by MASUDA, *loc. cit.*, p. 68, n. 1.

saṃghikas, the precursor of the Vijñānavādins' *ālaya-vijñāna*. Why was it called *ekarasa*? I have tried to ascertain the specific sense of the term by a comparison of passages where it occurs in ancient speculation. According to the parable of ChU VI, reality is *ekarasa* because of the invisible presence of *satya*, of the potential *ātman*; according to the NṛsiṃhottaratāpinyU the turīya is *ekarasa*, because the nāmarūpa reality is due to his first three aspects — as *ota*, *anujñātar* and *anujñā* — , whereas in virtue of his supreme indifference-aspect (*avikalpa*) the universe becomes avikalpa. *ekarasa* is thus the hidden link between the two opposite planes of existence, the potential immanence of salvation within Saṃsāra. And the same appears to be the purport of the term in Buddhist thought. According to the simile of Udāna V, 5 *ekarasa* is the character of the Buddha's teaching (leading from Saṃsāra to Nirvāṇa, and thus representing the potentiality of Nirvāṇa within Saṃsāra); according to the Mahāyānasūtrālaṃkāra (II, 3) it characterizes the Bodhisattva, who is active within Saṃsāra for the sake of Nirvāṇa, thus connecting in himself the "taste" of both the opposite planes. According to Nāgarjunā's Nirupamastava the Buddha knows the *aikarasya* of *saṃkleśa* and *vyavadāna*; and from his Cittavajrastava it appears that this *aikarasya*, this double potentiality, is the inherent quality of the citta.[39] In this sense the ālaya-vijñāna of the Yogācāra doctrine is an ekarasaskandha,

[39] See *Il Mito Psicologico*, pp. 350ff., 384f. According to the Mahāyānasaṃgraha comy. *ad* I, 10 (LAMOTTE, *Somme*, p. 25) the Tathatā (in which Saṃsāra=Nirvāṇa) is *ekarasa*, as it is constituted by the character common to all the dharmas (the latter being alternatively saṃskṛta and asaṃskṛta, or āsravadharmas and anāsravadharmas).

being capable of issuing in the two mutually exclusive aspects of reality, Error or Saṃsāra (as the *bīja* of differentiation [above, p. 75] and of the kleśas) and Illumination or Nirvāṇa (as the *Tathāgatagarbha*)[40]. The ancient Sautrāntikas also asserted the existence of *paramārthapudgalas*, and we may accept Dr. MASUDA's convincing supposition that the paramārthapudgala is the same as the "subtle consciousness", the ekarasaskandha. Finally, the fourth tenet of these Sautrāntikas : "a *pṛthagjana* also possesses the potentiality of becoming a Buddha", has to be considered in direct connection with the two points concerning the ekarasaskandha and the paramārthapudgala, between which it is inserted : the *āryadharma*, the potential Buddhahood dormant within the pṛthagjana, is nothing else than the ekarasaskandha, the subtle vijñāna liable to be transformed into the transcendent radiant universal vijñāna, into the *sarvajñatva* which is the essence of Bodhi.—The ālaya, anticipated in the Pudgalavādin's notion of the fifth and innermost kośa, was already conceived by the Mahīśāsakas[41] as the *saṃsārakoṭiniṣṭhaskandha*, uppermost (in space and time) on the ladder of Saṃsāra.

These few records and their implications point to the fact that in ancient Buddhism the *skandhavāda* was not always tantamount to the *skandhamātravāda* of the orthodox Hīnayānic position[42]; the contrary sectarian

[40] Cf. Triṃś.bh., p. 44; L-S, pp. 221ff., 62.

[41] According to Hiuan-Tsang, *Siddhi*, p. 180.

[42] Two years after the completion of the above study of the origin and development of the skandha-doctrine (of which an abridged version has been read at the 10th All-India Oriental Conference) I came across Mrs. C. A. F. RHYS DAVIDS' interesting article on the skandha-problem (*Towards*

opinions are consonant with the primitive import of the skandha-doctrine which appears in the ancient conception of the concentric bodies related to the successive cosmic layers and potentially containing as their innermost centre the body of transcendent infinite consciousness arising from the nirodha of nāma and rūpa. Such traces of the primitive skandha-ideology, along with the evidence of its survival, seem rather to foreshadow the Yogācāra theory of the potential immanence of Nirvāṇa in Saṃsāra — which will also have its counterpart in a *trikāya*-doctrine.

A History Of The Khandha-Doctrine, in Indian Culture, 1937, pp. 405-11, 653-62). The Author is mainly concerned with showing that the skandhas, as contrasting with the notion of "self", were introduced by the later exegesis, re-interpreting the teaching in a sense running counter to the Founder's intentions; hence she bases her argumentation on a series of old Nikāya-texts from whose narratives the references to the khandhas can be expunged without damage to the whole, and may thus be considered later insertions. The Author has noted the fact that "the newer five have been inserted into the older two" (p. 410), but does not raise the question whether the two had developed into the five. In fact, the assumption that in the older twofold division viññāna was originaly meant to be the "man" or "self", and that, on the other hand, the skandha-teaching was always bent on denying the "self", precludes any hypothesis of a genetic connection. The pattern of the "five" (it is taken for granted that the skandhas were always "five, no more, no less") is tentatively pointed out in the five senses.

The valuable statistics of the references to the five khandhas in the earlier Collections afford a gratifying corroboration of the conclusion I have the honour to share with Mrs. RHYS DAVIDS, namely that the doctrine of this pentad as constituting man can by no means be claimed to belong to the earliest strata of the Buddhist teaching.

IX

It is interesting to note that, in order to defeat the irrational position of the Pudgalavāda, the orthodox Skandhamātratāvādin of the KV. makes use of the same analytical proceeding as is employed in the Nikāyas to show the utter lack of any connection between the Tathāgata and the mundane nāmarūpa reality (e.g. SN. III, p. 109). But his conclusion is different: if the "inexpressible" pudgala cannot be grasped by any definition bearing upon the skandhas, it is because he does not exist at all, because he is a mere verbal assumption. Later exegesis interprets in this sense also the Sutta-passages relevant to the Tathāgata, taking "*Tathāgata*" to be an equivalent of *satta,* a term rendering the conventional concept of a personal unit. This peculiar interpretation is obviously an expedient, rendered necessary by the one-sided rationalization of Hīnayānic exclusivism from the point of view of contingency. It is clear that for the exclusivistic speculation based on the fundamental religious experience of Buddhism the Tathāgata in his proper reality of Nirvāṇa was not "a hare's horn", though his entity, being in no relation whatsoever with the anātman-reality of this world (cf. also SN. III, p. 117), was considered absolutely indefinable. But it is no less clear that for this religious speculation the reality of the Tathāgata could not be completely excluded from mundane existence;

although "in this life he cannot be grasped in his truth and reality", being utterly incommensurate with the skandhas constituting the mortal person of Gotama, still the very sense and possibility of Buddhist soteriology was based on his presence within contingency as teacher of the Dhamma and founder of the Way. This presence of the Tathāgata *quā* Dhamma is asserted in the Sutta-passages about *dhammakāya* as real immanent nature of the Tathāgata[1] in which his Wayfaring disciples partake as "born" and "fashioned" of it, as true sons and heirs not of his mortal food-body, but of his Doctrine-body[2]. The thesis opposing the fallacious *rūpakāya* and the true *dharmakāya* of the Leaders, as set forth in the famous Prajñāpāramitā-stanza and endorsed by Nāgārjuna, is but a consequential ontological formulation of this standpoint. This Dharmakāya of the Buddhas as L e a d e r s , as active within contingency, is by no means the transcendent static Dharmakāya of the later trikāya-doctrine. Neither is it meant to be identical with the transcendent reality, dharmatā, which in the last line of the stanza is said to be absolutely unknowable and inconceivable, whereas the preceding line emphatically asserts that "the Buddhas ought to be conceived *quā* Dharma, for the Leaders are dharmakāyas". This dharmakāya, which, according to the Mahāprajñāpāramitāśāstra, "is possessed of an immeasurable and limitless upright figure, of infinite brightness and infinite voice", is directly reminiscent of the unsensuous cosmic aspect of the Upanishadic Teacher and saviour : of the soteric Skambha as cosmic embodiment of the higher brahman, the enlightening

[1] *E.g.* DN. III, p. 84.
[2] *Ibid.*, and MN. III, p. 29; SN. II, p 221.

Doctrine. Prof. De La Vallee Poussin is therefore right in stating that this *dharmakāya* stands for the same thing as the *sambhogakāya* of the *Siddhi*[3]. But if considered in their ideological contexts, the two are not equivalent. There is an essential difference between the underlying conceptions. The absolute exclusivism of the Prajñāpāramitā, and of Nāgārjuna's doctrine, does not imply, does not even admit of, any direct relation of continuity between this dharmakāya and the transcendent *dharmatā*[4]: with the Mādhyamikas the teaching does not by any means originate from the dharmatā – or the Buddha *quā* Bodhi – who is eternally silent (see above, p. 72f. and n. 10); people perceive the immanent Mahāpuruṣa-image and hear the sounds of the Doctrine according to the quality of their aspirations. The preaching is a manifestation of the *svamanojalpa* (Dharmasaṃgītisūtra[5]). This means, in other words, that the immanent Doctrine-body is nothing else but the *citta* itself in the process of its purification (a tenet like-

[3] *Siddhi, App.*, p. 777.

[4] The views of the Prajñāpāramitāśāstra on the dharmadhātujakāya, partly contradictory in their successive formulations, seem to diverge from this classical standpoint and to incline towards the Yogācāra conception.

[5] Quoted in the Śikṣāsamuccaya; see La Vallee, *Siddhi, App.*, p. 797f.

The Yogācāra version of this notion differs significantly: the manifestations of the Buddhas in conformity with the aspirations of the beings have their source in a quality inherent to the nature of the former (*yathādhimuktiprakāśaguṇaḥ, yathādhimuktisambhinnabuddhakṣetrapradarśanaguṇaḥ*, M.-Saṃgr. II, 3, 14 and 17: Lamotte, *Somme*, p. 136). Ultimately however the difference resides only in the doctrinal formulation; in fact, from the fundamental cittamātravāda

wise propounded in the Cittavajrastava[6]). It is only *saṃvṛti* and has no causal or genetic connection with the *paramārtha*. There is therefore no ground for conceiving the latter as a *kāya*[7]. With the Yogācāras on the contrary the transcendent essence of Bodhi, the ultimate aim of the Teaching realized as the Way, is again held to be its source and archetype[8]; here again the yogic awareness of the irrational connection between the opposite planes of reality as experience fully asserts itself in the theoretical construction. This monistic construction again supplies a ground for the representation of Dharmatā = Bodhi = Nirvāṇa as a *kāya*, which had been anti-

standpoint of this school the Buddha-manifestations cannot be understood to be "external".

[6] St. 1. Cf. st. 2, 6. See *Il Mito Psicologico*, p. 387.

I may additionally refer to similar views expressed in the Samādhirājasūtra, three chapters of which have been published since the completion of the present study in the excellent ed. of Dr. K. REGAMEY (Warsaw 1938). See XXII, 7: *dharmakāyaprabhāvitāś ca buddhā bhagavanto na rūpakāyaprabhāvitāḥ*; 9: *tathāgatakāyaḥ śatapuṇyanirjātayā buddhyā ekārthanirdeśo animittaḥ* (= *arūpaḥ*, cf. the terminology of the L-S)...*adṛśyaś cakṣurpathasamatikrānto dharmakāyaḥ prajñātavyaḥ*. In view of the above remarks it is clear that I cannot agree with Dr. REGAMEY's identification of this *dharmakāya* with the "Absolute" (Introd., p. 23).

[7] It can be reached only by total elimination of any dynamic experience, by not experiencing any *vikalpa*; the Teaching, being constituted by *vikalpas*, is only *saṃvṛti* and as such incommensurable with Reality. But this stern exclusivistic position (represented by the kārikās), which consequentially does not admit of any Tathāgata-conception, is only one side of the Mādhyamika movement, its theory; the other side of it is yoga-practice, which gives rise to ideologies closely related to the cittamātravāda. See *Il Mito Psicologico*, p. 384ff.

[8] See above, p. 74.

cipated in the proto-Canonic conception of the Buddha's amṛtakāya attained by the arhat in nirodha. On the other hand the Dharmatā, identical with the Dharmakāya of all the Buddhas, is considered as ultimate source from which nāmarūpa existence has derived through differentiation or saṃkleśa and to which it returns through indifferentiation, unification or vyavadāna. The Yogācāra conception of the Buddhakāyas thus extends the purport of this notion from its primitive doctrinal range, confined to soteriological problems, to the field of ontology. This new approach, by increasing the evidence of the connexion between the old Buddhological dyad and the primitive climax of three types of kāyas as representing the three modes of existence, favours a structural assimilation in the wake of syncretistic developments turning the former into a triad. The basic triadism of Yogācāra Buddhology is structurally modelled on the nāma-rūpa scheme: but the additional component owes its structural position in the triad to an adjustment of its intrinsical value. The original Nirmāṇakāya was not simply a "docetic" replica of the human personality of the Buddha, of the *caturmahābhūtikakāya* of the Pāli Scriptures, the *rūpakāya* of the Prajñāpāramitā stanza. It did not actually belong to the sensuous plane. The tenet of the Lokottaravādins that the Buddhas have only manomaya bodies[9] (*rūpa*[10]) was no

[9] That is why in being born they do not injure their mothers (Mahāvastu, ed. SENART, I, p. 218; Lalita-Vistara, p. 67: a popular biological application of the doctrinal tenet). They are *aupapāduka* beings (Mahāv. I, p. 145).

[10] Mahāvastu II, 20, 16. *rūpa* used in this sense is evidently synonymous with *kāya*. On the other hand, *kāya* in the strict sense of "physical frame" is a synonym of *rūpa* as used in the compound *nāma-rūpa*, sometimes also styled *nāma-kāya* (e.g.

innovation; it was in conformity with the ancient conception of the Buddha as dhammakāya. (Only against the background of the later dogmatic developments of the Buddhological problem does it stand out as heterodox. Such conservative "heretics" also opposed the restriction of the scope of the doctrine and of the career to mere nirodha and lowered the dignity of this Canonical ideal of arhatship[11], thus in a sense anticipating the Mahāyānist profession of a "higher" aim and a "higher" way).

It is quite self-evident that the logical systematization of the ancient doctrine, as dominant in the Suttas, could not, as in fact it did not, admit the existence of different Buddha-bodies, but of one only, namely of the *dhammakāya*. We have seen above that the conception of this body, though it did not fit in with the theoretical view of the Tathāgata's absolute transcendence (excluding his connection with any skandhas, even with the soteric dharmaskandhas), could nevertheless not be

Sutta-Nipāta 1073). *rūpa* in the latter sense consists of the four gross elements (see SN. II, p. 3, MN. I, p. 53). But in the contexts dealing with the conception of a supersensuous rūpa, no more distinguishable from nāma and analogous to the *amūrta*, *aśarīra* rūpa of the Upanishads, the term rūpa obviously conveys the wider notion of a "body", regardless of its substance, which is specified by the adjective or the first part of the compound term. Thus the conception of an ārūpya rūpa is not self-contradictory, but if referred to the conception of nāma-rūpa it implies the passage to a higher, less differentiated plane, where only the differentiation of nāma (consciousness-personality) subsists. Therefore no different "places" are assigned to the ārūpya-spheres, though they represent different stages of consciousness, as *place* is concomitant with sensuous shape.

[11] See *Il Mito Psicologico*, pp. 360-364.

dispensed with, as it accounted for the Buddha's mystic presence in the cosmos implied by the fundamental datum of the Teaching. This Doctrine-body is manomaya, as it consists solely of elements of the nāma-sphere, and can therefore be perceived only by the *dibba-cakkhu*, which is a privilege of the confirmed disciples, the srotaāpannas[12], of those who have entered upon the Way: they perceive it, for they are coessential with it. Thus however the fact of the Master having been perceived as a nāmarūpa personality by the yet un-"converted" disciples was not accounted for. The problem does not concern Gotama's human personality. The survival of the individual Gotama as such after the cessation of upādāna on the night of the bodhi is irrelevant for the original position of Buddhistic thought (though it will become a problem in dogmatics); in any case this individual has nothing in common with the Tathāgata, as we see from the dialogues concerning the question of the Tathāgata's post-mortal condition (SN. III, p. 109, DN. II, p. 68); whereas the same cannot be said of the *dhammakāya*. But how was the fact to be explained that with regard to the yet un-converted that individual assumed the function of the dhammakāya? That the problem did arise and its solution was at least attempted is evidenced by the famous passage of the Mahāparinibbāna-Suttanta describing the Buddha's appearance in the assemblies of the different sets of beings, every time in a shape corresponding to theirs. This amounts to an explanation of the sensuous personality of the Teacher as an illusory reflection of the dhammakāya, not unsubstantial, but drawing its sensuous consistency from the differentiated perceptions of the audience. It di-

[12] The sotāpanna is *dhammadasa*, Vimānavatthu 16, 11.

stinctly foreshadows the conception of nirmāṇakāyas[13]. A nirmāṇakāya is thus at the outset conceived as a rūpa-like reflection of the dharmakāya, consisting of pure nāma, in the minds of beings abiding on the nāmarūpa plane; not as an independent body, nor even as separate from the dharmakāya — for, as the Sutta-passage significantly implies, the listeners, though perceiving it, do not recognize the Buddha: in fact, it is possible to "know" the Master only in his proper form of dharmakāya. This original Nirmāṇakāya is thus by no means co-ordinated with nāmarūpa reality: like the Buddha-body of the Lokottaravādins it is, in itself, manomaya, and is perceived in its real nature as soon as the Way is entered upon.

The Mahāyāna records, so far as they are not concerned with constructive issues, show a quite analogous conception of the Nirmāṇakāyas' relation to their noumenic originals, the Sambhogakāyas: their nature, the essence of their function, belongs to the latter[14], the form of their appearance to the yet mundane perception of the vaineyas, whose eventual sublimation to supersensuous vision reveals beyond the fictitious shape the real, purely psychic (manomaya) nature of the Doctrine-body, the Sambhogakāya. The difference between the Doctrine-body of the old Sutta-records and that of Mahāyāna resides only in the dogmatic divergency of the ideals of emancipation set forth by the two Canons: while the former shows the way to Nirvāṇa, the latter shows the way to

[13] As distinctly as does the tenet of *lokānuvartana* formulated in the Mahāvastu.

[14] See e.g. the notion of the *nirmitabuddhas* as propounded in the L-S: the Tathāgata does not consist in them, but he is not apart from them either (p. 242. Cf. n.$_{18}$).

Sambodhi. Structurally, their functions are parallel and co-ordinate in a common sphere of existence; being exponents of the Way, they both belong to the intermediate sphere. But the attempt at synthetizing the two *yānas* in the 'greater' career, as first carried out in the doctrine of the Saddharma-Puṇḍarīka (that it was novel at the time can be gathered from the emphatic assertion, repeated over and over again in this text, that there is in truth only o n e *yāna*[15], namely the way to Buddhahood) and then put into a system by Asaṅga and Vasubandhu, brings about the structural collocation of the Mahāyānic Doctrine-body above the Hīnayānic one: the perfection of the Śrāvaka-career, achieved on the level of the inferior āśrayaparāvṛtti, is only the starting-point of the second and higher part of the Way[16], leading to the superior āśrayaparāvṛtti or bodhi. As a consequence of this arrangement, the Hīnayānic Doctrine-body — the Buddha of the Śrāvakas, now degraded to the rank of a mere Nirmāṇakāya[17] — is displaced from its natural position to the nether sphere of nāmarūpa.[18]

[15] See e.g. pp. 40, 41-43, 69, 186. Cf. also L-S, p. 204, st. 117.

[16] If the process is stopped at this point, only *pratisaṃkhyānirodha* ensues but no *sarvajñatā* (cf. *Siddhi*, p. 662).

On the two āśrayaparāvṛttis in relation to the two careers, Triṃś. 29-30 and bh , see below, n.72.

[17] According to the L-S, the Buddha preaching the Hīnayāna-doctrine is the *nirmitanirmāṇabuddha* (p. 56).

[18] The trikāya climax, thus evolved in accordance with the triadic ascensional scheme of the *nāma-rūpa* system, also maintains the other aspect of this scheme, namely the inward progression: the MSA. (IX, 62a) intimates that the Svabhāvikakāya is inherent in (or encompassed by, *tacchliṣṭa*, cf. SYLVAIN LEVI'S restitution of the correct reading in vol. II, p. 86n.) the Sāmbhogya, and from the bh. to 63 it appears

This constructive expedient derives its plausibility from the trend of the intervening developments in Hīnayāna dogmatics. From the point of view of the structural ideology whose agency we have seen reflected in a variety of theories, it is clear that the sphere in which a doctrine is delivered must correspond to the sense or "level" of its teaching. The doctrine of *cittamātratā*, delivered by the Sambhogakāyas to assemblies of Bodhisattvas, structurally implies the elevation of the level of reality to the sphere of pure citta, i.e. to the ancient arūpa-sphere, styled *rūpaloka* in the tetradic classifica-

that the Nairmāṇika in its turn is only an extraversion of the Sāmbhogya, the character of the former being *parārthasampatti* as opposed to the *svārthasampatti*, the character of the latter.

This classification is strikingly analogous to the division of the Sambhogakāya into Svasambhogakāya and Parasambhogakāya, and might well be its source. The Svasambhogakāya would then be originally the Sambhogakāya itself, the Doctrine-body of the Boddisattvayāna, "fulfilling its own aim", namely sambodhi, whereas the Parasambhogakāya would be originally the Doctrine-body of the Śrāvakayāna, fulfilling "the foreign aim", mere nirvāṇa. Such a classification is in agreement with the definition of the Sambhogakāya (first parāvṛtti) as *twofold vṛtti* in the bh. to st. 14 (*abhisambodhiparinirvāṇadarśanavṛttyā dvayā vṛttiḥ*).

But as the classification under *sva°* and *para°* was shifted to the plane of the Mahāyānic Sambhogakāya alone, its original sense was naturally no more applicable and a new interpretation was needed. The sense of *para°* was now referred to the Bodhisattvas and that of *sva°* to the Buddha himself, in utter disagreement with the sense of *sambhoga*, which implies "common fruition of" (or "common participation in") the Doctrine and can be logically referred only to the recipients of the revelation of Dharma (and such was the case since the Pāli notion of *dhammasambhoga*) as united (through its mystic

tion. As already stated above, the archaic Buddhist doctrine (discernible in the oldest strata of the Nikāyas) stands out, in the purely psychological setting of its problems and purport of its aims, and in the psychical nature of its operative factors, as a cittamātratāvāda *avant la lettre;* it even explicitly professes this standpoint (e.g. in Dhammapada 1). Naturally, therefore, the sphere of its enunciation, and of its actualization (taking place, as must be remembered, in dhyāna), was understood to be that of *nāma = dharma* or *citta*. But at the time of the Mahāyānist criticism the Hīnayāna doctrine had turned to the pluralistic theory of *dharmas* such as we know it from the systematical writings, a theory evolved on the ground of realistic ontology, and far more alienated from the primitive attitude than the Mahāyānic constructions, whose source was a return to yoga. It is therefore by no means surprising that in their new classification of the teaching the Mahāyānist systematizers placed the Śrāvaka doctrine, with the Nirmāṇakāya preaching it[19], on the lower contingent

fruition) with its immanent source – but not to the transcendent undifferentiated Dharma.

The inference that the Svasambhogakāya is in the original sense of the relevant conception the Body of the Mahāyānic Teaching is corroborated by the evidence that even in Hiuan-Tsang's description (*Siddhi*, p. 705) it is still characterized by the thirty-two lakṣaṇas and the eighty vyañjanas, which, according to the description of the Abhisamayālaṃkāra (VIII, 12 – agreeing with the ancient notion of the embodiment of the Doctrine in the Mahāpuruṣa) characterize the *sāmbhogika kāya*, the Body of *mahāyānopabhoga*.

[19] The peculiar term *nirvāṇakāya*, used instead of *nirmāṇakāya* by Fa-t'ien (CHAVANNES, *Les inscriptions chinoises de Bodh-Gāyā*, RHR 1896, p. 20, Skt. rest. by SYLVAIN LEVI), is likely to have its origin in this speculative identification of

level of nāmarūpa, and figured the passage from the Śrāvaka-truth to the Bodhisattva-truth by an elevation of the assembly from the earthly level to the height of the heavenly Gṛdhrakūta (which seems to symbolize the Akaniṣṭha, the unity-plane of the Sambhogakāyas, the summit of 'rūpaloka'). From the doctrinal point of view this transition is stressed by the solemn assertion that the doctrine taught so far "has not been mendacious, for the Buddhas know the nature of the three dhātus[20]".

The surprising thing is rather that they did not avail themselves of the technical possibility offered by the tetradic dhātu-system, counting *two* intermediate spheres, for the location of the two doctrines and of the corresponding Buddha-bodies (which could have prevented the confusion, otherwise inevitable, between the nirmāṇakāya and the *caturmahābhūtikayāya*). This secondary system must therefore have had, at the time of the Saddharma-Puṇḍarīka, but little authority in Mahāyāna circles. Only an isolated and late evidence of its having directly effected the construction of a tetradic Buddha-climax can be gleaned from Yun-chou's inscription, actually distinguishing the Buddha's human personality from the Nirmāṇakāya[21], and thus extolling four Buddha-bodies.

The classical types of the tetradic Buddhology, elaborated in the Asaṅga-school, seem to have been produced in deference to formal, rather than ideological, postulates. Their very divergency makes it evident that they represent alternative solutions of the task of adapting the earlier triad to a later tetradic plan. One of these

the Buddha preaching the goal of Nirvāṇa to the Śrāvakas with the Mahāyānic Nirmāṇakāya.

20 S-P, p. 311ff. Cf. pp. 139-140.

21 See CHAVANNES, *loc. cit.*, p. 10f.

solutions is obtained by once more applying, in a new sense, and now to the Sambhogakāya alone, the earlier distinction of the two kinds of activity of the Doctrine-Body, that for the *s v a-artha* (Sambodhi) and that for the *p a r a-artha* (Nirvāṇa), already inherent in the ideological distinction of the two Doctrine-Bodies in the *trikāya*-ideology; it results in the series Svabhāvikakāya =Dharmakāya, Svasambhogakāya, Parasambhogakāya, Nirmāṇakāya, compendiously explained by Hiuan-Tsang (*Siddhi*, pp. 104ff.)—but without throwing any satisfactory light on the meaning of *svasambhoga* (cf. above, n. 18, *ad finem.*). The other solution, adopted in the Abhisamayālaṃkāra (Ch. VIII), is effected by a subdivision not of the Sambhogakāya but of the Svabhāvikakāya, the criterion being the analysis of the doctrinal notion that this Body is, on the one hand, eternally *pre-existent* in its transcendent purity, and, on the other, *attained* through the complex of the factors of purification and enlightenment. In the former aspect it is called Svabhāvikakāya, in the latter, Dharmakāya.

In the context dominated by the *cittamātratā* standpoint the constructional co-ordination of the Nirmāṇakāya with the nāmarūpa plane did not essentially modify or obliterate its original character. In its new position it definitely preserves the stamp of subjective experience; its specific nature is always considered as only provisional, conditioned by the immaturity of the vaineyas—hence in a character analogous to that of its Hīnayānic precursor, conceived, not as a variety of objective individual phantoms of the preaching Buddha, but as the various objectifications of the Preaching itself—of the Dhammakāya—in the individually perceiving minds of the yet immature beings.

From this point of view the Body adorned with the

32 lakṣaṇas seems to have been evaluated by the oldest speculation : in some of the lakṣaṇas blurred characteristics of a cosmic body are still discernible[22] ; such as they are, they may have been fixed long before the rise of any Buddhistic speculation : but their queer appearance could be successfully explained as a distorted perception of the cosmic Mahāpuruṣa-hypostasis of the Dharma through the inadequate medium of sense-bound vision.

The genesis of the conception of the Nirmāṇakāya is pre-Buddhistic : it can be traced as far back as the BĀU, where we find the idea of a "self-fashioned" (cf. *svayam nirmāya*) body of the vijñānātman, produced in the *sandhya sthāna* of sleep (IV, 3, 9), coalescent with the creation of a phantom-world (10) and moving at will (12); a body not strictly individual, but capable of appearing as a manifold series of individuals (*rūpāṇi kurute bahūni* etc., 13): this body, one and manifold, is truly "intermediate" between the sensuous individually limited body of the waking condition and the yonder one-and-all personality of dreamless sleep (cf. 9 : *idaṃ ca paralokasthānaṃ ca, sandhyaṃ tṛtīyaṃ svapnasthānam*). In itself it is not sensuous, for the vijñānamaya puruṣa has resorbed the functions of the senses (*śukram ādāya*, 11 ; cf. further *sa etās tejomātrāḥ samabhyādadāno* IV, 4, 1); it is a body consisting solely of mind-elements and coincident with nāma = vijñāna.

[22] Thus e.g. the distinctive feature that his feet adhere to the soil without leaving any interstice whatsoever adumbrates the absence of any *discontinuity*, and is a trace of the notion that his feet, like those of the Vedic and Upanishadic Puruṣa, are the earth itself; the wheel-like circles on their soles indicate that they are co-extensive with the earth-maṇḍala; the light-emanating circle between his eyebrows indicates that his third, non-human, "hidden" eye is the sun.

The analogous proceeding of *nirmāṇa* in waking consciousness produces the yogic manomayakāya. This idea of *nirmāṇa* underlies also the proto-Buddhistic acceptance of the term, as evidenced in the Suttas, where it is referred to the manomayakāya (with its iddhis of becoming multiple and again one, of appearing and disappearing at will, etc.) and implies its objectification. It equally underlies the early Mahāyāna notion of the Nirmāṇakāya, as evidenced in the L-S (p. 72 f., etc.), where this yogic personality of the Bodhisattva (to which the same faculties are ascribed) is nowise distinguished from the manomayakāya : in fact it is said to be obtained by the awareness of the world as cittamātra, i.e. by the elevation of experience = existence to the level of pure citta. It is even indiscriminately denoted by either of the two terms (cf. p. 73 and p. 137).

In the oldest Upanishads there are also references to such yogic manifestations of the mind-body; thus e.g. in the last (26th) khaṇḍa of the VIIth Adhy. of the ChU, designed on a pattern of kramayoga[23]. In the recapitulation of the items recurrent in the climax of the preceding khaṇḍas, another item is added, *avirbhāvatirobhāvau* (26, 1), which is also an iddhi of early Buddhistic yoga. And it is in connection with this item that the following phrase occurs in the sequel: *sa ekadhā bhavati tridhā bhavati pañcadhā bhavati saptadhā navadhā caiva punaś caikadaśa smṛtaḥ śataṃ ca daśa caikaśca sahasrāṇi ca viṃśatiḥ*. Hereupon the text mentions *āhāraśuddhi, sattvaśuddhi, dhruvā smṛti* and *sarvagranthīnāṃ vimokṣa*, leaving no doubt that also the above description refers to a yoga attainment. Now these indefinitely multiplied persons of the yogin, appearing and disappearing at will,

[23] See *Il Mito Psicologico*, p. 65f., n. 2.

are said to be within the range of his possibilities when he has realized the *mahiman*, the cosmic extension of his being to ātman-reality. These apparitional bodies are plural, seemingly individual reflections of the universal body.

The connecting, intermediate plane, to which the dream-fashioned body pertains, is called in BĀU IV, 3 *tṛtīya sthāna*. When the Yājñavalkyan doctrine of the three stages of consciousness corresponding to the triadic construction of reality was remoulded in the later Upanishads in consonance with the tetradic scheme of the yoga-process (we have seen that tetradic constructions of the stages of consciousness had been previously current in contexts of Yoga-technology in connexion with the psycho-physiologic centres and the corresponding dhātus), the *tṛtīya sthāna* was counted as 'third' in the sequence of four and was conceived as the yogic inversion of the svapnasthāna (now reckoned as *dvitīya*), namely as the unification of the manifold experience (converse to the multiplication of the individual consciousness-unit in the svapnasthāna) through its convergence towards the totality-centre, realizing the identity with the saviour Īśvara – whose characteristics anticipate those of the Sambhogakāya.

The identification of the dream-puruṣa, "fashioning" (*nirmimāṇaḥ*) his manifold shapes at will, with the cosmic All-deity appears for the first time in the KU (V, 8), whose teachings of yogic theism, closely related though not concordant with its teaching of Absolute Identity, try to enforce the interpretation of contingent dynamism as ultimately coincident with yogic dynamism.

The nirmāṇakāya of the Upanishads is thus, not a 'fictitious' or 'artificial' body, but the nāmakāya disengaged from the rūpakāya; not subject to the laws of nāma-rūpa, but maintaining a free relation to the reality of this nether sphere, in whose regard it is capable of self-multiplication – or rather of apparitional variety in the nāma-rūpa prism –, while it is one in its supersensuous totality-aspect orientated towards the transcendent sphere. It is perceptible only in the forms it chooses for its apparitional abode, not in its own nature (cf. BĀU IV. 3, 14 *ārāmam asya paśyanti, na tam paśyati kaścana;* this is quite consonant with the conception outlined in the Dīgha-text. The topmost *anta* to which the vijñānamaya puruṣa soars in abandoning the apparitional multiplicity of the svapnasthāma, at the limit of the sphere of transcendent unity [19], anticipates the Akaniṣṭha of Buddhism).

In fine: as regards the kāya-conception, the Buddhology of the Pāli Canon represents a phase in which the primitive notion of two kāyas (attributing to the Buddha a transcendent Amṛtakāya and a Dharmakāya soterically active in contingency) is reduced to an implicit admission of the one kāya indispensable in the economy of salvation; the logical incompatibility of even this conception with the theoretical view of absolute disconnexion between Saṃsāra and Nirvāṇa accounts for the half-hidden position of this connecting kāya in the background of the orthodox creed, while the transcendent amṛta-body is altogether banished from the latter's range bounded by the *avyākṛtas.* At the stage of the Mādhyamika-theory this one-kāya Buddhology is even further attenuated, its validity being necessarily reduced to that of yoga-saṃvṛti. Only the programmatic re-instauration of a continuity between Saṃsāra and Nirvāṇa in the Vijñānavāda creed could again postulate the character of a "body" for the transcendent reality, as the supreme archetype of the immanent and active Doctrine-body. The new term coined from the new standpoint for this revival of the proto-Buddhistic amṛta-kāya is *svabhāvika-kāya*, denoting the Tathāgata's transcendent essence as it is in itself (in its pariniṣpanna-svabhāva), while its reflection in the Body of the Teaching, of the Way, has only a *paratantra*-reality. True to the methods of Indian doctrinal innovators, the Vijñānavāda teachers, seeking to establish the validity of their theory by proving its antiquity, adopted traditional and current terms for their revolutionary conceptions: thus, the transcendent *svabhāvikakāya* was also styled *dharmakāya;* what was meant by the term was however no more the Doctrine, but the transcendent *dharmatā,* the reality of Nirvāṇa.

Whereas the theory of the Trikāya appears thus to have resulted from an ideological synthesis establishing the sequence between the transcendent Dharmakāya and the two contingent Dharmakāyas, distinguished in virtue of the distinction of two levels of the Teaching according to the twofold ideal of nirodha and bodhi, the later factitious four-kāya-theories were determined by the growing influence of the ancient tetradic scheme. The basic datum is the tetrad, the distinctions devised to fill it vary: they are brought about by splitting up either the transcendent kāya, according to the two terms under which it is now known (*svabhāvikakāya* and *dharmakāya*), or the Sambhogakāya (*svasambhogakāya* and *parasambhogakāya*[24]). Later

[24] See above, n. 18. The *Saddharmapuṇḍarīkaśāstra* (quoted by LA VALLEE, *Siddhi, App.*, p. 799) has both alternative solutions. Its subdivision of the *Ing-kāya* or "correspondence-body" into *parama* and *hīna* visibly answers to the

texts[25] also show a tendency to adapt the kāya-doctrine to the pentadic series of the Jina-skandhas. The doctrine of the five Jīnas is probably not unconnected with the latter (*v. supra*, Ch. VIII, n.27).

As personification of the Teaching and of the Way, the Sambhogakāya naturally belongs to the intermediate sphere, the upper unsensuous stratum of the cosmos. Several texts, pre-eminently the L-S, record its particular location on the Akaniṣṭha-plane (the Mādhyamikas place in the Akaniṣṭha their Dharmakāya, the Doctrine-body). In this old evidence the Akaniṣṭha is still clearly conceived as the "highest" region of the cosmos (*paraṃ sthānam*, L-S, p. 215, st. 3d); according to the classical cosmology it is however only the topmost region of *rūpaloka*. But the conception that it is the upper limit of the cosmos is maintained; its disagreement with the dogmatic dhātu-structure is explained away on the score that above the Akaniṣṭha there is no *sthāna* (AK. III, 72ab; i.e. no "place", the ārūpyas being "placeless", 3a). In reality, the Sambhogakāya has ārūpya qualities : it is all-pervading and omnipresent.

The Sambhogakāya, teaching gradual ascension to Buddhahood by gradually overcoming differentiation, by a progressive unification of reality in consciousness and by an age-long activity of conversion of the creatures (i.e. by their absorption and unification in the body of the Doctrine), is itself a *nascent* unity : neither absolutely

older classification of the Doctrine-body according to the two Vehicles. The second body of the tetrad thus constructed is called Vipākakāya and seems equivalent to the Dharmakāya of the Abhisamayālaṃkāra.

25 Non-tantric comy. to Nāmasaṃgīti : LA VALLEE, *Siddhi*, *App.*, p. 802.

one, such being only the transcendent Dharmakāya, nor yet really differentiated in the variety of its manifestations[26]. It is conceived as a cosmic body[27], present in all the regions at the same time[28] (a tenet already formulated by the Mahāsaṃghikas, forerunners of the Sambhogakāya-doctrine; see KV. XXI, 6; according to Vasumitra[29], the Mahāsaṃghikas held that the body of the Tathāgata is infinite), permeating every tiniest parti-

[26] The treatise on the Buddhaguṇas in the M.-Saṃgr. contains at II, 33, I, 14 the statement that a Buddha is *avikalpita-śarīra,* and at II, 33, II renders the same point by the phrase *yathādhimuktipradarśanaguṇaḥ.* LAMOTTE (*op. cit.*, p. 135) translates the first by "ses corps ne sont pas imaginés". As, however, the notion of "imaginary" is regularly expressed in the terminology of these texts by *parikalpita,* and *vikalpita* as regularly renders the notion of "differentiated" or "discriminated", it seems that the phrase would be more adequately rendered by "his bodies are not differentiated", which in fact agrees with the second formulation as well as with the comy. *ad* 33, 14 (p. 139). Although the contingent Buddha-bodies are realized in manifold ways by the many beings in accordance with the latters' aspirations – on the uppermost cosmic plane of the Doctrine, on the plane which is more properly their own, they are one undifferentiated body.

[27] It is the Mahāpuruṣa body, the perception of which is tantamount to the attainment of its form of existence; see MSA. XX, 49: *satpauruṣyam prapadyante tvāṃ dṛṣṭvā sarvadehināḥ, dṛṣṭamatrāt prasādasya vidhāyaka,* and bh. (cf. the cosmic body of *samprasāda,* Mdh. 246_{33}). A significant recurrence of the proto-Buddhistic notion that the *dibbacakkhu* and the *dhammakāya* are simultaneous and coessential attainments.

[28] Cf., *i.a.*, M.-Saṃgr. II, 33, I, 10 *sarvalokadhātuprasṛtakāyaḥ* (with its complement of omnipresence in time, I, 9 *tryadhvasamatāniryātaḥ*); II, 10 *sarvalokadhātuṣu sambhoganirmāṇakāyapradarśanaguṇaḥ.*

[29] I, 6, Chin. vers., MASUDA, *op. cit.*, p. 19.

cle of being; on the fundamental assumption that all the dharmas are of consciousness-essence, this ultimately amounts only to the statement that the Sambhogakāya as cosmic consciousness-body is present in every manifestation of consciousness: but, whereas these manifestations are many – in regard to the sphere of nāmarūpa –, it is not many in them, it is their potential unity; this unity is actualized in its own sphere, that of the active dharma. In this sense it is stated in the passage of the Bodh-Gāyā inscription of Yun-chou relevant to the Sambhogakāya (CHAVANNES, RHR 1906, p. 11) that "the original dust is on all sides purified of its contamination; a mutual harmony penetrates the rivers and the mountains". The cosmic omnipresence of the Sambhogakāya is not a presence in the multiplicity of the nether world, but an elevation of this multiplicity to the world of potential universal unity, to the anāsravadhātu. "As space is always omnipresent – says the MSA. (IX, 15) – thus it (sc. the *buddhatva* of the Sambhogakāya) is always omnipresent[30]; as space is universal in the multitude of forms, thus it is universal in the multitude of beings". And the bhāṣya interprets: "The buddhatva's universality in all the creatures is ascertained by the fact that in absolute truth it admits in itself all the beings". So the omni-presence is in truth an omni-absorption. Even the comparison used intimates this kind of relation: in fact it is not space that is in the forms but rather the forms that are in space; thus also this buddhatva is in the beings inasmuch as the beings become unified in it. Ākāśa is not divided by the multitude of forms, for in itself – i.e. in its own,

[30] Cf. M.-Saṃgr. II, 33, I, 20 *ākāśadhātuparyavasānaḥ*, he "terminates space".

form-less sphere, in the ākāśadhātu – it is one and infinite; but in this sphere the rūpas do not exist as such. While the presence of the one ākāśa in the many rūpas is structurally accounted for by the 'downward' derivation of the rūpas from ākāśa, the presence of the one anāsravadhātu (= the ākāśadhātu 'reversed' or provided with a tendency opposite to that of cosmic evolution)[31], of the sphere and the essence of the Sambhogakāya, in the many beings, is accounted for by the elevation of the beings to the embracing unity of the anāsrava sphere. This unity is that of the Doctrine: in this sense the L-S states that the Saddharma is comprehended by embracing all the beings (p. 195). It is neither the absolute, transcendent condition of unity achieved in the buddhatva of the Dharmakāya nor the merely latent unity present in every ālayavijñāna (the Tathāgatagarbha), but the process of its actualization; the Sambhogakāya is the Body of Unification – the hypostasis of the perennial activity of enlightenment whereby the universal unity is progressively realized. The peculiar position of the Sambhogakāya as intermediate between unity and plurality is eloquently explained in the texts by its functional character: the nature of the Sambhogakāya is entirely rendered by its *kriyā*, which implies "before" and "after" (= lower and upper limit of the psychic process). As the countless sunrays, commingled while in the sun-disk, even in their separate activities are operative towards a unity of effect, that of illumining the world,

[31] Also the Samādhirājasūtra stresses the ākāśa-like nature of the Doctrine-Body; XXII, 9: *atyantākāśasvabhāva;* 14: *sameti so 'ntarikṣeṇa* (here the use of the term *antarikṣa* instead of *ākāśa* is obviously suggested by this *dharmakāya's*

so the various activities of the Buddhas in the anāsravadhātu (which encompasses them from their beginning to their end, 21cd) coincide in the common effect of Illumination (IX, 29-30). As the sunrays coincide in the unity of the sun, their fountainhead, so the Sambhogakāyas are *one* in the effect and accomplishment of their kriyā (leading upwards to the fountainhead of Enlightenment) — though they are *many* in its performance (61). Hence this Buddhahood, though in itself uncontaminated by any āvaraṇa, cannot be conceived as either pure or impure, inasmuch as before and after are distinguished in it (22) : impure owing to its multiplicity in the *before*, it is pure in virtue of its unity in the *after*, in the accomplishment of Illumination[32]. In fact, in the *amaladhātu* the Buddhas are neither one nor many : (they are one) being bodiless like space (the limitless unsensuous Sambhogakāyas coincide in the anāsravadhātu), but (they are many) in conformity to their several bodies in the before (26). All these references point to a vision of the Sambhogakāya as a cumulative organism of spatially coincident units manifested through a synchronous

peculiar position in the intermediate sphere) No doubt but this body corresponds to the Pāli *dhammakāya* on the one hand, to the Sambhogakāya of the Asaṅga-school on the other it is *śatapuṇyanirjāta*, XXII, 9, cf. 14; *dharmanirjāta*, 9; invisible to the *māṃsacakṣus*, 17, cf. 9 — but visible, evidently, to the *divya-* or *dharmacakṣus* —, and rendered accessible to earthly vision as the body adorned with the lakṣaṇas (19; obviously the Nirmāṇakāya as reflection of the Doctrine-Body) by means of the Buddhas' "magical faculty and miraculous transformations" (Dr. REGAMEY's trsl., p. 90; the phrase *anubhāvād vikurvitaiḥ* is probably meant to render the concept of the lokānuvartana).

32 The rather cursory bh. on this st. does not render its obvious meaning; cf. however the bh. on st. 77, *ad finem*.

variety of functions in unceasing (cf. 20) harmony throughout the ages: midway between the irreducible plurality of becoming and the static unity of transcendent Being, it visualizes the notion of soteric convergence. This concept of the noumenic personality of the Doctrine as Unifying Body is implied in the term *sambhogakāya*, "body of convergent fruition." The concept is already familiar to Upanishadic-Epic thought, where it is connected with the ideologies concerning *bhoktar* and *bhogya*. The *bhoktar* is the kṣetrajña or vijñānātman, the *bhogya* is the *kṣetra*, the body in which he is incorporated and in a wider sense all the living experience which comes to him through this body. Under other denominations, they are classified as *jñāna* and *jñeya*. But unlike the term *bhogya*, the term *jñeya* implies also a postulate: if "rightly" (*samyak*) known by the jñāna freed from its veil of ajñāna (or avidyā, asamyag jñāna or pravṛtti; from the *śatru kāmarūpa*, the notion of whose function as "veiling" [*ā-vṛ*] the jñāna is most emphatically elaborated in the Gītā, III, 38-43), it reveals itself as the higher brahman. The relevant notion of Vijñānavāda is quite analogous. *jñeya* is the ālayavijñāna (Triṃś.bh., p. 44, st.) inasmuch as it is the source of all contingent experience both of avidyā and kleśas, but also inasmuch as its correct unitary cognition in the *svadhātusthānayoga* (see below, pp. 180ff.) brings about the sarvajñatā. The undoubtedly intentional bilaterality of the concept of *jñeyāvaraṇa* points to this alternative. As juxtaposed to *kleśāvaraṇa* the meaning of the term is obviously "the veil of the objectively cognizable". Thus jñeyāvaraṇa is a synonym of avidyā or subject-object consciousness, the "veil" which impedes the realization of all-consciousness or bodhi-jñāna. When however the double veil is removed, the jñeya is rightly cognized as the universal object (the Tathatā) coincident with the universal jñāna (Triṃś.bh. p. 44, I, 5), and sarvajñatā or bodhi is realized (I. 18). The rightly knowing kṣetrajña of the Gītā is the immanent Īśvara himself: *kṣetrajñaṃ cāpi māṃ viddhi sarvakṣetreṣu*[33], says Kṛṣṇa, the divine Teacher of yogic jñāna. But this immanence is not to be understood as actual on the plane of the unenlightened beings; Gīta VIII, 12 explains: although all the conditions of existence derive from the creator-Puruṣa, He—the saviour-Puruṣa—is not in them, but they are in him. They are in him inasmuch as they are elevated to his own plane, to the sphere of the higher brahman, which is also compared with ākāśa (IX, 6). The participation in the God's "own" nature is determined by knowledge; as inherent in the human form, he is "dis-regarded" by the blinded ones, ignorant of his higher Īśvara-nature, their plane being that of the *prakṛti āsurī, mohinī*: but those whose plane is that of the *daivī prakṛti*, participate (*bhajanti*) in Him, are incessantly united with Him by bhakti in upāsana (IX, 11-14; *mām eva ye prapadyante māyām etāṃ* [the *guṇamayī māyā*] *taranti te,* VII, 14, is therefore to be understood quite literally: the accession to the God's own plane, on which "they are in him" [12, above], is a "going beyond" the sphere of the lower Prakṛti). Those who participate in him by bhakti (*ye bhajanti tu māṃ bhaktyā*) are in him and he is in them (*ibid.* 29); their plane is common: it is the soteric jñeya (*jñeyam...yaj jñatvāmṛtam aśnute*), the higher brahman (XIII, 12), the saviour's omnipresent Body—the same as the omnipresent body of the creator Īśvara, but opposite in its functionality (apparent in all the indriyas and also free

[33] Cf. *sarvasya cāhaṃ hṛdi san niviṣṭo* XV, 15.

from them, within the beings and beyond them, moving and immovable, proximate and far away: 14-15). Undivided in the beings it stands as if divided (16a). In this body (*dehe 'smin*) Maheśvara as its bhoktar is called *paramātmā* (22). Those who have reached its plane by having acceeded (*prapadyante*) to Him, the "great Refuge" (Śvet.U III, 17), those who "partake" in it by bhakti, are fellow-bhoktars of this omnipresent bhogya. This union with the saviour Īśvara on the plane of yogic bhakti is a real *sambhoga*, and the omnipresent, "undivided though divided" Body of the *dharmāvaha bhageśa* is a full-fledged Sambhogakāya, *avant la lettre*. According to the traces of primitive Buddhist doctrine in the Pāli scriptures, the accession to the Refuge, to the Buddha's Doctrine-Body – represented in visibleness by the Saṃgha of the disciples –, is effected in the consummation of the initial upāsana, by which the passage to the higher sphere is brought about. Reborn in the *dhamma* – integrated in the *dhammakāya* –, the disciple partakes in the common fruition of dhamma (*dhammasambhoga*[34]). It may be significant that in such a classical Mahāyāna treatise as the MSA. the great *śaraṇa* is identified with the Sambhogakāya (celebrated in ch. IX), the Body which guides the beings in the sphere of the True Doctrine[35] to the Yonder Shore (IX, 10) and which is found in the *vyāvṛtti* of all the tendencies and in the dawn[36] of accomplishment (11). In it the (aspect of) bīja of both kleśa- and jñeyavṛttis, unceasingly inherent (in the ālayavijñāna) since time immemorial, is

[34] Cf. Vinaya, ed. OLDENBERG, IV, p. 137.

[35] This active "guiding" Body is the *dharmakāya* in the oldest meaning of the term (see above, pp. 139f.).

[36] *abhyudaya*, the "rise", as of a luminary.

thrown off and dispersed by the fullest proceedings of all-abandonment; this *buddhatva* is arrived at in the attainment of a new āśraya (*āśrayasyānyathāpti*) associated with the choice qualities of the *śukla-dharmas*, by virtue of the very pure *nirvikalpajñānamārga*, great in its aim (12). Standing on its height the Tathāgata looks down as standing on the most excelse great mountain of the world, pitying those who find satisfaction in Quiet (the arhats), not to mention those who find satisfaction in becoming (the worldlings) (13). This pinnacle of the world is doubtless the Akaniṣṭha[37], the unity level of the Sambhogakāya, the plane which, according to pre-Hīnayānic conceptions, is attained by the srotaāpanna at the upper end of the ascending line started by his accession to the Refuge.

The AK. (VI, 37cd.) names the *akaniṣṭhaga* as one only of several kinds of anāgāmins (its subdivision of the anāgāmin category into seven sub-categories [37-38; similar subdivisions in AN. IV, pp. 72ff.; Vis.-m., Pugg.-paññ.] bears very obviously the stamp of scholastic elaboration), and as one of two types of *ūrdhvasrotas* — the distinction of the *ūrdhvasrotas* into *akaniṣṭhagas* and *bhavāgragas* being evidently dictated by the same reason which led to the distinction of two nirodhas (see above, p. 100, n.6), namely the need of taking into account the

[37] The anāsravadhātu, the sphere of the convergent kriyās of the Sambhogakāyas, is obviously figured in the shape of a pyramid (a notion conformable to old cosmological conceptions), at whose top-point, reached in the consummation of the processes of enlightenment, the Sambhogakāyas coincide in the unity of the "after", in their common fountainhead, direct ectype of the Dharmakāya.

Cf. the *bhūtakoṭiprabhāvita tathāgatakāya* of Aṣtas.pr.pār. 94, 11.

ārūpya superstructure — ; in the simpler classifications of the Suttas any *uddhaṃsota* is *akaniṭṭhagāmi*: the two terms always recur as an inseparable couple of epithets[38] : (*uddhaṃsoto hoti akaniṭṭhagāmi*). The results of our analysis of the primitive notion of the anāgāmiphala (pp. 102ff.) show that its bearer was originally *ūrdhva-srotas ex definitione*, his sphere being the upward stream of the Dharma, psychically actuated in the progression of the four ancient dhyānas. The upper limit of this sphere, bordering on the transcendent plane of the arhattvaphala, is the fourth dhyāna. As the level of the Akaniṣṭha bounds the region of the fourth dhyāna (a notion accepted also in dogmatics, cf. AK. III, 2bd, Bh.), it is clear that the primitive anāgāmin was, as such, *akaniṣṭhaga*. On this level his final transfiguration or bodhi, his attainment of the transcendent āśraya identical with the Buddha's amṛtakāya (subsequent to his participation in the dynamic dharmakāya by virtue of the āśraya-parivṛtti in the Way-attainment[39]), was censed to take place. This notion is still preserved in early Mahāyāna records. A stanza of the Sagāthaka-portion of the L-S avers that bodhi takes place in the Akaniṣṭha (774, p. 361); another stanza of this collection (38, p. 269) declares the Akaniṣṭha to be the region of *nirvikalpa* (i.e. of the upekṣā-stage of dhyāna: upekṣā = nirvikalpa-jñāna according to MSA. XVIII, 61, bh.;

[38] Already noted by LA VALLEE, JRAS. 1906, p. 446ff., *Les cinq espèces d'Anagāmin*.

[39] The terms are used in this connection only by Yaśomitra, but they render a traditional notion recorded in the AK.: in IV, 104cd we meet with the remark that the srotaāpanna has a new personality which is "beyond" (*atyantam*) the old one, and elsewhere (VI, 41c) the same is said of the anāgāmin. It is the mārga-body of the Sautrāntika (II, 55d).

avikalpa is used in the sense of upekṣā in the Nṛsiṃhott.U). According to the Mahāyānaśraddhotpādaśāstra the Bodhisattvas obtain on reaching the Akaniṣṭha the most venerable and excellent body of the Universe[40], i.e. obviously the Sambhogakāya[41] in its supreme—structurally topmost—form of Totality.

The Buddhistic conception of Akaniṣṭha thus corresponds to the conception of the brahmaloka in the metrical Upanishads teaching a kramamukti. Located at the upper limit of the tṛtīya sthāna, this brahmaloka is the "uppermost" abode of the Īśvara in his saviour-aspect, the plane of "totality" where his unsensuous cosmic body is manifested (in the primitive Buddhistic conception borne out by the Mahāgovinda and other Suttas this topmost and all-embracing region is still named brahmaloka[42]): the same notion appears in another stanza of the L-S (p. 215, st. 3), where the Akaniṣṭha is called *maheśvaram paraṃ sthānam*[43] (its radiance being moreover described by the old Vedic term *vi-rāj*). As the infinite multitude of the Īśvara's forms is reduced to unity on the plane of the brahmaloka, thus also the many manifestations of the Sambhogakāya[44] are reduced to

[40] SUZUKI, *Awakening of Faith*, p. 125.

[41] Described *loc. cit.*, pp. 100ff.

[42] Cf. DN. II, pp. 238ff., I, p. 249; MN. II, pp. 193f. See *Il Mito Psicologico*, p. 302.

[43] In the Samādhirājasūtra the Doctrine-personality of the Buddha is called *lokanātha*.

[44] The manifestations of the Sambhogakāya are in the original sense as many as the cittas in which its teaching is realized; such was undoubtedly the symbolic purport of the scenes of *mahāpratihārya* introducing the doctrinal exposition in older Mahāyānic Sūtras. The motif of the countless rays of light emitted by the Buddha, each of them, according to the

their essential unity on the Akaniṣtha-plane (cf. above, p. 156ff.). The many sambhogakāyas converge towards and coincide in this top-point, which is the limit of the transcendent Dharmakāya sphere.

We have seen that the remnants of the proto-Buddhistic kāya-doctrine in the Pāli Canon imply a connection between the two successive stages reached by the disciple (the entrance on the Way and the attainment of arhatship) and the Buddha-bodies personifying the Way and Nirvāṇa, i.e. the *dharmakāya* and the *amṛta-kāya*. On the other hand, we have seen that the suppression of the last-mentioned and the dimmed half-admission of the dhammakāya in the dogmatic Buddhology of the Suttas resulted from the main trend of the evolution of Hīnayāna, namely from the rationalization of the exclusivistic standpoint. Consequently, the tenet of the *dharmakāya* was deprived of its transcendental implications and came to be considered as a mere allegorical formulation of the fact that after the Master's final disappearance the body of the Sayings was left to guide the later generations of disciples. The picture of the early vicissitudes of these notions may be completed by observing why the connection between the Way-attainment and the dhyānic body of the dhammaja was tentatively, though unsuccessfully, effaced in the extant texts, so that it can be only detected through comparing scattered allusions. The reason was obviously that this ideology was closely connected with

S-P, bearing a Buddha-manifestation seated on the lotus-throne (=the throne of the Sambhogakāya, see the Bodh-Gāyā inscription of Yun-chou, CHAVANNES, *loc. cit.*, p. 13) should, in these contexts, be interpreted in terms of the simile MSA. IX, 61 (above, p. 159f.).

the ancient conception of the religious career as a process of imitation of, and progressive assimilation to, the Buddha, in a word as a career of bodhi. As in the Hīnayāna it was turned into a career of nirodha (essentially different from that of the Buddha not only in the end, but also in the means, the determinant factor of dhyāna having been relegated as inessential), the ideology containing the evidence of the disciple's progressive assimilation to the Tathāgata was consequentially and intentionally obliterated. The *kāyavāda* deviated into the *skandhamātravāda*, the purport of its sequence as an ascensional and centripetal climax was forgotten along with its connection with the process of deliverance.

The Mahāyānic branch, whose fundamental divergence from the Hīnayāna consists precisely in its conception of the Career as a *yāna* towards bodhi, naturally perpetuated and developed the doctrine of the kāyas and maintained the notion of the correspondence and connection between the successive stages attained by the Way-faring disciple and the kāyas of the Buddha.

These stages are, as we have seen, hypostases of forms of experience structurally superposed to the normal pṛthagjana experience located on the plane of nāmārūpa.

If, as the Hôbôgirin directly states, and the texts indirectly imply, the three kāyas are connected with the three *svabhāvas*, the latter must be closely related to the old three-dhātu scheme.

The Yogācāra theory of the three *svabhāvas* or *lakṣanas* is quite obviously another version of the doctrine of the two truths, *saṃvṛti* and *paramārtha*, admitted by the Hīnayāna schools as well as by the Mādhyamikas. To say that it is a development of this doctrine would be too much: it is in fact the very same conception, reformulated in its original structural triadism by the Vijñānavāda, admitting the continuity between Saṃsāra and Nirvāṇa denied by the Śūnyavāda.

For both the Hīnayānists and the Śūnyavādins *saṃvṛti* is the common, conventional way of perceiving reality, "veiling" the correct mode of its perception, its *paramārthasatya*. The contexts of these doctrines show that the point of view from which this distinction of "truths" is established is not ontological, but soteriological. Here the compound *paramārthasatya* does not mean "the truth of the highest object", of Nirvāṇa (both doctrines in fact deny the "cognoscibility" of Nirvāṇa, and the term is not applied to a cognition of transcendent things, but to the correct cognition of contingency); it means "the truth conducive to the highest aim" (not *paramārthasya satyam*, but *paramārthādhigamaṃ satyam*). As to the contents of paramārthasatya the different forms of exclusivism naturally differ. From the Theravāda point of view, as it already emerges in the Suttas, the existence of entities is only "nominal", while the saṃvṛti perception takes them for objective units: their paramārtha truth is the perception of their "nominality", for "they consist only of changeful elements of experience (*dhammā*)", rising and disappearing in causal connection; the only datum permanently graspable in them is their impermanence itself, the causal connection, the pratītyasamutpāda. This point of view is originally a determined cittamātratāvāda *avant la lettre* (see above); the assertion of the "nominality" of objectively defined entities is to be taken quite literally, they are only "*nāmas*", various conformations of experience, of psychic essence. The perception of this character of reality reveals the vicious circle of grasping and thus leads to detachment and appeasement – it is therefore paramārthasatya; the content of this perception is the pratītyasamutpāda. But by the very power of this perception, if, of course, it is not a mere adopted notion but a "realization" (*sacchi-kṛ*), its content is reversed, it is "made true" not in the form of "dependent production" but in its inverted form of dependent cessation (see above, p. 59); thus the paramārtha-perception leads to the "highest aim", Nirvāṇa.

The systematized exclusivism of the Madhyamaka does not admit of any "Way" as such : the transcendent, and only, reality is not *attained*, but unveiled in the instant and by the sole virtue of the cessation of the erroneous perception : therefore the paramārthasatya of the old Sutta-viewpoint can be only saṃvṛti from the Madhyamaka-viewpoint – though a higher saṃvṛti – ; the only paramārthasatya is the non-"perception" of any form of contingency whatsoever, the complementary aspect of the realization of the inconceivable tattva. The perfection of this paramārthasatya coincides with the paramārtha itself, in the fulfilment of that method of psychical elimination of contingency (with its theoretical reflection in the prasaṅga-method of intellectual elimination) which is so characteristic of this school. The pratītyasamutpāda is an *anutpāda*, and is thereby identical with the unborn transcendent Tathāgata-essence. The adequate perception of the essence of contingency is no more interpreted in the sense of the ancient context, as the latter's *nivṛtti*, but as its *apravṛtti*, and thereby as the very realization of Nirvāṇa. It is an apravṛtti of nāmas[45] : in fact the pratītyasamutpāda is a process

[45] Chandrakīrti, quoted in STCHERBATSKY, *Nirvāṇa*, p. 209.

of "nominal" production; the original import of this notion is clearly illustrated by Nāgārjuna's assertion (Cittavajrastava) that the saṃsāra is only vikalpa of the citta[46], while the elimination of the vikalpa is deliverance (cf. Mādhyamikavṛtti, p. 524: nirvāṇa is *sarvakalpana-kṣayarūpa*[47]). Only in its banishing the idea of a process from the conception of deliverance does the new position differ from the oldest one; moreover, that idea is not utterly banished, but admitted as a lower degree of truth, as the *yogasaṃvṛti* eventually conducive to the

[46] The scholastic point of view had turned the dharmas into "things", into objective "elements of existence", and thus the assertion of the "nominality" of the pratītyasamutpanna had assumed another meaning: it stated the *fictitious* character of the compound units, whose objective reality however consisted in their components. The original yogic attitude in its Mahāyānic revival reacts to this ontological innovation by the apparently novel teaching of the *dharma-śūnyatā:* dharmas, too, are only nominal, i.e., according to the new interpretation, only fictions. Fictions arising from what, effected by what? The sheer "negativism" of Nāgārjuna's dialectics does not formulate any reply, but the doctrinal implications of Nāgārjuna's lyrics make it quite clear: the vikalpas are fictions of the citta – which however can also rend its self-made veil. The citta or pratītyasamutpāda is not essenceless to the same extent as the citta-made differentiations (pratītyasamutpanna). The Vijñānavāda develops this position (as rendered by the distinction between the *māyā* and the *māyākṛta* in MSA. XI, 15) into a new monism: the fictitious or nominal differentiated reality, the *prajñapti* (*pratityasamutpanna* or *parikalpita*), is the product or fiction of the noumenic process, the *vijñapti* (*pratītyasamutpāda* or *paratantra*), which in itself is only the dynamic saṃkleśa of the static vijñāna (*anutpanna* or *pariniṣpanna*).

[47] Cf. also the wording *sarvakalpanopaśama arūpa nirvāṇa*.

paramārtha standpoint; this saṃvṛti is the vyavadāna process leading to paramārtha[48], or rather revealing it – *tattvarūpam abhidyotayati*[49] – by effecting the vyāvṛtti in the saṃtāna[50]. (In a similar manner the S-P adopts the Hīnayānic paramārtha-conception in a subordinate and provisional rôle: the Śrāvaka-truth is not mendacious, but true on a lower plane).

Thus the "way", indispensable in the yogic economy of Mahāyāna Buddhism, is indirectly admitted again without formally encroaching on the ultimate theoretical issues of Mādhyamika exclusivism.

The twin doctrines of the double truth-perception and of the triple nature of reality are repeatedly met with in the Upanishads, either in close connection with, or as implicit in, the doctrines of *satya* (examined above, pp. 19-40). According to BĀU II, 3, of the two contingent manifestations of brahman the 'shapeless' one, the amūrta rūpa represented by prāṇa and hṛdākāśa = vijñāna, is the superior, because it is capable of actualizing its faculty of satyasya satyam in its translation to the plane of the unutterable, "higher than which there is none". This criterion of comparative evaluation produces the incisive formulation of the tenet in the MaitriU: *yan mūrtaṃ tad asatyam yad amūrtaṃ tat satyam*. That shapeless reality of prāṇa, which is *karman* in both the senses – worldly and yogic –, and may be considered as amṛta inasmuch as it is conducive to amṛta, – is "veiled" by the satya of the nāmarūpa plane (BĀU I, 6). Similarly, according to ChU VI, the reality of particularized perception represented by names

48 Mādhyamikavṛtti, p. 126.

49 Subhāṣitasaṃgraha quoted by LA VALLEE, *Siddhi*, p. 550

50 *Ibid.*

as differentiations of Vāc can be reduced to the right perception of the fundamental cosmic tri-unity as the starting-point of the dynamic processes of differentiation, to the *satya ḳat'exochen*, and this way of perception of the more real satya of things is soteric, being conducive to the realization of *sat*.

Furthermore, according to ChU VIII this satya, the *brahmapura* (1, 5), is the locus of all the kāmas and of their "con-formations" (*saṃḳalpa*) experienced as reality in everyday consciousness, and does not perish with the individual[51]. It possesses the potentiality of *satyāḥ ḳāmāḥ* and *satyāḥ saṃḳalpāḥ*, conducive to the realization of ātman, but themselves not liable to be realized as long as they are veiled by anṛta (3, 1–2). The unveiling is the perception of the true nature of reality, not as reflected and dispersed in the passing show of nāmarūpa, but as centred in the hṛdākāśa, in the pure nāma-sphere; here it is manifested as the essence of karma-causality[52] (1, 5 *yathā hy eve h a prajā anvāviśanti* etc....-6 *ḳṣiyate;* cf. Muṇḍ.U II, 1, 5, evolution of concrete contingency – of the *nāmarūpaṃ brahma* I, 1, 9 – from satya along the lines traced by the pañcāgnividyā), apt however to turn into an instrument of deliverance from such causality in producing the ātman-knowledge through satya-desire (6 *tad ya ihātmānam anuvidya...ḳāmacāro bhavati*).

[51] We have seen that it corresponds to the ālayavijñāna, whose nature is that of the pratītyasamutpāda or paratantra (cf. *i.a.* M.-Saṃgr. I, 20).

[52] By virtue of this knowledge-conquest of the psychic mechanism of causality the manifestations of reality conform to the knower's wish (2, 1–10). The same is stated with regard to the Bodhisattva's *cetovaśitā* as first degree of dhyānic mastery (M.-Saṃgr. II, 14, 4a).

In this way the adequate satya-perception results in the samprasāda stage of satya, which in attaining the supernal Light "comes forth" (*abhiniṣpadyate*) in the *svarūpa* of the transcendent ātman-brahman (3, 4). Thus the satya as amūrta rūpa, contingency as perceived in its essence of pure "name", partakes both in the sphere of nāmarūpa-satya or anṛta into which it develops in the "veiled" form of common waking experience, and in the sphere of the *abhiniṣpanna svarūpa,* of *sat,* to which it leads when its function is inverted. This is rendered by the pseudo-etymological analysis of the term *satya* into three component syllables: "*sat* is the immortal, *ti* the mortal (cf. BĀU V, 5, 1: *ti*=anṛta), by *yam* it connects both (cf. BĀU II, 3: *yat*)" (3, 2). The same notion is found in Muṇḍ.U III, 1, 6: satya is the divine path leading from anṛta or nāmarūpa-satya (cf. I, 1, 9 *brahma nāmarūpam...tad etat satyam*) to the "highest abode of satya".

In the Vijñānavāda doctrine of the three *svabhāvas* or *svarūpas* of reality this conception appears again: the *parikalpita-svabhāva* or *nāmarūpa*[53] experienced in common consciousness is the final effect and false objectification of the vikalpa[54] or causal evolution of the citta (vijñānapariṇāma), of the pratītyasamutpāda or *paratantra-svabhāva*[55]; the *pariṇiṣpanna-svabhāva* is realized by the "pure" paratantra when it ceases to imagine[56], i.e. by

[53] *nāma-nimitta* in the terminology of the L-S. *parikalpita* is the conjunction of nimitta and nāma (p. 131, st. 193).

[54] Also called *saṃkalpa:* see L-S, pp. 68, st. 134; 227; 229, st. 6; MSA. XI, 39.

[55] Cf. L-S, p. 225.

[56] Cf. MSA. IX, 78cd: *sarvathā 'nupalambhaśca upalam-*

the supression of pariṇāma, whereby the vijñāna "comes forth" (*niṣ-pad*) in its static transcendent essence.

Thus the paratantra partakes by its double potentiality (as sāsrava and anāsrava[57], i.e. as pravṛtti and nivṛtti) both in the parikalpita and in the pariniṣpanna. It is *saṃkleśa-vyavadāna-nibandha*: this Mahāyāna notion (Candrakīrti, *ad* Mādh.-kār. XV, 11, p. 274f.; cf. M.-Saṃgr. II, 28[58]) is the counterpart of the Upanishadic *sat-ti-ya — ubhe yacchati.*

In the Yogācāra context, where the ecstatic cognition of the paramārtha is again put into a series with the contingent modes of cognition, the paramārthasatya is, on the one hand, paramārthasya satya (the aim, realization of the Tathatā), on the other, paramārthādhigama satya (the Way, progressive realization of the vijñaptimātratā). The soteric Śrāvaka-truth being counted apart

bhaḥ paro mataḥ; bh: *yā parikalpitena svabhāvenāvidyamānatā saiva paramā vidyamānatā pariniṣpannena svabhāvena/yaśca sarvathā 'nupalambhaḥ parikalpitasya svabhāvasya sa eva parama upalambhaḥ pariniṣpannasvabhāvasya.*

57 Only as sāsrava it is called *abhūtaparikalpa;* as anāsrava, i.e. during the process of its cessation, the kalpa is neither *bhūta* nor *abhūta,* and when this process is accomplished, it is, obviously, no more *kalpa* at all, but the *(akalpa) lokottara jñāna,* the pariniṣpanna. (See MSA. XI, 31 bh).

58 It is Saṃsāra by its *parikalpitabhāga,* Nirvāṇa by its *pariniṣpannabhāga.* Inspite of the appearance created by these terms the conception cannot be interpreted as that of an impossible simultaneity or co-existence of Saṃsāra and Nirvāṇa. The same treatise (II, 23) in fact explains that the svabhāvas, though inherent in the paratantra, never coincide, as they are reciprocally exclusive conditions or aspects (see also II, 32).

from the latter, as yogasaṃvṛti efficiently counteracting the lokasaṃvṛti, the satyas are in the Yogācāra synthesis implicitly four.[59]

If the two alternative aspects of the paratantra be counted separately, the resulting tetrad reveals its structural analogy with the ancient Buddhist scheme of the four satyas: the parikalpita corresponds to the duḥkhasatya, the paratantra of pravṛtti to the samudayasatya (or pratītyasamutpāda anulomam), the paratantra of nivṛtti to the mārgasatya (or pratītyasamutpāda pratilomam), the pariṇiṣpanna to the nirodhasatya.

The Epic Upanishads also distinguish three svabhāvas respectively perceived: (a) by common subjective consciousness, (b) by concentrated consciousness able to see the underlying essence of contingency (the pravṛttilakṣaṇadharma or samyogalakṣaṇotpatti), or by dhyānic consciousness, whose coincidence with its object is also the inversion of the latter's orientation (into nivṛttilakṣaṇadharma), (c) in ecstatic universal consciousness.

The first is also named *paribhāva*, "enclosing" or "outer" reality (Mdh. 238$_6$d)[60]. Its foremost character is

[59] The theories elaborated by the Vijñānavāda scholastics regarding the relations between the two satyas and the three svabhāvas, as recorded by Hiuan Tsang and studied by LA VALLEE, *Siddhi*, p. 549ff., are rather a show of scholarly subtility than the evidence of further doctrinal developments.

[60] The underlying notion of concentric svabhāvas—which so obviously points to the connection with the archaic notion of concentric kāyas (still surviving, cf. above, n.$_{18}$) is evidenced in the Vijñānavāda conception as well: thus Hiuan-Tsang states that the parikalpita is *on* the paratantra and the parinispanna *in* the paratantra (*Siddhi*, p. 611).

dvaya or *dvandva*[61], the inherent duality of its nature, to which its multiplicity is due (cf. e.g. Mdh. 239_{20} : [*bhūtāni*] *svabhāvenaiva vartante dvandvasṛṣṭāni bhūriśaḥ*). This is not truly real, therefore 238_3 states "unreasonable is he who considers (reality) in regard to its svabhāva without (having produced) the bhāva (concentration of consciousness)." The latter enables one to see, not the mere surface of concrete sensuous contingency (the paribhāva-svabhāva), but the svabhāva constituting its cause. Our text goes on ($_4$): "But even those who in concentration (*ekāntabhāvena*) perceive the cause (of reality) as due to svabhāva (the causal svabhāva underlying the sensuous one), do not attain anything, even if they purify the stalk and its core". Ever since this image was inaugurated by the KU (VI, 17), the stalk represents the sensuous body, its inner core the unsensuous consciousness-body, the potential ātman. "Purification" in these texts always means nivṛtti, progressive cessation of the dynamism. The texts repeatedly warn against mistaking common, temporal nivṛtti, such as it takes place in natural periodic involution—only to be followed by a new process of pravṛtti—, for the supernatural yogic nivṛtti which is definitive, "a way of no return", and conducive to the transcendent condition; if artificially brought about, the former is a false yoga (styled *tamorūpānubhūti* in Nṛsiṃhott.U IX) and produces catalepsy and eventually death, but no realization of the ātman. Our text continues: "Those who, taking their stand on this aspect (*pakṣa*) (namely concentrating on causal creating svabhāva), realize involution (*nivartanti*), have yet little wisdom, for by cognizing the causal

[61] Cf. the Mahāyānic conception of the *dvayalakṣaṇa* of parikalpita.

svabhāva they do not attain the *śreyas;* in fact the svabhāva consisting in the manas whose essence is karma and moha (the pravṛttilakṣaṇadharma), (when concentrated upon in the involutional process) leads (only) to death" ($_{5,6}$). The factor whose presence or absence constitutes the criterion for distinction between the two nivṛttis is the cosmic expansion of consciousness concomitant with its concentration, with its withdrawal from the senses at the outset of the process : a foreboding – in the very midst of contingent life – of transcendent universal consciousness. The passage from this initial point of the process to its terminal point is conceived as a progressive elimination of contingent consciousness. When that initial factor is absent, only unconsciousness can be the final result. The mere ekāntabhāva, namely withdrawal of the consciousness from sensuous experience to its own sphere, brings about the perception of the supersensuous svabhāva, which is the Cause (*kāraṇa*), the intrinsic law of elementary becoming (cf. $219_{7,41}$) : not the pravṛtta svabhāva, but the pravṛtti-svabhāva or pravṛttilakṣaṇa-dharma, "the svabhāva-stream by which the world is incessantly carried hitherward" (236_{13} *svabhāvasrotasāvṛttam*[62] *uhyate satataṃ jagat*), the samyogalakṣaṇotpatti (Upanishadic equivalent of the Buddhistic pratītyasamutpāda). But if the ekāntabhāva is concomitant with the initial stage of dhyāna, i.e. if it is accompanied by the sukha (cf $195_{14\text{-}22}$) of the yogin who "perceives all the beings in himself and himself in all the beings", the causal svabhāva therein apprehended is characterized by the opposite lakṣaṇa, by the *kṣetrajñasya*

[62] Similar is the agency attributed to the pravṛtti of the ālayavijñāna as creative paratantra, which *vartate srotasaughavat*.

svalakṣaṇa (217$_9$), the svalakṣṇa of tapas = yoga (*ibid.*$_{16}$); its agency results in *karmanivṛtti* (*ibid.*$_{11}$), it is the nivṛttilakṣaṇa-dharma.

The kāraṇa-svabhāva, which is also called the "higher" one, *para svabhāva*[63] (202$_{3,5,13}$), and does not reside in the single causes and effects, but is to be found in the reduction of contingency to the intrinsic omnipresent law that pervades it and determines its course, is thus, in its alternative orientation, *sarvahetu* and *paramātmakarin* (cf. *ibid.*$_7$). The paramātman, "produced" by the para svabhāva achieving its nivṛtti, or rather revealed out of its transfiguration, – the *abhiniṣpanna svarūpa* of the ChU – is called *parama svabhāva*. The "production" is only a revelation, for this doctrine assumes the parama svabhāva's eternal immanence in the contingent vijñāna. Its revelation is progressively brought about by the purification (nivṛtti) of consciousness; the first stage of the process is effected by the withdrawal from sensuous perception to pure noumenic perception; it is the buddhi-stage (cf. 203$_1$), where the parama svabhāva, though yet "distant", is rendered "proximate" (*ibid.*$_{10}$; cf. *pratyakṣatām eti sa dharmadhātus* MSA. VI, 7cd). This turning-point is obviously the condition of aiśvarya (cf. above, p. 153), to which also our chapter 238 refers in concluding its teaching of the three svabhāvas (st. $_{21\text{-}25}$). It consists in the full mastery of the śabdabrahman and hence implies the unfailing promise of the highest attainment.

Thus the dhyānic cognition of the para svabhāva as consciousness alone, free from the *dvaya* of the paribhava, i.e. its realization as nivṛttilakṣaṇadharma (the

[63] It is obviously identical with the "higher brahman".

satyasya satya of the old Upanishads), is exactly parallel to the Yogācāra's soteric recognition of the vijñaptimātratā, realizing the paramārtha-orientation of the paratantra as anāsrava, free from the *dvaya* of parikalpita.

The recognition of the vijñaptimātratā of reality (eliminating the prajñaptisatya, the parikalpitasvabhāva, the experience of the nāmarūpa-plane) is *eo ipso* an elevation to the plane of pure vijñapti, of pure nāma (cf. L-S, p. 96, st. 156a),—a parāvṛtti, as the vijñāna "returns" from its imagined alienation to its own sphere (*svadhātu*). The condition in which the ensuing process of purification or cessation takes place is therefore called *svadhātusthāna* (MSA. XI, 33) or *nāmni sthāna* (*ibid.*, bh., XI, 6; Triṃś.bh., st. quot. *ad* 25) or *cittasya citte sthāna* (MSA. XVIII, 66).

By concentrating on the awareness of *cittamātra* (MSA. VI, 7ab) or *nāmamātra* (XI, 48 and bh.; Trimś.bh. p. 42), and thus elevating reality-experience to the level of pure nāma or manojalpa (MSA. XI, 6, etc., see above, p. 90), the adept, having soared to the ārūpya sphere (where only nāmopādāna is left, Trimś.bh. p. 19), obtains by virtue of this parāvṛtti an omnipresent āśraya (*sarvatragāśraya* MSA. XI, 44), infinite and of pure jñāna-essence (*jñānānantāśraya* Triṃś.bh. p. 44[64]). The new parāvṛttyāśraya thus obtained on reaching the samādhi-level is, according to the L-S (pp. 50, 80-81, 125f., 136-37), his *manomayakāya* or *māyopamasamādhikāya* (Māyā being the dynamic ālayavijñāna [=the paratantra[65]] in both its opposite func-

[64] Ms. reading, see ed., n. 4.

[65] The parikalpita is *māyākṛta* (MSA. XI, 15 and bh.).

tions, and the present meditative condition, wherein cittamātra is realized, being a "residence in the svadhātu", i.e. in the ālayavijñāna = citta = nāman, this samādhi-body is "Māyā-like"). It is no more liable to restrictions of time and space, it is endowed with the yogic powers, it is conformable to the ārya(= Bodhisattva)-assemblies (which take place in the intermediate region, see above, p. 149), it is used for accomplishing the vow of enlightening the many (L-S, pp. 139, 81): it thus clearly appears to be the Bodhisattva's cosmic Doctrine-body[66] corresponding to, or coincident with, the Buddha's Sambhogakāya[67]: it is the Mahāpuruṣa-body adorned with the 32 lakṣaṇas.

The *nāmni sthāna* is by no means a novel invention of the Yogācāra: it is a replica of the *tṛtīya sthāna*, outlined in the Śvet.U (see above pp. 50, 153), in which the adept identifies himself with the cosmic body of the Īśvara as Teacher and Saviour (even the simile of the mirror, used in the Upanishadic passage, reappears in the Buddhistic Śāstra and is commented upon by the words: *ādarśaḥ cittasya dhātau sthānaṃ samādhir yad etatpūrvaṃ nāmni sthānam uktam*, XI, 42 bh.[68]). Like

[66] The *dharmakāya bodhisattva* of the Mahāprajñāpāramitāśāstra; cf. LA VALLEE, *Siddhi, App*., pp. 779ff.

[67] Cf. ROCKHILL, *The Life of The Buddha*, p. 201, quoting the Bkaḥ-hgyur: "the sambhogakāya is discernible in the whole air of a bodhisattva...the Sambhogakāya is the samādhi inherent to all the buddhas..."

In the sphere of the Sambhogakāya the peculiar unity-plurality ratio obtains also with regard to the Bodhisattvas. They are potentially *ekāśrayāḥ*, for their cosmic perception is common and their activities are blended in the unity of the common effect (MSA. IX, 85).

[68] The MSA. (IX, 67-69) agrees with the authorities

the tṛtīya sthāna, it is the condition of dhyāna, in which the nāmarūpa-reality is reabsorbed in, and transposed to the plane of, pure nāma, consciousness being reverted upon itself (the definition of dhyāna as *sthitiś cetasa adhyātmam* XVI, 25a definitely confirms this conclusion)[69]. The dhyānic process (whose sphere was the

followed by Hiuan-Tsang in considering the *ādarśajñāna* as the essential characteristic of the Sambhogakāya (see *Siddhi*, pp. 708f., 712).

[69] The notion is a familiar item of the yoga speculation recorded in the Mdh. (cf. above, p. 88). *manasi sthāna* (also *citte* or *sattve sthāna*) is a current designation of the dhyānic condition, in which the svabhāva's return to its primordial ātmic reality — begun by its withdrawal from sense-perception, tantamount to the nivṛtti of the elemental plane (cf. $205_{14,15}$) — is finally performed. It is the second and concluding part of the pratyāhāra of reality in the buddhi as in its essence and fountainhead (194_{18}). When, having gone beyond sensation, having transcended the *karmaguṇa*, the buddhi functions on the manas-stage alone, then the brahman is attained or discerned in the samādhi of dhyānayoga: this is the outset of the way towards pralaya (194_{25}, 204_{17}, 205_{10}).

Even the image of the mountain referred to in this connexion by the MSA. (above, p. 164) — the mountain-top being the unity attained in the consummation of the nāmni sthāna, at the upper limit of the sphere entered by virtue of the first āśrayaparāvṛtti — recurs in the Mdh. in an analogous connexion: *dhyānena paramaṃ kṛtvā...āhatya sarvasāṃkalpān sattve cittaṃ niveśayet, sattve cittaṃ samāveśya tataḥ kālañjaro bhavet* ($247_{7,8,9}$). The *guṇavatī buddhi* has descended like water from this mountain, 205_{11}; cf. KU IV, 14). The manasi sthāna — the condition in which the buddhi, having abandoned sense-perception, is turned upon itself — is the sphere of the budhyamāna or kṣetrajña (whose *samyak*-orientation realizes his potentiality of cosmic omnipresence; cf. above, p. 96, n. 54), midway between the state of *apratibuddhatva* — in which he cannot be distinguished from, and

original sphere of the Way, see above, pp. 100f., 104) is a progressive ascension in which the contents of the consciousness of the first dhyāna (*vitarka, vicāra* and *prīti*) are gradually eliminated; same is the case with the nāmni sthāna, in which the residual nāmopādāna (*vijñaptāv upalambhaḥ* Triṃś.bh. p. 42, st.), the *trividhālambana-lābha* of XI, 7 (cf. *trividhaśca saḥ* XVI, 26b)[70] is gradually eliminated. At its culminating point the transition to the *nopalambha dhātu* (Triṃś. bh. *ibid.*, 2nd quot. st.; cf. MSA. XI, 47f., and bh.), the final advent of bodhi (cf. MSA. VI, 7-10 and bh.), actualizes the transcendent Dharmakāya. The whole process, whose lower and upper limits are marked by the two āśraya-parāvṛttis, takes place in the anāsravadhātu, described in the IXth ch. of the MSA. (in the verses relating to the

(according to the dynamic monism of this yoga-conception) is actually identical with the buddhi spellbound by sense-experience – and the state of *buddhatva* in which he is undistinguishable from and identical with the transcendent *buddha,* the 26th. The Mokṣadharma notion of the Budhyamāna thus in a way anticipates the Mahāyāna notion of the Bodhisattva As against the monism of this dominant yoga school of the Epic, the then revolutionary doctrine of Pañcaśikha (expounded in Adhy. 218, 219) asserts the exclusivistic position peculiar to the Hīnayāna: the condition-entity realized on the manas-stage of the reversed consciousness-process (*sthito manasy yo bhāvaḥ*), held to be the ātmic kṣetrajña by the teachers of the adhyātma (namely by the asserters of the triple svabhāva, of the potential ātman-character of dynamic reality), is only the nivṛtti-manifestation of the anātmic buddhi, whose sole essence is karman. (See *Il Mito Psicologico*, pp. 272-8).

[70] The three forms of knowledge, *śruta-*, *cintā-* and *bhāvanāmaya*, referred to in XI, 7, are represented in dhyānic consciousness by *vitarka, vicāra* and *prīti:* XVI, 26 bh.

Sambhogakāya and to the sublimation process whereby it is attained, 12-36) as the soteric inversion of the ākāśadhātu[71]. The notion of the coessentiality of ākāśa and vijñāna is obviously still familiar to the late Mahāyāna author. According to IX, 47 the vyāvṛtti (=first parāvṛtti, see above, p. 80) whose name is *ākāśa* consists in the perfect manifestation of the thought-entity, in the limitless expansion of the Wayfaring body. The nāma freed from sensuous rūpa is manifested in the spacelike jñānāśraya penetrating anywhere at will (*cintitārthasaṃṛddhi* is explained in the bh. by *gaganagarbho bhavati*, *gatirūpa* by *yatheṣṭagamanād ākāśīkaraṇāc ca*). This realization is an event of samādhi, as is evidenced by XVIII, 60cd: as a "Return to limitlessness" (*ameyaparāvṛtti*) this elevation to the anāsravadhātu is the attainment of limitless *vibhutā* in the coalescence with the pure āśraya of the Buddhas (IX, 48); the *buddhānām amalāśraya*, interpreted by the bh. as *buddhānām anāsravadhātu*[72], is

[71] The conception of the anāsravadhātu thus obviously reiterates the proto-Buddhistic conception of the contingent *dharmadhātu* (=*anāsravadharmasaṃtāna*), the sphere of *dhammasambhoga* (see above, p. 62, 163ff.). The two āśrayaparāvṛttis forming the lower and upper limits of the anāsravadhātu are anticipated in the two upāsanas, issuing respectively in srotaāpatti and bodhi (above, p. 103f.).

[72] Hiuan-Tsang seems to have misunderstood the intricate wording of the conception formulated in the last couple of stanzas of the Triṃśikā, whose exact sense is very definitely but not all too explicitely rendered in Sthiramati's bhāṣya. The stanzas of the MSA. provide us with useful supplementary evidence. The couple of stanzas Triṃś. 29-30 appears to be correctly rendered as follows: "The aśrayaparāvṛtti is twofold owing to the abandonment of (two) *dauṣṭhulyas* (29cd; namely: abandonment of the kleśāvaraṇa

obviously the Sambhogakāya, the pure Doctrine-Body, that form of Buddhahood which, according to st. 4, consists of the white (= anāsrava) dharmas – or of all the dharmas (unified) and none of them (singly) – the *dharmakāya* of the oldest conception, defined by Yaśomitra's phrase *anāsravadharmasaṃtāno dharmakāya aśrayaparivṛttir vā*.

The second and higher part of the Bodhisattva's career is determined by the progressive sublimation of dhyāna; on the upekṣā stage, which is *nirvikalpa jñāna*

– parāvṛtti of the Śrāvakas etc., which realizes only the *vimuktikāya* –, and abandonment of the jñeyāvaraṇa – parāvṛtti of the Bodhisattvas, realizing the Buddha's Dharmakāya): that one (*asau*) is a cittaless anupalambha, whereas this one (*tat*) is a jñāna lokottara (ab)[1]; that one (*asau*), incognoscible (as the citta is no more, cf. a), propitious and steady, the blissful *vimuktikāya* (of the Śrāvakas), coincides with the anāsravadhātu (as realized by the Bodhisattvas) (30abc), (whereas) this one (*ayam:* the one of the second parāvṛtti which implies abandonment of the *jñeyāvaraṇa;* not cittaless, but realized as *nirvikalpa lokottara jñāna*) is the Mahāmuni's Body called Dharma" (30d).

In interpreting the anāsravadhātu as the transcendent Dharmadhātu Hiuan-Tsang misses the point, as can also be seen from the MSA. stanzas: in the Dharmadhātu no *kriyās* can take place; moreover, from the bhāṣya to 51 it appears that the anāsravadhātu is the sphere proper to the Bodhisattvas. According to XI, 44 bh. the anāsravadhātu constitutes the āśraya of the Bodhisattvas as well as that of the Śrāvakaarhats and of the Pratyekabuddhas.

A perusal of the L-S affords abundant evidence that this old Mahāyāna text considers the anāsravadhātu as the

[1] It is a more perfect kind of *anupalambha*, implying awareness (*vidyamānatā*) of the parinispanna (MSA. IX, 78cd, bh.).

(XVIII, 61 bh. = *niṣkalpanajñāna* VII, 2a, realized in the second parāvṛtti, *manaso parāvṛtti* IX, 41-42[73]), he attains the supreme perfection of power, i.e. bodhi.

Thus the Bodhisattva-career is structurally anticipated in the old triadic scheme of the disciple's progress to bodhi along the path of the dhyānic ascension. The only substantial difference between these two closely related ideologies, the proto-Buddhistic and the Mahāyānic, concerning the basic structure of the Career, consists chiefly in the fact that the primitive Wayfarer was expected "not to linger" in the arūpa (Itiv., see above, p. 109) — in the Mahāyānic anāsravadhātu —, but to proceed forthwith to the nirodhadhātu conceived as Bodhi = Nirvāṇa, whereas the Bodhisattva deliberately "lingers". This difference is in its final analysis due to the one great innovation of Mahāyāna Buddhism; only faint and indefinite foreshadowings of the hetero-soteric

intermediary sphere in which the ascension towards the Dharmakāya takes place. See e.g. p. 134: *yadā teṣāṃ, mahāmate, sarvadoṣavāsanāḥ prahiṇā bhavanti dharmanairātmyāvabodhāt tadā te vāsanadoṣasamādhimadābhāvād anāsravadhātau pratibudhyante;* (and now only are they able to progress towards the Dharmakāya:) *punar api lokottarānāsravadhātuparyāpannān sambhārān paripūryācintyadharmakāyavaśavartitāṃ pratilapsyante.* The anāsravadhātu is attained along with the eighth bhūmi, the stage of the first āśrayaparāvṛtti, on whose level the Śrāvaka's career is achieved in nirvāṇa, while the Bodhisattva's career continues: *ato na parinirvānti, śrāvakapratyekabuddhās tu samādhisukhenāpahriyante, atas tesām tatra parinirvāṇabuddhir bhavati.*

[73] The twofold parāvṛtti (1, of *indriyarūpa* and 2, of *citta*) is referred to in MSA. IX, 41-42 by the terms *pañcendriyaparāvṛtti* and *manaso parāvṛtti;* the second results in nirvikalpa-jñāna.

ideal can at best be traced in the extant evidence of proto-Buddhistic thought.

Not only the psychological scheme of the career was fully anticipated, but also the connection of its two main landmarks with the two original Buddhakāyas (cf. *supra*, p. 167f.). The vyāvṛtti was represented by the srotaāpatti, in which the saṃsārasrotas of the āsravas originating from the micchā paṇihita citta (later designated as *vijñānasrotas* or *saṃtāna*) was turned into the anāsrava srotas (*anāsrava-dharma-saṃtāna*), into the actualization of the Dharma by the sammā paṇihita citta. Regenerated to partake in the Buddha's upward-leading *dharmakāya*, the disciple obtained the manomayakāya of the anāgāmin, the ūrdhvasrotas, the akaniṣṭhaga; the conception of this transfiguration preluded to the Mahāyānic conception of the first āśrayaparāvṛtti as accession to the plane of the Sambhogakāya, whereas the disciple's second transfiguration, his bodhi in which he was censed to attain consubstantiality with the Buddha's amṛta-body, anticipated the conception of the second āśrayaparāvṛtti whereby the Bodhiṣattva is consubstantiated with the transcendent Dharmakāya.

Still, as many centuries had elapsed between the disappearance of this conception from the dogmatic surface of Buddhistic doctrine and its reappearance in the Yogācāra theory, it would be – to say the least – hazardous to consider the latter as an amplified doctrinal reiteration or reinstatement of the half-forgotten ideology of primitive Buddhism, eclipsed by early dogmatic revisions. But the more natural explanation is pointed out by the evidence of our survey, concerning the native ground of the ever recurrent triadic scheme which underlies these two historically distant ideological climaxes as well as so many other characteristic doctrinal items of Buddhism, both in its earliest strata and in its Mahāyānic revival — and not of Buddhism alone. In fact, the constant and explicit references of the Yogācāra texts to the three main stages marking the psychic ascent from common consciousness to all-consciousness, as disclosing the essence of the three kāyas, make it obvious that the newly formulated theory is but a new reading of psychological data — belonging, not to any half-extinct dogmatic tradition, but to the living tradition of yoga. Uninterruptedly active along the unbroken line of Indian speculation descending from the Ṛgveda to the Mahāyāna — as a broad surface-stream in the most productive periods, as a powerful underground current when engulfed under the dogmatic accretions of materials accumulated in its course — , the Yoga-movement is constantly accompanied by the fundamental structural scheme of *nāma-rūpa*, underlying the various and complex soteriological constructions of its successive systems. This psychic climax of three modes of experience, translated into an existential climax of three modes of reality, is the mould in which the trikāya doctrine has been recast into its final shape, which is organic notwithstanding its syncretistic genesis. And this accounts for its peculiar ideological criterion. Only thus is it in fact explainable that the Nirmāṇakāya was co-ordinated with the nāma-rūpa-plane of individual sensuous experience, on account of its being perceived in manifold individual shapes by the adepts of the teaching of substantial dharmas and of individual deliverance; while the original domain of the Doctrine-Body, the "unifying" intermediate sphere of the dhyānic process, was reserved to the Sambhogakāya, the progressively realized functional unity of all the Buddhas — who are one in the spatial coincidence of their unsensuous cosmic personifications of the Doctrine and in the temporal continuity of its perennial kriyā, but manifold owing to the dynamic diversification of the nāma, to the various formulations of its identical essence – ; the Sambhogakāya being the entity instituting the progress to sambodhi through the age-long "service to the many beings", i.e. through the elevating absorption of the multiplicity into the unity of the Doctrine. And that the ultimate fulfillment of that yogic process of unification, the attainment of all-consciousness in Bodhi, is conceived as the return to the transcendent plane of the primordial and eternal unity, to the Dharmakāya, in which no distinction whatsoever obtains between the unuttered archetypal Dharma and the "own Form" (*svarūpa*) of the unmanifest Mahāpuruṣa Tathāgata : where the one Nāma coincides with the one Rūpa.

INDEX

OF TERMS AND NOTIONS

Notions represented by several synonymous terms are referred to under the English renderings of the former, the terms being cited in brackets alongside with the respective groups of passages. Under English headings also are surveyed the component elements of principal ideologies, and are classified according to import and aspect in the same way as the notions appearing under their covering Skt. and Pāli terms. Partial synonymity, parallelism, or close and constant interrelation are indicated by cross-references ("cf.v.", "cf.vv."). To correlated opposites this procedure is applied only in cases where the evidence is not directly conveyed by the word-formation. Prominent technical terms are noted throughout; the relevant passages being seldom repeated under the comprehensive survey-headings, some of the latter's counter-references are strictly complementary items. Passages where the notion occurs without the term are mostly quoted in brackets. Particularly important passages are noted in italic figures. Structural co-ordination is marked ||.

Current abbreviations: q.v., q.v.v., q.s.v., q.s.vv., q.e.s.v. = *quaere vocem, quaere voces, quaere sub voce, quaere sub vocibus, quaere eadem sub voce*; cf.v., cf.vv., cf.s.v., cf.e.s.v., = *confer vocem, confer voces, confer sub voce, confer eadem sub voce*; cet. = *cetera*; id. = *idem*; Up., Ups. = Upanishadic, Upanishads; Bsm., Bst. = Buddhism, Buddhist; canon. = canonical; orig. = original; inf. = inferior; sup. = superior; transc. = transcendent; pot. = potential; imm. = immanent; cosm. = cosmic; cosmog. = cosmogonic; psych. = psychic; sot. = soteric; consc. = consciousness.

To avoid splitting the index the order of the Latin alphabet has been adopted.

A

*abhijñā*s 88, 94n.53. 123n.21
acosmism 38f., 66f.
cf. v. Identity (absolute)
adhyātma 86ff., 183n.69
°*yoga* 52
cf. vv. *svabhāva*, consciousness
Aditi 3&n.4, 32
cf. vv. *Virāj, Vāc*, Ocean
ahaṃkāra 44, 86
cf. vv. *cakra*s, *guṇa*s, consciousness (self-)
aiśvarya 50, 179
cf. vv. *Īśvara, Puruṣa* (cosmic), *kramamukti, tṛtīya*
ajñāna q.v. *avidyā*
ajñātāvīndriya 115
akaniṣṭha 149, 154, *156, 164-167*
°*ga* 164f., 187
cf. vv. *arūpa, rūpadhātu* (canon.), cosmos (summit of —), 1st *āśrayaparāvṛtti*
akṣara 14, 37; 39; 95
(=Om q.v.)
amṛta (Immortal, °ity, plane or sphere of 3f., 7f., 9, 10f., 12 f., 14, (16), 17f., 19, (21, 23, 27), 29f., 32; (33: immanent), (36); (=*satya*) 38; 39&n.26; 40, 46, (50, 63, 68f., 91, 98), (°*dhātu*) 109, 111, 115, 130, 154; 172, 174, (177), 189.
Cf. vv. *ātman, Nirvāṇa, ānanda, nirodha*, con-

sciousness (transc. all-), *Tathatā, sat, Vāc* (unuttered)

— -essence in contingency 6f., 9 f., 13n.24, 31f., 113, 133f.& n.35 ;

cf. vv. *dharma* (soteric), Doctrine

°*kāya* 109, 111, 114, 130, 154, 165, 167, 187 ; cf. vv. *kāyas, kośas*

anāgamya 102, 104

anāgāmin q.s.v. *phalas*

anāsrava 60, 77, (96), 175&n.57

— *cetovimukti* 104, 121 ; cf. v. *vimukti*

°*dharmas* 120, 127 (three), 135n.39, 164, 185. Cf. v. unification

°*dharmasaṃtāna* 62, 80, (93), 184n.71, 185, 187

°*dhātu* 76f., *158ff., (amaladh°)* 160, 164n.37, 183f. &n.71, 185f.&n.72. Cf. vv. *dharmadhātu* (sot.), *arūpa* (-sphere)

anātman q.v. *nairātmya*

anāvṛtti (27), 177 ; cf. vv. *phalas, avaivartika, parāvṛtti,* sublimation

°*dharma* 105&n.13 ; *(=anāgāmiphala)* 102&n.7

Androgyne 3f., (5), 11f.&nn.20,22, 19, 21, 23, 33, 37, 51, 95

anna 36 ; *(āhāra)* 152 ; °*maya* (P. *āmisa)* q.s.vv. *rūpa* (sensuous), *Tathāgata*'s *rūpakāya ;* cf. vv. *kośas, attapaṭilābhas* s.v. *skandhas*

anṛta 29f., 41, 76n.18, 83f.&n.35, 173f. ;

cf. vv. *nāmarūpa,* °*satya*

an-ṛta=amṛta 32

antarabhāva 114, cf. v. *(pratisaṃdhi) vijñāna*

anutpāda 59, 170

°*panna* 32

anutpādajñāna 127

apocatastasis 11, 14, 20, 23f., 25, 27, 29, 32, 37f...129, 189

cf. vv. enlightenment, descent & ascent, *parāvṛtti*

apratibuddha (abuddha) 86, 182n.69

°*tâ* 96n.54

arhat q.s.v. *phalas*

arūpa (7), 10, 11f.&n.20; 19; *(amūrta)* 19f., 27f., 31, 33, 39, 41ff., 53, 61n.9, 96n.54, 172, 174 ; 20 *(=nāma, ākāśa),* 35n.24 *(cidrūpa);* 40&n.26, (46), 57, (64), 69, (72n.10), (84n.36), 96, 108f., 113f., 132, 141n.6, 143n.10, 160 *(adeha),* (162f.)

°*in* 108n.3, 116, 133

— -sphere (8ff.), 20, 28, 29f., 35n. 24, 38, 40, 47, 49f., 53, 58, 60, 62, 63n.14, 46&n.15, 66n. 16, 68, 73, 76, 81, 84f. (=sphere of *nāma),* 88 *(manasi sthāna),* 90, 94f.; (precanon.) *97ff.,* 100, 105f., 109, 111, 114f., 130, 143n.10, 146, 147, 151 *(sandhya sthāna),* 152, 153 *(tṛtīya sthāna),* 156, 157n.26, 158f., 160n.31, 163 f., 166, 180f., 181 *(cittasya dhātu),* 182&n.69, *(=anāsravadhātu)* 186&n.72 ; 188

°*dhātu* (canon.) q.s.v. *ārūpyadh°*

Cf. vv. *dharma* (sot.), Doctrine, *manomaya, ākāśa, anāsrava*

°*dhyānas* q.s.v. *dhyāna*

aśabda q.s.v. *śabda*

asaṃskṛta 58ff.&nn.6, 7 ; 64f.n.15 ; (°*āḥ*) 107 ; 135n.39
ascent q.vv. descent & ascent, *parāvṛtti*, sublimation, *srotas*
assimilation (to soteric & progressively to transcendent reality) 49f., 74, 84n.35, 92, 103f., 111, 157&n.27, 168
cf. vv. enlightenment (process of —), *dhyāna*, *upāsana*
asti — nāsti 52f.n.5, 144 ; cf. v. *avyākṛta*
asti ca nāsti ca 89
aupapāduka 105, 142n.9
autonomy q.v. *svatantra*
avaivartika 81&n.31 ; cf. vv. *phalas*, Way, sublimation, *parāvṛtti*, *anāvṛtti*
avidyā 27, 48, 55, 62, 91&n.51, 92, 112, 161 (=*ajñāna)*
°*dhātu* q.s.v. *ṇāmarūpa* (sphere of —)
avijñapti q.s.v. orientation
avikalpa (14), 35n.24, 47, 135 ; *(nir°)* 164(*-jñāna-mārga)*, 165, 185 f. ; 166, 175n.57 *(akalpa)*. Cet. q.s.v. *jñāna* ; cf. vv. *sākṣin*, *upekṣā*
avinipātadhamma 102&n.7, 103f. Cf. vv. *anāvṛtti*, *anāgāmin* s.v. *phalas*, *avaivartika*, Way, sublimation
avyakta 87, 89f. *parama* — 24. Cf. v. *brahman*
avyākṛta 70n.4, 154. Cf. v. *asti — nâsti*

Ā

ākāśa 20 (sheer *nāma*, sphere of) ; 29, 33 *(brahman)*, 45 ; 59n. 7, 60, 64n.14, 90, *95*, 97, *(°ātmā)* 108, 131f., *158f.*& nn.30-31, 160, 162, 184
°*dhātu* 20, 30, 65n.15, 159, 184. Cf. vv. *dhātus*, *arūpa* (-sphere), *ārūpya*
hṛdākāśa (6), 20f., 28&n.18, 29f., 34 ; 36 ; 44f., 46, 63f.n.14, 83f., 84n.35, 90n.48, 95, (131), 132, 133, 172f. Cf. vv. *vijñāna*, *cakras*
ālaya (Up.) 46 ; °*vijñāna* *75f.*, 76n. 18, 77&n.22, 78f., 81, 83f., 85, 87&n.42, 91, 134f., 136, 159, 161, 163, 173n.51, 178 n.62, 180f.
lower and higher — 46, 77, 84f. Cf. vv. consciousness, *vijñāna*, *citta*, (*hṛd*)*ākāśa*
ānanda 18, 32f., 39, 46, 84 ; *(°maya ātman)* 35, 37, 133
potential — 32, cf. v. *ātman* (potential)
Cf. vv. consciousness (transc. all-), *ātman*, *amṛta*, *ekībhāva*, Androgyne
ārūpya-dhātu (canon.) 57, 76, 97f., *99f.*, 101n.6, 105f., 116f., 128, 165, 180
āyatanas of — 143n.10, 156
ākāśānantya° 60
vijñānānantya° 60
akiñcānya° 100n.5
naivasaṃjñānāsaṃjñā° 100n. 5, 101n.6
saṃjñāveditanirodha 100f.n.6, 110, 118 ; cf. vv. *nirodha*, *sākṣin*
Cf. v. *dhyāna (ārūpya-*°s)
ārya 78, 101n.6, 115, 181 *(Bodhisattva)*

°*dharma* 136, cf. v. *tathāgata-garbha*
°*mārga* q.s.v. Way
°*satyas* q.v. *satyas*, four, s.v. *satya*
°*skandhas* 115, 126f.
Cf. vv. orientation, sublimation, *vyavadāna*, *nivṛtti*, Way
āśraya 46, 76f., 77n.22, 80, 84f., 87n.42, (plural & one) 181n. 67, 185n.72
°*parāvṛtti* s.v. *parāvṛtti*
parāvṛttyāśraya: inf. 90, (112, 164), 180f.
sup. 91, (111, 165)
sarvatraga° 77, 180 ; cf. vv. omnipresence, body (cosmic consc.-)
citta° 77n.24, cf. v. *manomaya-kāya*.
Cf. vv. *nāmarūpa* (indiv.), *arūpa*, *ālaya*
āsrava(s) 104, 111, 187
°*dharmas* 135n.39; cf. s.v. *dharmas*
sa° 175&n.57 ; cf. v. *anāsrava*
āvaraṇa q.v. veil
ātman 15f., 19, *20f.*, 24f., 29, 34, 35f., 41, 66f., 69, 70n.4, 84 n.35, 85f., 88, 90, 95 ; (sphere of —) 27, 69, 130f. ; 131, 132f., 153, 163, 173f., 177, 179, 182f.n.69
immanent — 15, 86, 179
potential — 18, 26, 30, (49), 83f., 132f., 134, 135, 137, 177, 183 n.69
mahān — 96n.54
— as saviour god 40, cf. v. *Puruṣa* (sot.)
four *pādas* of — 34. Cf. v. *smṛtyu-pasthānas*
atta-paṭilābhas q.s.v. *skandhas* (three)
Cf. vv. *Puruṣa* (transc.), *Vāc* (transc.), *amṛta*, *Nirvāṇa*, Androgyne, consciousness (transc. all-), *brahman* (transc.)

B

bhakti q.s.v. love (soteric)
bhavāgra 97, 100f.n.6, 164n.37 (*bhūtakoṭi*)
°*ga* 164
Cf. vv. cosmos (summit of —), totality (cosm.), *akaniṣṭha*, *arūpa*, *ārūpya*
bhoga (*upa*°) 115, (*sam*°) 147n.18, 161, 163 ; (*mahāyānopa*°) 148n.18
dhammasambhoga 147n.18, 163, 184n.71
svasam° 147n.18, 150
parasam° 147n.18
bhoktṛ 13n.23, 161, 163
bhogya 161, 163
Cf. vv. participation, assimilation
bhūmis: first 81n.31
eighth 80, 186n.72
śuddhādhyāśaya° 80
pramuditā 78, (80)
Cf. v. Way (stages of —)
bhūtātman 87. Cf. v. *kṣetrajña*
bīja 34n.24, 75, 76n.18, 77, 78n.25, 85&n.39, 86, 136, 163
bird, (°s), 7, 8f., 10n.19, 12&n.23, 14, 44
Cf. vv. light (-rays), *Skambha*, *manas* (divine & mortal)
bodhi q.v. enlightenment

Bodhisattva 77n.23, 78, 80f., 81f.n.31, 94n.53, 135, 147&n.18, 149, 152, 166, (180), 181 &n.67, *(dharmakāya°)* n.66, 183n.69, 185&n. 72, 186f.
°*yāna* q.s.v. Way
career of — 184f., *186f.* Cf. e.s.v.
bodhyaṅgas 112, 119f.
body: of gross elements 15, 29, . . . 92, 95, 118, 120, 134, 142, 149, 177 ; cf. v. *rūpa* (sensuous). Contemplation on — q.v. *smṛtyupasthāna*, 1st
unsensuous: *(yogāgnimaya śarīra)* 17f., 20, 50, 134 ; *(prāṇaśarīra)* 39, 95, 108 ; *(ākāśaśarīra)* 33; *(aśarīra)* 19, 95 ; *(nirāśraya liṅga)* 46 ; *(amūrta rūpa)* 98, 132 (etc., q.s.v. *rūpa, mūrta & amūrta)* ; *(ārūpya, vijñānamaya)* (61n.9), 108, 113, 133, 143n.10, 177 ; (of *nirmāṇa*, Up.) 151, 153 ; *(manomaya)* q.e.s.v. *(rūpa, kāya)*
cosmic consciousness-body: 6 &n.12, 12n.24 *(tanū)*, 14, 16f., 19, *29*, 31 ; *(kālavatī & lokavatī tanū)* 34; 43f. ; 50, 53, 54 *(śivā tanū)*, 55, 84n.36, 93&n.52, 94f., 139, 151&n.22, 153, *157 &nn.26, 27, 28* ; 158, 160, 162f., 166, 180f., 184, 188f. Cf. vv. omnipresence, totality, unification
three cosmic (& microcosmic) bodies 35n.24, 47 ; (triune c.b.) 25f., 42, 47, 173
four bodies of *turīya* 35n.24
five b. *(kośas)* 35f., 37f. Cf. v. *kośas*
seven b.: 34n.24
transcendent all-consciousness-body, q.s.vv. *amṛtakāya, nirodha°, nirvāṇa°, dharma°, prajñā°* ; cf. vv. consciousness (transc. all-), *ānanda, ātman,* Androgyne
Cf. vv. *kośas, skandhas, kāyas*
brahman 21 etc. passim
transcendent — 17, 21, 24, 27, 32f., 36, 38, 69, 70f.&n.5, 86, 88, 95, 133, 174
cosmogonic — 25n.15, 26f., 29f., 39, 41 ; ("lower") 48 *(śakti)*, 55, 96. Cf. v. *(pravṛttilakṣaṇa)dharma*
soteric — 27, 30, 36f., 39, 41 ; ("higher") 40, 47, 48 *(śakti)*, 49, 53f., 55, 88, 90n.48, 91f., 94f., 95f., 139, 161f., 179n.63, 182n. 69
Cf. vv. *dharma* (sot.), *vidyā*, Doctrine, *(nivṛttilakṣana)dharma, satya* (sot.), *setu, Vāc* (sot.)
contingent, microcosmic — 21f.& n.7, 23 *(Kuṇḍalinī)*, 27, 29 *(hṛdākāśa)*, (its twofold potentiality) 30 ; 32, 37f., 39, 108, 133, 173f. Cf. vv. *satya* (four aspects of —), *Vāc* (uttered)
two forms of — 42, 44, cf. v. *rūpa (mūrta & amūrta)*
three stages of — 33
five stages of — 35
four aspects of — q.v. *satya* (4 asp.)

brahmaloka: transcendent 24, 36, 39n.26 ; q.vv. *amṛta, dhātu* (fourth)
summit of cosmos 30, 40, 92*f*., 166. Cf. vv. cosmos (summit of —), *dharmaja*
heart-° 30, (37, 39), 83, 173 *(brahmapura)*
brahmabhāva (°bhūya) 54
brahmavidyā q.s.vv. *vidyā, jñāna*, knowledge (sot.), Doctrine
brahmacakra 71
brahmakāya 71, 92; cf. v. *dharmakāya*
brahmanirvāṇa q.s.v. *Nirvāṇa*
Brahmán 38, 93&n.52
brahmarandhra (18), 23, 46 ; cf. v. *cakra*s
brahmavihāras 85, 93f.&.n53
Buddha q.v. *Tathāgata*
buddha (Up.) 88, 96n.54, 183n.69 ; (orig. import of term in Bsm.) 104, 111
buddhatva, °tā 70n.4, 127 (three *jñāna*s, id. & five *dharmas*); 146, 156, 158ff., 164, (170); (Up.) 183n.69; 185; cf. vv. *tathatā*, enlightenment, *kāyas (Buddha-°)*: *Sambhoga°*, *Dharma°*
buddhi 44, 86, 88 ; *(śubhā)* 53, 96, 141n.6 ; 182f.n.69. Cf. vv. *citta, vijñāna*
stages of — 88, 182n.69
1. phenomenic perception 88, 182f.n.69
2. noumenic perception 88, 89, 179, 182n.69
3. ecstatic *(ātman)* perception 88
Cf. vv. *svabhāva, parāvṛtti*
budhyamāna 96n.54, 182f.n.69
Cf. vv. *kṣetrajña*, enlightenment (process of —)

C

caittas 131f.
cakras
three + *brahmarandhra*: 22&n.11, 23, 33, 153 ; (‖*dhātus*) 22 ; 3rd: (10&n.16), 23 ; 2nd: 18, 20f., 23, 28ff. ; 1st: 22, 23
(four – — 33)
(five – — 37f.)
six – — 34n.24
Cf. vv. *guṇas, dhātus*, consciousness (stages of —), *kośas*, inward-upward progression
cakṣus 19
three:
divya° 95, 114f., 144, 157n.27, =*dharma°* 114&n.10, 160n.31
prajñā° 114f.
māṃsa° 114, 160n.31
cākṣuṣaḥ puruṣaḥ 10n.16, 17f.n.5, 19. Cf. vv. *puruṣa (rūpa-°)*, *prāṇa*
causality q.s.v. *karman, pratītya-samutpāda, pravṛtti*
cetanā 107n.1, 131. Cf. v. *saṃskārāḥ*
cetovāśitā 173n.52
citta 46 ; 79, 84f., 87n.42, 88, 91, (=*saṃjñā*) 119f., 166n.44, 171&n.46, 181, 182n.69
Cf. vv. *vijñāna, buddhi, manas*
— *viśuddha* (=*sattva v°*, *buddhi v°ā*) 48, 53, 85, 96
— *samyakpraṇihita* 62, 76n.18,

79, 85f., (88ff.), 91, 113, 140, (179, Up.), 187
— *upakliṣṭa* 58f., 63
— *mithyāpraṇihita* 76n.18, 79, 85, (88), 113, 187
Cf. vv. descent & ascent, orientation, *vyavadāna*
— *prabhāsvara* 58, 62f., 68, 85, 113
Cf. vv. *vijñāna* (transc.), consciousness (transc. all-)
— *ādiśuddha* 59, 63, 85, 113
— 's *aikarasya* 135
°*kāya* (61n.9), 120, 125, 130. Id. *manomayak*°, *nāmak*°
°*mātra(tā)* 152, (175), 180f.
°*vāda* 140f.n.5, 147, (pre-can.) 148, 169 ; (in Yogācāra) 150, 180
Cf. v. *vijñānavāda*
°*sya citte sthāna*, q.v. *nāmni sthāna*
acitta 46, 185n.72 ; cf. vv. *aprāṇa*, *avijñāna*
cognition, modes of — q.s.vv. subject-obj. exp., *ekībhāva*, consciousness
consciousness:
essence of the real (4f., 26f., 29), 63 f., 65n.16, 82, 87n.42, 148, 158, 182n.69 ; cf. vv. *vijñāna(vāda)*, *citta(mātratā)*, *dharma*(s), *adhyātma*, *svabhāva*(s)
common, waking, discriminating — 5, 13, 22, 30, 34, 75, 90, 91, 151, (158), 161, (168), 173f., 176, (182n.69), 188. Cf. vv. *vikalpa*, subject-obj. experience, *nāmarūpa* (sphere of —), *citta (mithyāpraṇihita)*
pluri- — 22&n.11, (60f.n.9), 150f., 152f., 160, (163) ; cf. vv. *iddhi*, dream, personality (pluri-)
unsensuous, concentrated — 13f., 17f.n.5, 46, 151, 176ff.
self- — 18, 22f.&n.11, 26&n.16, 28, 31 *(aham)*, 48, 81f., 92, 131. Cf. vv. *avidyā*, *ahaṃkāra*, *nāmarūpa* (sphere of —), *vijñāna(maya puruṣa)*
cosmic — 14, 15f., 26, 29, 48, 53f., 85, 93, 153, 158f., 161f., 178, 181n.67, 188. Cf. vv. omnipresence, body (of cosmic consc.), unification
soteric — 14, 17, 48, 53ff., 156, 164, 176, 188. Cf. vv. knowledge, ("higher") *brahman*, *dhyāna*, love, *dharma* (sot.)
transcendent all- — 5f., 16f., 18f., 23, 28, 48, 51, 54, 58, 63, 68, 71, 72n.8, 74&n.12, 75, 82, 85, 95, 113f., 120, 133, 161f., (173), 185n.72, 188f. ; *(sarvajñatā)* 83, 136, 146n.16, 161f. Cf. vv. *ātman*, enlightenment, *citta (prabhāsvara)*, *Nirvāṇa*, *dharma (°tā*, — transc.)
potential 18, 23, 28, 82, 137, 161, 165, 175, 176, 178. Cf. v. *ātman* (pot.)
transfiguration of — 49, 55, 113 ; cet. q.s.vv. sublimation, reversal, assimilation..., *vyāvṛtti*, *parāvṛtti*, *yoga*
"subtle" — , *ekarasaskandha*, q.s. v. *skandhas*, cf. v. *ālayavijñāna*.

three stages of — (22&n.11), 33f., 88, 96n.54, (98f.), 114f., 151, 153, 168, 188. Cf. vv. *buddhi* (stages of —), *svabhāvas*, triads, *dhātus* (three)
contingent (*guṇas*) 44, 84
four stages of — 22ff., 34, 41, 153 Cf. vv. *tṛtīya, turīya*, tetrads (primary), *cakras* (three + *brahmarandhra*)
— -functions q.vv. *prāṇas, indriyas*
cosmos
manifestation of — 3f., 7ff., 14, etc., cf. vv. *nāmarūpa* (cosm.), light (cosm.)
structure of — 7, 10, 11nn.19, 20, 13n.24, 20, 22, 23f., 29, 34, 50... cet. cf. s.v. *dhātus*
summit of — 5n.7, 7, 12, 14, 23, 39n.26, 40, 61n.9, 92f., 100n.6, 164&n.37, 182n. 69. Cf. vv. *akaniṣṭha, brahmaloka* (cosm.), *naivasaṃjñānāsaṃjñāyātana* s.v. *ārūpyadhātu* (canon.); *nirodha*, totality, *ṛta, bhavāgra*
current, stream 61, 81, 92, 104&n.10, 165, 178&n.62, 187, q.vv. *nāmarūpa* (indiv.), *saṃtāna (vijñāna°, anāsravadharma°)*; cf. vv. descent & ascent, *saṃsāra*, Way, *dharma* (sot.)

D

descent and ascent (psychic & cosmic) 4; 5n.7, 7, 9f., 13f.&n.25, 14, 18, 20f., 24, 30f., 36f., 43f., 48, 71, 77n.23, 79, 81, 84n.35, 89f., 91f., 95f., 102f., 113, 129f., 132, 134, 158f. Cf. vv. orientation, sublimation, *parāvṛtti, citta* (*samyak- & mithyāpraṇihita*), *pravṛtti, nivṛtti*, apocatastasis
— soteric 7, 9, 14, 74f., 91f., 141
desire q.v. *kāma*
dharma
transcendent, one: 4f., 8f.&n. 15, 11, 12n.20 ; (46), *51f.*, 55, (=*Nirvāṇa*) 61f., 63, 65, 67, 68, 70f.&n.5, 72f. (unuttered Doctrine), 74, 78, 81f., 94, 104, 148n. 18, (159), 189 ; (*Dharmatā*) 73f., 76&n.20, 139f., 141f. Cf. vv. *Nirvāṇa, amṛta, ātman*
soteric: 7, 9, 10ff.&nn.19,20 ; *53ff.*, 71, 73, 75, 79, 81& n.29, 90n.49, 91f., 94, 103, 106, 109, 115, 139, 148, 158f., 163, 165, 185, 187f. Cf. vv. *vidyā, brahman* (sot.), Doctrine, knowledge (sot.), *satya* (sot.), *manas* (divine), unification
°*cakra* 71, 81n.31
dharmas (pl. °*āṇi*, °*āḥ*) 8, 13n.24, 32 ; (*pṛthag*°) 42, 46, 51, 55 ; *63f.*, *65&n.16*, 72, 78, 81f., 85, 87n.42, 91n.51 ; (*aikarasya* of —) 135n.39; (precan. & canon. theory of —) 148 ; 158, 169, 171 n.46, 188. Cf. vv. *nāmāni*, differentiation
— of Teaching 72, cet. q.s.

v. Doctrine
anāsrava-°s 119f. ; (three) 127 ; (*śukla*-°s) 164 ; 185 ; q.s.v. *anāsrava*
— -duality 44; cf. vv. *dvaya*, subj.-obj. exp.
°*nairātmya* q.s.v. *nairātmya*
pravṛttilakṣanadharma 55, 88f. 90, 176, 178
nivṛttilakṣanadharma 55, 88f., 90 ff., 176, 179
dharmya 52ff., 55. Cf. *nāmarūpa* (sphere of)
dharma-rūpa, binomium (& *nāma-rūpa*) 56-60 ; later import 64
dharmakāya (transc.) q.s.v. *kāyas Buddha*-°) ; (imman.) q. e.s.v. &s.v. Doctrine (-body); three *dharmakāyas* 155
dharmadhātu q.s.v. *dhātus*
°*cakṣus* q.s.v. *cakṣus*
°*jñānakṣānti* q.s.v. Doctrine
°*gati (lokottarā)* 78, cf. v. Way
dharmaja, °*nirmita* 92, 139, (157n. 27), 167, (187)
°*nirjāta* 160n.31 ; cf. *ekaja* 9, 11n.20, *prathamaja ṛtasya* 5f., (12), 17, 31, *bhūtakoṭiprabhāvita tathāgatakāya* 164n.37. Cf. vv. totality, cosmos (summit of —), assimilation
dharmaskandhas (three) 115, cet. s.v. *skandhas*; cf. v. *tathāgataskandhas*
dharmatā q.s.vv. *dharma* (transc.), *(dharma-)dhātu* (transc.)
dhāman (hypercosmic) 8, 9n.15, 53. Cf. vv. light (transc.), *dharma* (transc.), *amṛta*, *Nirvāṇa*.
°s 7f., 18, 42. Cf. vv. light (cosm.), *tejas*, *dharmas*, differentiation
°s and *rūpas*, binomium, 7, cf. vv. *nāma-rūpa*, binomium, *dharma-rūpa*, binomium
dhātus, *lokas*, spheres of existence 4, 13nn.24,25; 20, 83, 128n.23
three (2 & 3rd) (20), 27, 33, 52f., 60, 98f., 100, 109, 162f., 168. Cf. v. triad
four (3 & 4th) 22f., 24&n. 13, 25, 31, 33f., 41f., 43, 44, 60, 69, 97f., 99f., 116ff., 121n.19, 130f., 149, 153, 156. Cf. vv. *trailokya*, tetrads, *vyāhṛtis*
from three to four 99, 116, 125&n.24
five 35f., 128n.28, (contingent) 131f. Cf. v. pentad
six 57, 60, 63f., 97, *132* ; (3×2 11n.20). Cf. v. hexad
sixth 129
seven 34f.n.24. Cf. v. heptad
dharmadhātu (two °s) 60, 61f.
transcendent: 62, 73, 82, 97, 179. Cf. vv. *dharma* (transc.), *Nirvāṇa*, *amṛta*
immanent: 60, 62, 65f.n. 16, 68, 93, 107, 158, 160, 165, 184n.71. Cf. vv. *dharma* (sot.), *arūpa*, *anāsrava*, Way

— °*jakāya* 140n.4. Cf. v. *dharmaja* s.v. *dharma*
dharmadhātu (canon.) 64
rūpadhātu q.s.v. *rūpa*
ārūpyadhātu q.v.
kāmadhātu q.s.v. *kāma*
svadhātu q.s.v. *sva°*
dhātus||*skandhas* 116f., 128ff.&n.28
||*kāyas* 117f., 125&n.23, 128ff., 137
||*cakras* 22
vedana°, *sañña°*, *saṅkhāra°* 128n. 28
vijñāna° q.s.v. *vijñāna ; ("dhātu" =ālaya-vijñāna)* 87n.42
dhyāna 34f.n.24, 49f., 85, 88, 90ff., 93n.53, 97f., 100ff., 106, 109, 111, 113f., 115f., 120, 122f. &n.21, 124, 126, 133f.&n.35, 148, 168, 173n.52, 176, 179, 182&n.69, 183n.70, *185f.*
sphere of — 99f., 104n.11, 118, 123 n.21, 125n.23, 148, 165, 182&n.69, 188. Cf. v. *arūpa*(-sphere)
formula of — 113, 120, 122ff.n.21, 125
body of — 113, 122f., 124n.22, 126 n.24, cet. cf. s.v. *manomayakāya*
rūpa-dhyānas 93f.n.53, 97, 99, 100 f., 104, 116, 119, 121, 122 &n.21, 124, 125f.&nn.23, 24, 165
first: 99, 102, 104, 122, 178, 183
second: 122
third: 113, 121f., 122f.n.21, 125
1st–3rd: 113, 122, 123n.21
3rd & 4th: 113
fourth: 94n.53, 100n.4, 101n. 6, 104, 113f., 117, 121, 123f.n.21, 124f., 165, 185
ārūpya-dhyānas: 60, 97, 100, 121, 125
first: 60
second: 60
third: 100n.5
fourth: 100n.5, 101n.6
Cf. v. *ārūpyadhātu (āyatanas* of —)
rūpa° + *ārūpya°* 97f., 100&n.4, 110, 121
dhyānas||*vimokṣas* 121
— ||*smṛtyupasthānas* 122
differentiation 2f., 4f., 7f., 10, 12f., 14, 15f., 21&n.8, 25, 27, 28f., 32, 37ff., 43 *(sakala)*, 46, 48, 51, 55, 66, 73, 75, 77, 83, 85, 87, 136, 142, 156, 171&n.46, 172f. Cf. vv. *vikalpa*, *pariṇāma*, unity and multiplicity
indifferentiation q.v. unification
dissimilation (& concealment) 4, 5, 7, 75, 84n.35, 133. Cf. vv. veil, assimilation
Doctrine, soterical 26, 39, 49f., 61f., 71ff., 74, 78, 82n.31, *91f.*, 94ff., 103f., 109, 114, 135, 139f., 140 *(nirmāṇa)*, 141& n.7 ; 143, 144f., 147n.18, 148ff., 157n.26, 159, 163, 188 f. Cf. vv. *dharma* (sot.), *brahman* (sot.), *satya* (sot.), knowledge, *Vāc* (sot.), Way
— , (worldly & soterical) 55, 90
— , (levels of —), 147ff., 155
(two Doctrines) 145f., 148ff.
— -body (54), 70n.4, 71, *92ff.*, *139f.*, 144 ; (Hīnayānic & Mahāy.) 145f., 147n.18,

149f. ; 150 ; 151, 155, 156 &n.24, 157n.26, 159f.&n. 31, 163, 181, 185, 188. Cf. vv. body (cosmic consciousness-), *setu, Skambha, Puruṣa* (sot.), unification, assimilation, *kāyas (Buddha-°)*

dharmajñānakṣānti 78

dream 22, 34&n.24, 41, 151, 153f. (=*dvitīya sthāna* 153)
Cf. vv. consciousness (pluri- ; three & four stages of —), *nirmāṇakāya* s.v. *kāya*

duḥkha (13n.24), 18, 86, 114
°*satya* q.s.v. *(ārya)satyas*

dvaya, dvandva 44, 177, 179f. Cf. vv. subject-object experience, consciousness (self-, waking), *vikalpa*

dyads
(the contingent and the transcendent real) 32 etc.
(Buddhakāyas) 142, 154

dynamism (psychic & cosmic) 51-54, 66, 75, 80, 81n.31 ; (opposite aspects of —) 79n.28, 134, 172, (identical) 153 ; 141n.7, 177, 183n.69. Cf. vv. descent & ascent, orientation, *pravṛtti, nivṛtti,* reversal, *pravṛttilakṣaṇadharma* & *nivṛttilakṣaṇadharma* s.v. *dharma*

E

ecstasy q.vv. egression, consciousness (transc. all-), *parāvṛtti* (2nd), *ānanda*, enlightenment (event of —), lightning

egression *(ut-sthā ; niṣ-pad ; vi-nir-gam ; nir-vā ;* etc.) 5&n.8, 11, 14, 15f., 23, 45, 46f., 50 f., 91, 134, 174f. Cf. vv. *cakras*, sublimation, *yoga, dhyāna, dhātus*, cosmos (structure of — , summit of —)

ekībhāva (union of principles of *nāma* & *rūpa)* (10n.16), 18&n.5, 19ff., 23, 28, 34, 37f., 40, 44, 47, 49, 95. Cf. vv. *(satyasya) satya, cakra* (2nd, s.v. *cakras*, three + *br.), ākāśa (hṛd°)*

elements
four: 68, 107n.1
five: 36, 63n.14, 131f.
six: 63, 97. Cf. v. *dhātus* (six)
body of — 92, cet. q.s.v. body (of gross elements), *rūpa* (sensuous). Cf. vv. *skandhas, kāyas, kośas*

elimination 37f., 77&n.23, 104, 119, 120, 122&n.20, 131ff., 164, 170f., 178, 183. Cf. vv. *nivṛtti*, sublimation
— only 111, 133, 141n.7, 143, 177f. Cf. v. *vimukti* (without *bodhi)*

emanation 20, 25, 32, 39, 89, 129, 132. Cf. v. *pravṛtti*
— , soteric 8ff., cf. v. *dharma* (sot.)

enlightenment
(event of —) 5f., 9, 10f. &n.19, 12, 14, *(pratibodha, bodhi, sambodhi)* 16&n.3, 42, 50, 81, 100n.5, 144, 146, 147n.18, 150, 155, 161 f., 165, (175), 183, 184n.71, 187, 189. Cf.

vv. egression, *parāvṛtti* (2nd)
(Gotama's) 74n.12, 100, 101n.6
(plane & entity of —) 109, 136, 140f., 160f., 186. Cf. vv. *amṛta, buddhatva,* consciousness (transc. all-), *Dharma* (transc.), *Nirvāṇa*
& deliverance (process & activity of —) 7, 11f.&n.20, 13&n. 25, 14, 17f., 23 f., 27, 31, 34–37, 39&n.26, 42, 49f., 51, 60, 80f., 89f.& n.48, 91, 96, 101, 150, 154, 159f., 163ff., 168, 171 (no process), 173, 181, 182n.69, 186 &n.72, 189. Cf. vv. unification, assimilation, *dhyāna, yoga,* consciousness (sot. ; transfiguration of —)
two main stages: (*kramamukti*) 40, 50, 166, 179; q.v. *parāvṛtti*. Cf. v. *upāsana*
three & four stages, q.s.v. Way (four & five stages of —)
sambodhayitṛ 42, 95
sambodhiparāyaṇa 104
budhyamāna q.v.
Buddha q.v., & v. *Tathāgata*
bodhicitta 91 ; cf. v. *citta (samyakpraṇihita)*
Error 51, 136, 170. Cf. vv. Identity (absolute), *parikalpita* s.v. *svabhāvas* (three, Bst.)
evolution q.v. *pravṛtti*
exclusion, mutual
(evolution by —) 62, 130f.
(realization & thesis of —) 66f., *69 f.&n.4*, 75, 113f., 134, 138; (absolute) 140, 141n.7 ; 154, 167, 169f., 172, 183 n.69

F

fruition q.v. *bhoga (sam°, bhoktṛ, bhogya)*. Cf. vv. participation, imitation, assimilation
fruit q.s.vv. Tree, *phalas*

G

guide to Immortality: *(gopā)* 13f., *(netṛ)* 39&n.26, *(praṇetṛ)* 42f., 46 ; teacher (of *yoga*, inner —) 14, 49, 53 ; (in Ups. & in Bsm.) 91f., 95f., 162f., 181 ; *(Buddha* as t.) 61, 103f., 144 ; 139 *(nāyaka)*, 163&n.35, 167. Cf. vv. *Puruṣa* (sot.), *manas* (divine), *prajñā* (pure), *brahman* (sot.), *dharmakāya* (imm.) s.v. *kāyas (Buddha-°)*, Doctrine (-body)
guṇas (25), 44ff.&n.5, 84, 86f., 89, 96 n.54, (162), (182n.69). Cf. vv. *cakras, skandhas, dhātus*

H

heptad 34n.24 (from triad & tetrad)
hexad (element-layers + transcendent sphere) 36 ; *ṣaḍdhātu* (origin of —) 132, cet. q.s.v. *dhātus*

I

iddhi 106, 109, 114, 123n.21, 124, 152, 160n.31, 181
Identity, absolute (doctrine of —) 38f., 51, 67, 71n.4, 153.
 — , supreme *(parama sāmya)* 95. Cf. vv. consciousness (transc. all-), *Puruṣa* (transc.)
imitation 111, 168. Cf. vv. assimilation, enlightenment (process of —)
Indha-Indra 17f., 19, 38, 44, 47, 134. Cf. vv. *prāṇa*, orientation, *ekībhāva*
individuum 15, 17f.&n.5, 19, 21f.&n. 8, 26f., 61n.9, 76f., 86f., 150f., 169, 171n.46, 173, 188; (— & cosmos 21f.n.8, etc., passim). Cf. vv. *nāmarūpa* (individual), *skandhas*
 individuation q.s.vv. differentiation, *vikalpa, dharmas*, consciousness (self-)
indriyas 17f.n.5, 37, 162. Cf. vv. unification, consciousness (waking)
inversion q.v. reversal
involution q.v. *nivṛtti*
inward-upward progression 35, 38, 46, (76), 108f., 113, 117f., 122n. 20, 128f., 132 (outward-downward) ; 137, 146f.n.18, 168, 176&n.60. Cf. vv. *kośas*, *kāyas*, *skandhas*, *dhātus*, orientation, descent & ascent

Ī

Īśvara (50), 53 *(bhageśa)*, (95f.&)n. 54, 153, 162f., 166(&n.43), 181
 Cf. vv. *aiśvarya, Puruṣa* (cosmic, soteric)

J

-ja : *eka°*, *prathama°*, q.v. *dharma-ja* s.v. *dharma*
 aja 11&n.20, 30, (170)
jalpa, ajalpa q.s.v. *śabda*
Jīnas, five: 128n.27, 156
jīva : *(-ātman)* 25f., 46 *(prāṇa)* ; 48 f., 86
jñāna 33, 35, 161f., 180. Cf. v. *prajñā (°ātman)*
 °āśraya 180, 184 ; cf. vv. consciousness (cosm.), body (cosm. consc.-), omnipresence
 nirvikalpa lokottara jñāna 175n.57, 185f.&n.72. Cf. v. *avikalpa*
 ādarśa-° 181f.&n.68
 three *jñānas (kṣaya°, anutpāda°, samyagdṛṣṭi)* 127
 four — 127f.n.27
 °āvaraṇa q.s.v. veil
 °rūpa 33, passim s.v. *āśraya (citta°, sarvatraga°, parāvṛtty°)*. Cf. v. *arūpa*
 jñeya 42, 161f.

K

kaivalya 50. Cf. vv. *aiśvarya, turīya, kramamukti*

karman (worldly & yogic) 31f., 89f., 172 ; *(pravṛtti)* (55) ; (sot.) 82n.31 ; 86 ; 131, 173, *(°nivṛtti)* 179 ; 183n.69
°*nāmāni* 16
°*lakṣaṇa* 78
°*guṇa* 182n.69
niṣpannak° 94n.53
Cf. vv. dynamism, orientation, *pratītyasamutpāda*
kāla 42ff. ; — and *akāla* 43f., 46 ; 96
trikāla 34, *(tryadhvasamatā)* 157n. 28. Cf. vv. *Skambha, Puruṣa* (cosmic)
kāma 18, 161 ; *kāmāḥ* 83, 173, etc.
satyāḥ — 29f., cf. v. *satya* (sot.)
°*cāra* 173, cf. vv. *svatantra, cetovāśitā.*
°*dhātu* 57, 76, *97ff.*, 128
*kāya*s 108–125 ; 128, 137
two & third (transc.) 108ff., 111, 113ff., 124, 130, 142 ; (without third) 112
three & fourth: 116ff., 119ff., 122n.20, 123n.21, 125, 130
& *skandha*s 108, 117f., 128, 129f.
& *vimokṣa*s 110f., 117ff.
|| *dhātu*s 109, 116f., 125n.23, 129, 137
|| *svabhāva*s 168, 176n.60
rūpakāya q.s.v. *rūpa*
nāma° q.s.v. *nāman*
manomaya° q.s.v. *manas*
vedanā° q.s.v. *skandha*s
saṃjñā° q.s.v. *skandha*s
mārga° q.s.v. Way (body of —)
samādhi° (=°*skandha*) 115f., 123 n.21 ; cf. vv. *manomayakāya* s.v. *manas, dhyāna* (body of —)
transc. *kāya* : 114, 130, *dharma°*, *prajñā°* 115, 120, 121f.&n. 20, *vidyā°* 112, *nirvāṇa°* 109ff., 112f., 124, *nirodha°* 110f., 115, 118, 121, 123n. 21, 125 ; *amṛta°* q.s.v. *amṛta*
vimukti° q.s.v. *vimukti*
kāyasākṣin q.s.v. *sākṣin*
*kāya*s *(Buddha-)* : (doctrine of —) 73n.10, 120, 127, 142, 154, 156, 157n.26, 167f.
one: 143, 154
(orig.) two: (56f.), 142, 154, 187
trikāya 137, 139, 142, 146 n.18, 150, 155, 188 ; (& *svabhāva*s) 168
four: 147f.n.18, *149f.*, *155*
— & *phala*s 167f.
Dharmakāya (transc.) 74, 76, (109), 111, 120, 127, 139, 141, 142, 150, *154f.*, 157, 159, 164n.37, 167, 183, 185f.n.72, 187, 189. Cf. vv. *Dharmatā*, enlightenment (plane & entity of —), *Nirvāṇa, amṛta, dharma* (transc.), *Puruṣa* . (transc.).
— (imm.) 54, 70n.4, 71, 92ff., 139f., 141n.6, 143ff., 147 n.18, 150f., 154f., 156, 160n.31, 163, 165, 167, 187 ; (°*bodhisattva*) 181 &n.66. (=*Sambhogakāya* q.s.v.)

— two immanent *Dharmakāyas* 145f., 149f., 155
Cf. vv. Doctrine (-body), *Puruṣa* (sot.)
Sambhogakāya 76, 81n.30, 140, 145, 146f.&n.18, 149f., 153, 155, *156–161*, 157n. 28, 159f.&n.31, *163f.*&n. 37, 166f.&n. 44, 181&n.67 (*Bodhisattva's*), 182n.68, *184f.*, *187ff.*
Nirmāṇakāya. 72n.10, (orig.) *142*, 144f., 146&n.17, 147n.18, 148f., 149n.19, *150ff.*, (Up.) 153f., 157n.28. 160 n.31, 188. Cf. v. *nirmāna*
Svabhāvikakāya 146n.18, *150*, *155*
amṛtakāya q.s.vv. *amṛta*, *Dharmakāya* (transc.)
Svasambhoga° 147f.n.18, 150, 155
Parasambhoga° 147f.n.18, 150, 155
vipāka° 155f.n.24
nirvāṇa° (=*Nirmāṇa*°) 148n.19
Buddha-body of the 32 *lakṣaṇas* 148n.18, 150f. ; cf. v. *lakṣaṇas* (thirty-two)
kleśāvaraṇa q.s.v. veil
knowledge, soterical 12, 15f., 25ff., 32, (*jñāna*) 33, 35, 39n.26, 49, (53f.) ; (*samyagjñāna*) 161f.; 173n.52, 180; (three forms of —) 183n.70
Cf. vv. *prajñā*, *satya* (sot.), enlightenment (process of —), *upāsana*, *vidyā*, Doctrine, (*nivṛttilakṣana*)*dharma*
kośas (31), (33), 35f., 38, (45), 46, 84, 85n.38, 108, 132f.
(orig. 3 extended to 5): 108, 132
fifth: (36, 38), 46, (in Bsm.) 133f., 136
— & *skandhas* 108, 132f.
Cf. vv. inward-upward progression, *kāyas*
kṣetrajña 86f., 161f., 178f., 182f.n.69. Cf. v. *budhyamāna*
Kuṇḍalinī 23. Cf. vv. *cakras*, egression, *Vāc*, *brahman*, *satya*

L

lakṣaṇa 89, cet. q.s.v. *dharma* (*pravṛtti* — °, *nivṛtti* — °). Cf. v. orientation
dvaya° 177n.61. Cf. vv. *dvaya*, subj.-obj. experience
3 -s (=*svabhāvas*) q.s.v. *svabhāva*
32 -s 148n.18, 160n.31, 181 ; *Buddha*-body of — q.s. v. *kāyas* (*Buddha*-°). Cf. v. *Puruṣa* (cosm., sot.)
leader (*netṛ*, *nāyaka*) q.s.v. guide to Immortality
light:
cosmic & psychic 3n.5, 4, 7ff., 10, 28, 31 (*ahar*), 42ff. (*Āditya*=*Kāla*) ; 46, 69, 151
Cf. vv. *dhāmas*, *dharmas*, *kāla*, consciousness (self-, waking —)
transcendent 3&n.5, 6, 7, 8f., 12n.20, 15, 24n.13, 28, 29, 39, 42, 45f., 69, 84&n.35, 174
Cf. vv. *dhāman*, *dharma* (transc.), *Virāj*, *amṛta*, *Nirvāṇa*, enlightenment

(plane of —), Ocean, *Vāc* (unuttered)
the two opposed 4, 8, 44, 69
soteric 8f., 10, 12n.20, 45f., 103, 139, 159f., 163&n.36, 166
Cf. vv. *dharma* (sot.), *brahman* (sot.), *satya* (sot.), *vidyā*, knowledge, *tejas*
— -rays 7, 9, 14, 159f., 166n.44.
Cf. vv. birds, unification
lightning 10f.&n.17, 19 ; 12n.20, 17, 39n.26, 45
Cf. v. enlightenment (event of —)
lokas q.v. *dhātus*
parama loka q.v. *amṛta*
lokānuvartana 145n.13, 160n.31
love (universal, soteric): 6, 54, 92 ; *(rasa)* 32; *(bhakti)* 53f., 162; *(maitri)* 92f. ; *(prīti)* 116, 122&n.21, 183n.70
Cf. vv. consciousness (cosmic), assimilation, unification, *ekībhāva, brahmabhāva, brahmavihāras*

M

manas 6n.9, 10n.16, 14, 44, 63, 75n. 14, 79, 85f., 87n.42 ; 88, 99, 178
(divine & mortal) 10, 12f.&n. 25, 14, 33, 91
manomaya : *rūpa* (33), 34n.24 *(sūkṣma)* ; 39, 50
— *kośa* 36 ; °*kāya* 73n.10, 92f., 94, 105f., 108f., 113f., (— *atta-paṭilābha)* 116f.; 118, 119 n.18, 122f.&n.21, 124 &n.22, 125, (125f.n. 24), 130, 142, 144f., 151f., (167), 180, 187.
Cf. vv. *arūpa*, body (unsensuous, cosm. consc.- —), *dhyāna* (body of —)
(sphere of —) 105f., cf. vv. *dhyāna* (sphere of —), *arūpa* (sph. of —), *rūpadhātu* (canon.)
manasi sthāna 88f., (161), (182f.) &n.69
Cf. vv. *nāmni sthāna* s.v. *nāman, dhyāna, upāsana, parāvṛtti* (1st)
mānasa puruṣa 39n.26 ; cf. vv. *manomaya*, guide, *Skambha, setu*
manojalpa q.s.v. *śabda*
manovijñāna 75n.14, 79
māyā 6, 34n.24, 50, 54, 171n.46, 180 f. Cf. vv. *Prakṛti, brahman* (cosm., sot.), orientation
°*kṛta* 171n.46, 180n.65
°*opamasamādhikāya* 180f., cf. v. *manomayakāya*
mukti q.s.v. enlightenment & deliverance (process of —)
kramamukti q.e.s.v. (two stages of —)
vimukti q.v.
mūrti q.v. *rūpa* (sensuous, *mūrta* & *amūrta* —), *Puruṣa (rūpa-)*
mūrta & *amūrta* q.s.vv. *rūpa, arūpa*

N

nairātmya, anātman, (°tā) 45n.5, 63, 66, 69f.&n.4, 113, 130, 133, 138, 183n.69
°*vāda* 131

dharma° 66, 186n.72
pudgala° 66n.20
Cf. vv. *ātman, nirodha*
nāḍīs 28 ; cet. q.s.vv. *(hṛd)ākāśa, suṣumnā*
nāman 2, 4f., 6&n.11, 16, 19ff., 25 &n.15, 26&n.16, 29, 63, 95, 97, 107f.n.1, 137
nāmāni 2, 3n.5, 4, 6ff., 8.n.13, 16, 19, 22, 37, 52, 63, 72f., 82, 95, 169, 170f., 172f. Cf. v. *dharmas*
nāmasaṃjñāvyavahāra 74 ; cf. vv. *vikalpa*, differentiation, *dvaya*, subject-obj. experience
nāma, sheer 20f., 27f., 33, 40, 50, 85, 90, 94, 98, 106, 108, 115, 119, 143n.10, 144, 148, 151, 173f. ; *(°mātra)* 180f., 182, 184 *(=vijñapti)* 77, (169), 171n.46 ; cf. vv. *parāvṛtti* (1st), *dharmadhātu* (imm.) s.v. *dhātus, arūpa*
nāmāni ("higher", "immortal") 5, 6, 13n.24
— (sphere of —) q.v. *arūpa* (sphere of)
— (one, transcendent) 2, 3&n.5, 8, 16, 19, 51, 189. Cf. vv. *Vāc* (transc.), *dharma* (transc.), *brahman* (transc.)
nāmni sthāna (53), 180–185 ; cf. vv. *manasi sthāna, (adhyātma)yoga, upāsana, dhyāna*
nāmakāya 108&n.3, 109, 111, 113, 124, 130, 153. Cf. vv. *manomaya(kāya), arūpa*
°skandha 108
°opādāna 76, 180, 183
nāmarūpa
(individual & cosmic) 1f., 4, 15, 20 f.&n.8, 25, 26&n.16, 27, 29, 49, 52f., 56&n.1, 57, 61, 63, 76f., 85, 90, 94, 97f., 107f., 144, 182.
(binomium) 1f., 19, *20*, 33, (& *dharma-rūpa)* 56–60; (later sense) 64 ; 97f., *107& n.1, 108*, 142&n.10, 146n. 18, 188f.
(sphere, level of —) 4, 15, 20, 25, 26n.16, 29, 31f., 33, 34f. n.24, 38, 42, 52f., 56&n. 1, 60, 62, 64, 68, 79f., 90, 91n.51 *(avidyādhātu)*, 97, 114ff., 135, 137, 142, 143 n.10, 145f., 149, 150, 154, 158, 168, 172f., 174&n.53, 180, 188. Cf. vv. *rūpadhātu* (precan.)
nirmāṇa (process, faculty of —) 106, 109, 113f., 124, 140, *152f.*, 160n.31. Cf. vv. *iddhi*, dream, *dhyāna*
°kāya (Up.) 151–154 ; (Bst.) q.s.v. *kāyas (Buddha-)*
nirmitabuddha 145n.14, 146n.17.
vāgnirmāṇa q.s.v. *Vāc*
nirodha : (viññānassa —) 68, 85, 114, 128n.28, 133, 170 ; 80f., 86, 110, 114, 133, 142f., 155, 168, 170 ; (=*kṣaya* of the *āsravas*) 104, 111f., 144
°samāpatti 80, 100n.6, 110, 121
two — °s *(asaṃjñisamāpatti & saṃjñāveditanir.)* : 101n.6, 164
— *°kāya* q.s.v. *kāya* (transc.)
— *°dhātu* 98, 109, 111, 186. Cf. v. *Nirvāṇa (-dhātu), amṛta*

°*satya* q.s.v. *āryasatyas* s.v. *satya*
°(=*kṣaya*°)*jñāna* 127
pratisaṃkhyān° 146n.16
Nirvāṇa (event, condition, reality of) 50, 52f.&n.5 (*mahān sāmparāya=nirupadhiśeṣa*), 55, 58, 59f.&n.7, 62, 67, 68, 69 (*abhisamparāya*), 70, 75, 81f., 91, 94&n.53, 95, 100, 104, 112, 114f., 121, 134, 136, 138, 141, 147n.18, 149 n.19, 150, 167, 169f. (*paramārtha*), 186. Cf. v. enlightenment (event, entity of —)
— without enlightenment q.s.v. *vimukti* (without *bodhi*)
potential — 79, 87n.42, 112f., (124), 134f., 137
parinirvāṇa 74n.12, 100&n.4, 105, 113f., 186n.72
brahmanirvāṇa 24, 50, 54f., 92, 96, 134
dṛṣṭadharman° 112.
"perception", "fruition" of — 115, cet. q.s.vv. *sākṣin, kāya* (transc.), *cakṣus* (*prajñā*°)
nirvāṇadhātu 24, 60, 62, 65, 93f.n. 53, 97f., 100, 109, 114, (165). Cf. vv. *amṛta, nirodhadhātu* s.v. *nirodha, dharmadhātu* (transc.) s. v. *dhātus*.
°*kāya* q.s.v. *kāya* (transc.)
N° & *Saṃsāra* : (exclusion) 154 etc., passim, cf. v. exclusion (thesis of —);
(continuity) 134f., 137, 141, etc. Cf. v. *yoga* ;
(identity) 67, 135n.39 ; cf. v. Identity (absolute)
nirvikalpa q.s.vv. *avikalpa, jñāna*
nivṛtti (36, 48), 49f., 76&n.18, 77n.22, 78, 79n.28, 81, 86, 88f., 91, 133, 170, 175, 177f. (temporal & yogic), 179, 182f.n. 69
°*lakṣaṇadharma* q.s.v. *dharma*
nivṛtatva 46, cf. v. *nirodha*

O

Ocean (hypercosmic Light- —) 3, 7, 13, 26n.16, 28, 32, 42, 61. Cf. vv. *Virāj, Vāc* (transc.), *Dharma* (transc.)
(psychic —) 30 (*salila*), 87
octad (from two tetrads) 121
OṂ (14), 43f., 45f., 47. Cf. vv. *akṣara, brahman, Vāc*
three moras 42f., cf. v. *śabda*
four — 34, 41 ; cf. vv. *aśabda, turīya*
unity 42 ; (soteric) 45, 46, 92, 95. Cf. v. unification
omnipresence 29, 50, 88, 93, 156, 157 &n.28, 158, 162, 180, 182n. 69 ; cf. vv. consciousness (cosmic), body (cosm. consc.-)
orientation (structural — of psychic factors) 13&n.25, 18, 30f., 48, 79&n.28, 82n.31, 84n.35, 85, 86, 89f.&n.48, 91f., 94, *103*, 134, 154, 161, 162f., 172 f., 176, 178f., 182n.69 ; (*avijñapti*) 65n.15, 107. Cf. vv. descent & ascent, reversal, *vyāvṛtti*, dynamism

P

pañcāgnividyā (39), 173. Cf. vv. *pratītyasamutpāda, pravṛtti*

paramārtha 141&n.7, 168f. ; (=*svārtha)* 147n.18, 150 ; 172, 175. Cf. vv. *amṛta, Nirvāṇa,* enlightenment (event & plane of —), *ātman*
°*satya 169f.*, 175. Cf. vv. *satya* (sot.), knowledge, orientation
paratantra q.s.v. *svabhāvas*. Cf. vv. *svatantra, pratītyasamutpāda*
parāvṛtti, parivṛtti, āśrayap° (Ups.) 49, 53, 182n.69 ; (Bsm.) 76 f.&n.22, 81, 87, (129), 164 *(āśrayasyānyathāpti)*, 182n. 69, 185, 189
two stages of — 76f.&n.22, 146n. 16, (Up. 29, 182n.69), 183 ff.&nn.71, 72, 186n.73. Cf. vv. *upāsana,* enlightenment & deliverance (process of — : two stages)
first 76f., 80, 85, 146, 147n.18, 184, 185f.n.72, 187. Cf. vv. *manasi sthāna, nāmni sthāna, arūpa*
second 76, 77&n.24, 146, 185f.&n. 72, 187, 189. Cf. vv. enlightenment (event of —), *Nirvāṇa*
parivṛttajanman 80, 105n.13
pariṇāma 75, 87, 174. Cf. vv. differentiation, *vijñāna*
pariniṣpanna q.s.v. *svabhāvas*. Cf. vv. *svatantra,* egression, enlightenment (entity of —), *Dharma* (transc.), *Nirvāṇa*
participation *(bhaj)*53,162f.,165,187
(bhuj) q.v. *bhoga*
Cf. vv. love (universal), assimilation, *śaraṇa*
pentad (from triad): *kośas* 35ff., 132; *āryaskandhas* 126f.
(from dyad): *skandhas* 130ff., 137n.42
elements||*kośas* 36
— ||*skandhas* 131f.
personality q.s.vv. *nāmarūpa, kośas, skandhas, kāyas,* body, consciousness, individuum
pluri- — 152f., 160, 163, 164n.37, 166&n.44, 188f. Cf. vv. consciousness (pluri-), dream
all- — q.s.vv. *Puruṣa* (cosmic, transcendent), omnipresence, consciousness (transc. all-), *ātman*
phalas, four 101f., 116 ; origin of — 105 ; primitive two: 102 ; *(āgāmin* 103ff.) ; original triadic scheme 104 ; & *Buddhakāyas* 167f
srotaāpanna 102&n.7, 103f.&n.11, 105, 115, 144&n.12, 164f.& n.39
°*āpatti* 103f., 116, 167, 184n. 71, 187
sakṛdāgāmin 103, 105, 116
anāgāmin 80, 102&n.7, 103f., 105 f., 110, 115f., 164f.&nn.38, 39, 187 ; *ūrdhvasrotas* 164 f., 187
arhat 81 (plane of °ship), 102, 104, 110f., 112, 115f., 120, 142, 143, 164f., 185n.72
prajñā (°*ātman)* 18, 20, cet. q.s.v. *vijñāna (°maya puruṣa, °ātman)* ; (=*prāṇa* 38) ;
pure *p*° : *(p° purāṇī)* 49, 53 ; 110, 115, 120, 126f., (three *jñānas*) 127
prajñāvimukti 104, 110f., 121, 126. Cf. v. *vimukti*

p.° + *vim*° 126 ; + *vimuktijñānadarśana* 126
prajñācakṣus 114f. Cf. v. *cakṣus*
°*kāya*, °*skandha* 115n.13, 120 f., 122n.20, 127n.26, 128 n.27
Cf. vv. *Vāc*, *vidyā*, knowledge, *brahman* (sot.), *dharma* (sot.), Doctrine
prājñā 34 ; cf. v. *suṣupti*
Prakṛti 50 (higher & lower) ; 89 ; *(āsurī & daivī)* 162. Cf. vv. *māyā*, *brahman* (cosmog., sot.)
pralaya 88, 177, 182n.69
prasaṃga 74, 170, (171n.46)
pratītyasamutpāda 58f., 62, 66, 169 ff., 171n.46, 173&nn.51, 52 ; 174, 176 ; (=*samyogalakṣaṇotpatti*) 90, 176, 178. (Buddhist formula) 108n.1
— — — *pratilomaṃ* 59, 170, 176
— °*samutpanna* 32, 170n.46
Cf. vv. dynamism, orientation, *pravṛtti*.
pratyāhāra 182n.69 ; cf. v. *nivṛtti*
pravṛtti 48, 75, 77n.22, 78f., 79n.28, 81, 85ff., 90, 129f., 132, 159, 161; 173f., 175, 177, 178& n.62. Cf. vv. emanation
°*lakṣaṇadharma* q.s.v. *dharma*
°*vijñānas* 75, 77&n.22, 81n.30
yoga-pr° 49f., 96 (*pravartaka*) & n.54
apr° 170
prāṇa 10n.16, 15, *17f*.&n.5, 19f., 21, 28f., 40, 46 ; (*vaiśvānara*) 34, 43, 134 ; (=*kāla*) 43
(soteric, yogic) 15, 23, 31, 45f., 50, 95, 134, 172 ; (=*prajñātman*) 38
°*maya kośa* 36
°*śarīra* q.s.v. body (unsensuous)
prāṇas 15f., 18n.5, 21&n.8, 27ff., 30. Cf. v. *indriyas*
— unified 15f., 28f., 31, 37. Cf. v. unification
aprāṇa 46
prīti q.s.v. love (universal)
pṛthagjana 78f., 101n.6, 102&n.7, 136, 164, 168
— -experience q.s.vv. *nāmarūpa* (sphere of —), consciousness (discriminating)
pudgala 133ff., 138 ; (three, seven, ten *p*°s) 110
°*nairātmya* q.s.v. *nairātmya*
paramārthap° 136
Cf. v. orientation
pudgalavāda 85n.38, 133-138
purification q.v. *vyavadāna*, cf. vv. enlightenment (process of —), unification, *anāsrava*, *nivṛtti*
Puruṣa
(universal & transcendent) 2f., 4, 6, 8, 12f.&nn.20, 22, 24 ; 14, 16, 19, 21, 23, 24, 33, 37, 40, 48, 54f., 92, 95f., 151, 189
(cosmic & cosmogonic) 3, 4, 5n.7, 6, 8, 10ff.&nn.18, 22 ; 15, 17, 25, 29, 39, 43, 48 (creator), 50 (*Īśvara*), 53, 96, 162. Cf. vv. *Skambha*, *prāṇa*, *Īśvara*
psychic: *rūpa*- — 10n.16, 17&n.5, 18, 19, 31, 43 (*mūrti*), 49 ; cet. q.s.vv. *prāṇa*, *Indha*; cf. v. *Skambha*
nāma- — 18, 27, 48; cet.

q.s.vv. *prajñātman, vijñāna(maya p°);* [=dream-*p*° 153, cet.s. vv. dream, consciousness (pluri-)]

(soteric) 17, 27, 39&n.26, 40, 41, 43, 48, 49f., 53ff., 92, 95 *(Īśvara)*f., 153, 162, 166, 181 ; *(Mahāp°)* 148n.18, 151&n.22, 157n.27, 181

four aspects of — 48

— as *tattva* 89f., 129

Ṛ

Ṛṣis (as cosmogonic powers) 3, 4, (5), 6f., 10&n.18

(the 6 & the 7th [soteric entity]) 8f., 11f.n.20

ṛta (order of —) 9n.15, 11n.19, 32

an-ṛta=amṛta 32

— (seat of —) 5, 7 ; cf. v. cosmos (summit of —)

— (first-born of —) q.s.v. *dharmaja*

R

rāśi 95, 129. Cf. vv. *kāya*s, *skandha*s

reintegration 6f., 11f.&n.20, 15, 19, etc., cf. vv. apocatastasis, unification, *parāvṛtti,* totality, consciousness (cosm., sot.), body (cosm. consc.-)

regeneration 5f., 8ff., 12&n.20, 13f., 23, 48, 163, 187

Cf. vv. enlightenment (process of —), *parāvṛtti* (1st), *parivṛttajanman* s.e.v., *dharmaja,* sublimation, unification, assimilation

return q.v. *parāvṛtti*

reversal 7, 43f., 46n.5, 76n.18, 82f., 85ff., 96n.54, 103, 113, 133f., 153, 159, 170, 174, 176, 187. Cf. v. *vyāvṛtti*

rūpa 2, 17n.5, 19ff., 25n.15, 29, 40 (term, & *kāya)* 142f.n.10

— , sensuous 6, 17n.5, 19ff., 28, 34 n.24 *(sthūla)*, 40, 41, 50, 57, 58, 60, 64, 65n.16, 68f., 76f., 92, 95, 106, 107 n.1, 118, 120, 139 *(āmisa)*, 161, 177, 184

— , unsensuous q.s.v. *arūpa*

(rūpakāya, °skandha) 64n.15, 108&n. 3, 109, 111, 113f., 122&n.20, 124, 128, 130, 139, 141n.6, 142, 149, 154, (160) ; (*oḷārika attapaṭilābha*) 116f. ; cf. v. body (of gross elements)

°dhātu (precanonical) *98ff.*, 109, 116; cf. v. *dhātu*s (three) (canonical) 57, 76, 93n.52, 97f., 99f., 105f., 117, *125&n.24,* 128, 130, 147, 149, 156 ; cf. v. *dhātu*s (four)

rūpāṇi 2, 4, 7, 8n.13, 11n.20, *(tanū* pl. 13n.24), 17n.5, 19, 29, 42, 65n.16, 88, 95, 151, 158f., (182n.69)

three *rūpa*s *(guṇa*s) 25f.

mūrta & *amūrta r°* 19, 27f., 30, 33, 42, (44), 95, 98, 108, 132, 143n.10, 172, 174. Cf. v. *arūpa*

eka°, viśva° (in sphere of *nāma= dharma)* 4, 6, 8n.13, 11& n.20, 13n.24, 28f., 41, 50, 53, (77), 84n.36 ; *(r° aiśvara)* 95 ; cf. vv. *Puruṣa* (sot.), totality, cosmos (summit of —)

—, transcendent 2, 3, 6 *(tanū)*, 16, 18f., 38f., 51, 55, 189; *(svarūpa)* 15f., 23, 44f., 50 f., 76, 84&n.35, 189; *(abhiniṣpanna sv°)* 174; *(avikalpar°)* 35n.24. Cf. v. *Puruṣa* (transc.)

Ś

śabda 41f., 46; (*=manojalpa*) 90, 180; *(svamanojalpa)* 140
°*brahman* 41f., 50, 85, 90&n.48, 92, 179
aśabda 41, 46, (72f.), (*=ajalpa*) 90&nn.48, 50
Cf. v. *Vāc* (sot.; unuttered); OṂ, *dhyāna, nāmni sthāna* s.v. *nāman*
śaraṇa 53, 103, 163
°*āgati* (°*prapatti, saraṇagamana*) 53f., 103, 163f.
°*ṃ gata* 104, (*=śraddhānusārin*) 105. Cf. vv. *phalas, upāsana*
śarīra q.vv. body (of gross elements), *rūpa* (sensuous)
sa° & *a°* q.s.v. *rūpa, mūrta* & *amūrta*
śīla 115f., 126
śraddhā 39n.26
°*anusārin* 105, 115. Cf. vv. *śaraṇa, upāsana, phalas*
śrāvaka; °s 77n.23, 80f., 146, 148f.& n.19, 172, 175, 185f.n.72
śubha 118, 120f., 124n.22.
asubha 118, 120.
śūnyatā 59, 70n.4, 74
°*vāda* 169. Cf. v. *prasaṃga*, exclusion (absolute, thesis of)
dharmaś° 171n.46, cet. s.v. *nairātmya*

S

salvation (career of) q.vv. enlightenment & deliverance (process of —), *vimukti*, id. (without *bodhi)*, Way.
samādhi 10f.n.19, (13f.,), 15, 39, 72& n.7, 110, 115f., 126, 180, 181&n.67, 182n.69, 184
— not conducive to supreme *sambodhi* 186n.72
°*skandha* 115f.
°*kāya* q.s.v. *kāya* (*samādhi°*); cf. vv. *manomayakāya* s.v. *manas, dhyāna* (body of —)
samāpatti q.v. *dhyānas (ārūpya-)*
9 — s 101n.6
asaṃjñis° q.s.v. *nirodhas* (two)
nirodhas° q.e.s.v.
sambodhi q.v. enlightenment (event, plane & entity of —)
saṃgha 103f., 163
saṃjñā q.s.v. *skandhas*
°*kāya*, °*dhātu* q.e.s.v.
Cf. v. *smṛtyupasthāna* (third)
saṃkalpa 19, 29, 44, 83, 173, 182n. 69; (*=vikalpa*) 174&n.54. Cf. v. *vikalpa*
satyas° 30, 36, 173
saṃkleśa 85, 135, 142, (160), 171n.46
— -*vyavadāna-nibandha* 175.
Cf. vv. orientation, *pravṛtti, citta (mithyāpraṇihita)*
samprasāda 15, 30, 84&n.36, 157 n.27, 174. Cf. vv. sublimation, consciousness (cosmic), body (cosmic consciousness-)
Saṃsāra 5n.7, 13n.23, 27, 55, 59, 67, 70, 75, 87n.42, 91, 95f., 136, 171, 187
— & *Nirvāṇa*: exclusion s.e.v.

(thesis of —), esp. 154 ; identity 67, 135n.29, cet. q.s.v. Identity (absolute) ; continuity 75, 134f., 137, 141, 154
saṃskāras q.s.v. *skandhas*
saṃskṛta 58, 135n.39
a° q.v.
saṃtāna q.s.vv. current, *vijñāna, anāsrava*
saṃvṛti 141&n.7, 168f. ; *loka°* 176 ; *yoga°* 154, 170ff., 176. Cf. v. veil
samyak & *as°* q.v. orientation
°praṇihita citta & *mithyāpr° c°* q.s.v. *citta*
°tva niyama 78
samyagjñāna 79, 161
°dṛṣṭi 127&n.26; cf. v. *jñānas* (three) s.v. *jñāna*
sarvajña, °tva q.s.v. consciousness (transc. all-)
sat (transc. form of *satya)* 24&n.14, 25, *(tyat, asat)* 32 ; 91, 173f. Cf. v. *brahman* (transc.)
(immanent *satya)* 32. Cf. v. *brahman* (cosmog.)
satta (conventional person) 138. Cf. v. *skandhas*
sattva (= *buddhi, citta)* 48, 86, 88, 96, 152
°śuddhi 152
°e sthāna 182n.69 ; q.vv. *nāmni sthāna* s.v. *nāman, manasi sthāna* s.v. *manas*.
Cf. vv. *satya, citta, buddhi* (& stages of —)
satya Ch. II (22&n.10, 24f., 28&n. 20, 29, 39) ; 42, 51, 83f.n.35, 135, 172 ;
(cosmic & cosmogonic) 22, 25, 27, 31, 39, 41f., 52, 173
(psychic) 26f., 28, 30, 39, 83f.n.35, 135, 174
(soteric) 26f., 28, 30, 39ff., (42ff.), 51, 76n.18, 83, 91, 172ff. Cf. vv. knowledge, Doctrine
(transcendent) 27, 40, 51 ; *(°tas)* 139 ; 174. Cf. vv. *sat, brahman* (transc.), *amṛta*
(nāmarūpa-s°) 31, 33; *(asatya)* 41f., 172; 173f. Cf. v. *anṛta*
(identity of *s°* & *amṛta)* 38. Cf. vv. Identity (absolute), *Saṃsāra* & *Nirvāṇa* (identity)
(four spects of *s°)* 27, 39, 51
satyasya s° 27f., 34, 36f., 172
sat + tyam 38
sat-ti-yam 30, 174f.
two *satyas*: *saṃvṛti°, paramārtha°*, q.vv. ; esp.: *168ff.*, 172, 176n.59
2 *saṃvṛtis* & 2 *paramārthas* 175f.
āryasatyas, four: 119f., 126 ; & *svabhāvas* 176
duḥkha° 65n.15, 176
samudaya° 114, (169), 176
nirodha° 60, (170), 176
mārga° 59, 60, 62, 65n.15, 169f., 176
saviour q.vv. *Puruṣa* (sot.), guide, *Tathāgata* (immanent), *Dharmakāya* (imm.) s.v. *kāyas (Buddha-)*
sākṣin 35n.24, 87f. ; *(kāya°)* 109f., 111f., 118, 121
senses q.v. *indriyas*
— , *dhātus* & *dhyānas* 99&n.3, 125 &n.24.
setu 30, 40, 54, 92. Cf. vv. *Skambha*, Way
Skambha 4, 5&n.7 *(uttānapad)*, 8&n. 13, 10&n.16, 11f.n.20, 12f.&

n.24, 23, (25f.), 31, 40, 41, 43f., (47), 53, 96&n.54, 139. Cf. vv. *Puruṣa* (cosm., sot.), Tree, *setu*, Way
skandhas 45f.&n.5, 57, 64n.15, 106&n.15, 107f., *117–137*, 117n.15, 136f.n.42, 143
five 107f., 108n.3; 126f., 128n.28 (*"dhātus"*), *130f.*
two 108f., 130
three (=*attapaṭilābhas*) 116f.&nn.15, 16 ; 122, 127
rūpa q.v. *rūpa* (sensuous, °*kāya*) ; esp. 64n.15, 106&n.15, 118 f., 120, 128, 130
vedanā 107, 118f., 120, 125, 128, 131f.
°*kāya* 118f., 120, 122&n.20, 125, 126n.24
°*dhātu* 128n.28
saṃjñā 107, 116ff., 119, (120), 128, 131f.
°*kāya* 117ff., 120 (*citta*°), 122&n.20, 124n.22, 125
°*dhātu* 128n.28
saṃskārāḥ 107f.&n.1, 128, 131f.
°*adhātu* 128n.28
vijñāna 70, 108&n.1, 128, 131f., 133. Cf. v. *vijñāna*
Cf. vv. *kāyas*, body (of gross elements ; unsensuous), *kośas*, *dhātus*
nāmaskandha (°*kāya*, orig. *vijñāna-sk*°) 108&n.3, 130
prajñā° q.s.v. *prajñā*
dharma° 115, 126, 143
samādhi° 115f.
ārya°s, *Tathāgata*°s q.s.vv.
ekarasa° 134ff.
saṃsārakoṭiniṣṭha° 136
skandhas||*dhātus* 116f., 128ff. ; 5 *sk*°s||3 *dh*°s 128
— & *kāyas* 118–125, 128–1
skandhavāda & *skandhamātravā* 130, 136f., 168
smṛtyupasthānas 118–125, 122n.2
first 118f., 120f., 1
second 119, 120f.
third 119f., 125
fourth 119ff.
— ||*dhyānas* 122, 125n.23
speech q.v. *Vāc* ; cf. vv. *dharmas* (of Teaching), Doctrine, *nāmāni*, *śabda*
srotas q.v. current & s.vv. *vijñāna* (°*saṃtāna*), *nāmarūpa* (indiv.), *Saṃsāra*, *dharma* (sot.), Way ; cf. vv. orientation, descent & ascent
ūrdhvasrotas 164f., 187. Cf. v. *anāgāmin* s.v. *phalas*
sthāna q.v. *dhātus*
tṛtīya — q.v.
manasi —, *nāmni* —, q.s.vv. *mānas*, *nāman*
svapna° q.s.v. dream
sandhya° q.s.v. *arūpa*
a° 143n.10, 156
subject-object experience: passim, esp. 44, 90, 161, 174&n.56, 176f. Cf. vv. consciousness (discriminating, waking), *dvaya*, *parikalpita* s.v. *svabhāvas*, *nāmarūpa* (sphere of —)
sublimation, superlation, elevation passim, esp. 20, 23, 28ff., 31 f., 33, 35ff., 38, 41, 44f., 46 f., 48f., 50f., 76, 89, 95f., 103 f., 109, 113f, 116, 126, 132f., 145, 147, 149, 158f., 162f., 164f., 180, 182&n.69, 183f., 185, 186n.72

Cf. vv. *vyavadāna*, orientation, enlightenment (process of —), *nivṛtti, parāvṛtti, dhyāna, upāsana*
sukha (of *samādhi* or *dhyāna)* 72n.7, 80f., 113, 122f.&n.21, 126n. 24, 178, 186n.72
suṣumnā 18, 46, 91. Cf. vv. *nāḍīs*, sublimation, *yoga*, egression, *brahmarandhra, Kuṇḍalinī*
suṣupta 34&n.24
°*i* 24, 83, 151
Cf. vv. consciousness (stages of —, three & four), *samprasāda*
sva-
°*dhātu* (28), 180; °— *sthāna*, ° — *sthānayoga* 161, 180; cf. v. *nāmni sthāna* s.v. *nāman*
°*citta* 49, 53 ; °— *dharmatā* 76n. 20
°*buddhi* 88. Cf. v. inward-upward progression
°*rocis* 3f.&n.5
°*sambhoga* 147n.18, 150 ; °— *kāya* q.s.v. *kāyas (Buddha-)*
°*artha (Sambodhi)* 147n.18, 150
°*rūpa* 15f., 19, 23, 44f., 50f., 76, 84 &n.35, 98n.2, 174, 189. Cf. vv. Androgyne, Light (transc.), *dharma* (transc.), *Puruṣa* (transc.), *ātman, rūpa* (transc.)
°*manojalpa* q.s.v. *śabda*
svam 28, 46
svayaṃkṛta=*sukṛta*, self-generation 32. Cf. vv. regeneration, *ānanda*
svabhāva (Up.) 86, 88, 182n.69
three °s (Up.) 176f.&n.60, 178f., 183n.69
pravṛtta s°=*paribhāva s°* 176 f., 178
para s° : *pravṛttis°*=*kāraṇas°* 177f., 179
nivṛttis° 178f
. — — — & twofold *satya* 172ff.
parama s°=*abhiniṣpanna svarūpa* 89, 174, 179
three *s°*s (Bst.) 89, *168*, 174
& *kāyas* 168, 176n.60
& two *satyas* 175f.&n.59
& *dhātus* 168
parikalpita s° (157n.26), 171n. 46, 174, 175&nn.56, 57 *(abhūtaparikalpa)* ; 176& n.60, 180
paratantra s° 32, 79, 89, 155, 171n.46, 173n.51, 174f.&n. 57, 176&n.60, 178n.62, 180f.
pure *p°s°* (of *nivṛtti)* 174f. &n.57, 176, 180
pariniṣpanna s° 32, 79, 89, 155, 171n.46, 174, 175&nn. 56, 57, 176&n.60
Cf. v. consciousness (three stages of —), *buddhi* (stages of —)
four *s°*s, & *āryasatyas* 176
svabhāvikakāya q.s.v. *kāyas (Buddha-)*
svapna q.v. dream
svara 47 ; cet.s. vv. *śabda*, OṂ
svargaloka 91, 98n.2. Cf. v. *dhātus*
svatantra (=*svadhā)* 13, 32 ; 46, 85. Cf. v. *paratantra* s.v. *svabhāva*

T

Tathatā 74, 76f., 79f., 84, 90, 135n. 39, 162, 175 ; *(tathatta)* 69& n.3, 131 ; *(tattva)* 170, 172
dharma-tathatā 59.

Cf. vv. *Dharma* (transc.), enlightenment (entity of —)
Tathāgata (& °s) 61, 70n.4, (silent) 71ff., 72n.7 ; 91–94, 100, 101n.6, 103f., 109, 111, 113, 124, 127, 128n.28, 135f., 138, 139f., 141nn.6–7, 142f., 144 ff., 147n.18, 149&n.19, 150, 154f., 157&nn.26–28, 160, 163ff.&n.37, 166f.n.44, 167f., 170, 181&n.67, 184, 185n.72, 187f., 189
— (immanent in contingency) 139, 142ff., 158–161. Cf. vv. *Dharmakāya* (immanent), *Sambhogakāya*, s.v. *kāyas (Buddha-)*
potential *T°* 136, cf. v. *T°-garbha*
Tathāgatagarbha 76n.18, 82, 136, 159. Cf. vv. *bīja*, *ālaya-vijñāna*, reversal
T° 's silence 72f., 140 ; cet. above, s.v. *T°*. Cf. v. *Vāc* (unuttered)
T°kāyas q.v. *kāyas (Buddha-)*
T° 's *rūpakāya* 139, 141n.6, 142, 144, 149
T°skandhas 126f.&n.27
teacher q.s.v. guide to Immortality
tejas (7), 25, 28&n.18, 30, 34, 44, 63 n.14, 95, 151
Cf. vv. *satya* (cosm., sot.), light (sot., cosm. & psych.)
taijasa 34
tetrads (primary) 22ff., 34, 36, 122f. &n.21, 125n.23, 153, 155
(secondary, from triads) *33*, 34&n.24, *97ff.*, 124n.22, *125* &n.23, 126, *149f.*, 155, 156 n.24 ; (from two dyads) 105, 175f.
theism, *yogic* 53, 153. Cf. vv. *Īśvara*, *Puruṣa* (cosm., sot.)
totality (cosmic) 14, 26, 37, 40f., 48, 52, 53, 93, 131, 153f., 157 n.26, 166. Cf. vv. cosmos (summit of —), consciousness cosmic)
— (transcendent) 9, 16, 33, 39, 41, 48, 52, 66, 69, 72f., 74f., 78. Cf. vv. *dharma* (transc.), *Puruṣa* (transc.), *Vāc* (transc.), Ocean, enlightenment (entity of —), *ātman*
trailokya 22, 24f., 31, 33f., 41f., 43f., 69, 88, 98&n.2, 112 ; cf. s.v. *dhātus* (four)
Tree, cosmic 5n.7, 7, 12&n.23, 14, 42, 46n.5. Cf. vv. *Skambha*, *setu*
top of — 5n.7, 12, 14
fruit of — 12&n.23, 14
triads (primary): passim, e.g. 33, 36, (88, 96&n.54), 98, 109, 114f., 124f., 126f., (130), 142, 153, 169, *186ff.* Cf. vv. consciousness (three stages of —), *dhātus* (three), *kāyas* (two & third), *svabhāvas*, *yoga*
(secondary): 127, (fr. dyads) 142, 146n.18 ; cf. v. *trikāya* s.v. *kāyas* (Buddha-)
— ism of Yogācāra Buddhology 142, 155, 169
tṛtīya 50, 151, 153, 166, 181f. Cf. vv. *-aiśvarya*, consciousness (four stages of —), *suṣupti*
Truth, Truths, q.s.v. *satya*
turīya 24, 41, 46 ; four bodies of — 35n.24, 135
°*-turīya* 35n.24, 47

Cf. vv. consciousness (four stages of —), *amṛta*, *Tathatā*, *Nirvāṇa*, *dharma* (transc.)

U

unification 7, 13f., 15f., 17f.n.5, 25, 27f., 31, 37f., 40, 42, 47, 55, 85, 93n.52, 94, 142, 153, 156, 158f., 160f., 166f., 185, 188f. Cf. vv. *vyavadāna*, *samādhi*, sublimation
— producing union q.s.vv. *ekībhāva*, enlightenment (process of —, two stages)
unifying Body 94 ; *(Sambhogakāya)* 161
unity & multiplicity 2f., 4f., 7f., 10, 13n.24, 14, 21f.n.8, 25, 27, 29 ; (no multiplicity) 38, 51 &n.4, 66f.; *(sakala & akala)* 43f. ; 52, 61, 63, 65, 78, 81f., 152f., 154, 158f., 160f., 166n.44, 181n.67, 188f.; etc., passim. Cf. vv. differentiation, unification, *dharma*s, *nāmāni*, *vikalpa*, *avikalpa*, *rūpāṇi*
upaniṣad 27
upāsana 16, 33, 39n.26, 42f., 44, 45, 49, 53, 103, 162 ;
two stages of — 104, 163, 184n.71. Cf. v. *parāvṛtti* (two stages of —)
upāsaka 104. Cf. v. *phala*s
upekṣā 93, 165f. Cf. vv. *avikalpa*, *dhyāna*s (*rūpa-*, fourth), *brahmavihāra*s
upekkhāsatipārisuddhi 104, 121

V

Vāc
(unuttered, universal & transcendent) 2f., 4, 5f., 7ff., 10, 11, 12, 14, 16f., 19, 21f., 25f., 32. (*aniruktam brahma*), 33, 34 (fourth mora), 36, 37, 41f., 47, 71, 72n.8, 74f., 78, 82, 90n.48 ; 133f. *(avācya kośa)* ; (silent *Dharma)* 71ff., 140, 189 ; 172. Cf. vv. *Dharma* (transc.), Ocean, Androgyne, *Aditi*, Light (transc.), *turīya*, (*a*)*śabda*
(uttered) 4f., 6f., 12, 14, 18, 21n. 7, 22, 32 *(niruktam brahma)*, 37, 41, 46, 48, 52, 74f., 173
(cosmogonic) 4f., 10, 22, 25f., 29, 42, 48. Cf. v. *brahman* (cosmog.)
(psychic) 18, 20f., 23 ; cet. cf. s.vv. *prajñātman*, *Virāj*, *Puruṣa (nāma-)*, *vijñāna*
(soteric) 7, 8, 9, 10f.&nn.16, 19 ; 12n.20, 14, 17, 41, (48f.), 71, 139f. Cf. vv. *brahman* (sot.), *dharma* (sot.), *śabda*, *prajñā (purāṇī)*, Doctrine
vāgnirmāṇa 72f.n.10, 140
Vehicle q.s.v. Way
veil & unveiling 8n.13 *(vavri)*, 9, 10f. &n.18 ; 12n.20, 14, *(apidhā)* 29, 173 ; *(ulbaniṣṇu)* 38, *(dharmya)* 52, 84n.35 ; 103, 174 ; *(āvaraṇa)* 119, 160 ; *(nīvaraṇa)* 120, 132f., *(ā-vṛ) 161*, *(saṃ-vṛ)* 169, 170, 171n.46, 172f., 174,

179. Cf. vv. dissimilation & concealment, *saṃvṛti*
kleśāvaraṇa 77n.23, 161, *(°āvṛti)* 163, 184n.72
jñeyāvaraṇa 161, *(°āvṛti)* 163, 185n.72
Vena 6. Cf. vv. love (universal), sublimation, inward-upward progression, *ekībhāva, Puruṣa*
vidyā 33, 39, 48f., 55, 91f. Cf. vv. *prajñā* (pure), Wisdom, *Vāc* (sot.), *brahman* (sot.), knowledge, *satya* (sot.), *citta (samyakpraṇihita)*
vijñapti q.s.v. *vijñāna*
°mātra(tā) 175, 180 ; q.s.v. *cittamātra(tā)*, *°vāda*. Cf. v. *nāma* (sheer)
— & *prajñapti* (138, 169), 171&n. 46, 180.
vijñāna
(°maya puruṣa) (17f.&n.5, 22), 27f., 30, 34, 64n.14; *(°ātman)* 35, 40, 108, 133, 151 ; 153f., 161, 172 ; 39 ;
— 57, 58, 62, 70, 84n.35, 91f., 95, 108, 114, 128n.28, 132, 137n.42, 171n.46 (*vijñapti*), 179, 184. Cf. vv. *prajñātman, buddhi, citta, ālayav°, nāman,* consciousnes (self-, pluri-).
— *°skandha* 70, 108&n.1, 128n. 28, 130ff., 134; cf. v. *vijñāna* s.v. *skandha*
°dhātu 60, 97f., 99, 128n.28. Cf. v. *dhātus* (six).
°saṃtāna 62, 68, 78&n.25, 83, 172, 187.
°pariṇāma 75f., 83. Cf. vv. differentiation, *pravṛtti.*
pratisandhi-v° 61n.9
ālaya-v° q.v.
*pravṛtti-v°*s q.s.v. *pravṛtti*
— (transcendent, static, radiant) 61f., 68f., 70, 85, 114, 128n. 28, 134, 136, 171n.46. Cf. vv. *Nirvāṇa* (entity of —), *citta (prabhāsvara)*, consciousness (transc. all-), *dharmadhātu* (transc.)
avijñāna 32, cf. vv. *acitta, aprāṇa*
the "eighth" *v°* 75&n.14, 86
v°sthitis 93n.52
mūla-v° 134, 136. Cf. vv. *ālayav°*, *ekarasaskandha*
vijñānavāda, pre-Canonical 68, 70, 82, 85, 148. Cf. v. *cittamātravāda*
vikalpa (13&n.25), 76, 78f., 81&n.29, 83, 141n.7, 157n.26 *(vikalpita)*, 171&n.46, 174&n.54 (=*saṃkalpa)*. Cf. v. differentiation
sarvakalpanakṣaya, °opaśama 171 &n.47
— *°nirvāṇa* 81
vikāra, vyavakāra 25, 45n.5, 129f. Cf. vv. differentiation, *skandhas, vikalpa*
vimokṣas 110, 117–122, 124 ; (Up.) 152
first 120f.&n.19
second 117f., 120f.&n.19
third 117f., 120f.&n.19, 125
4th–7th 121
eighth 121&n.19 ; q.v. *nirodhasamāpatti* s.v. *nirodha*
orig. four 121f.
— ||*dhyānas* 121f., 125n.23
vimukti (°tti) 125f. Cf. vv. *vimokṣa* (eighth), enlightenment & deliverance (process of —),

āryaskandhas s.v. *ārya*
cetov° paññav° 104, 121, 126
— *°jñāna* 126&n.25
(Śrāvaka's) v° (nirodha, nirvāṇa) without *bodhi* 80f., 111, 143, 145, 147n.18, 149n. 19, 150, 155, 168 (career of —), 186n.72, 188. Cf. v. elimination (only)
— *°kāya* 115n.13, 126, 185n.72
Virāj 3, 14, 18, 20, 23, 47 ; *(vi-rāj)* 166
Cf. vv. *Vāc*, (transc., sot., psych.), Ocean, Light (transc., sot.)
viśuddhi, pariśuddhi q.vv. *vyavadāna, nivṛtti*
viśveśvarya q.v. *aiśvarya*
vyavadāna 76, 85 *(śodhaya-)*, 86 ; 135, 142, 150, 152 *(śuddhi : āhāra°, sattva°,* etc.), 160, 172, 175 *(saṃkleśa-v-°nibandha)*, 177 *(pū-)*, 179. Cf. vv. enlightenment & deliverance, (process of —), *nivṛtti*, consciousness (stages of —)
vyāhṛtis (three) 22, 31, 33, 36, 41 (four) 24, 33. Cf. v. *dhātus*
vyāvṛtti, vyāvartana (43f.), *78*&n.26, 79f., 81&nn.29, 30 ; 87, 163, 172, 184, 187. Cf. v. reversal
— , (orig. & dogm. location of —) 78–81

W

Way *(pathyā)* 7, *(pathi)* 13f., (26), 91, 96; (*devayāna p.*) 39n.26, 40, 174 ; *(niyāna)* 7 ; *(sṛti saṃcaraṇī)* 18, *(saṃcāriṇī)* 46 ; *(gati)* 78, 88 ; *(adhvan)* 92, 95 ; *(mārga)* 59n.7, 60, 62, 70n.4, 78, 80, *91f.*, 94n. 53, *103*, 114, 139, 141, 146, 164 *(nirvikalpajñānamārga)*, 167, 170, 172 ; *(yāna)* 168, *(dharmayāna, brahmayāna)* 71 ; *([dharma]srotas)* 81n. 31, 104&n.10, 144f., 167 ; (*paramārthasatya*) 169f., 175; (orig. — to *bodhi*=to *Nirvāṇa)* 97, 100f., 104, 111, 115f., 126, 183, 186 ; (dogm. construction of dhyānic path) 97, 100, 120f., 126 ; *(Bodhisattva's)* 76–81, 180–187. Cf. vv. enlightenment (process of —), *vimukti* (without *bodhi*), *nivṛtti*
"higher" — 143 ;
(Bodhisattvayāna vs. *Śrāvakay°* 145f., 147n.18 ; (one continuous career) 146
body of — *(mārga)* 80, 112, 165 n.39, 184 ; *(Buddha's*= imm. *Dharmakāya)* 155f., 167
attainment of — *(srotāpatti)* q.s. v. *phalas*
Truth of — q.v. *(mārga)satya* s. v. *(ārya)satyas*, four
three stages of — 104, 109, 115, 126f., *186f.*
Wayfarer 130, 139, 168 ; Wayfaring body 184. Cf. v. *manomayakāya*
Wisdom 5 *(manīṣā)*, *(vidatha* pl.) 7 ; 10f., 12, 14, *(prajñā purāṇī)* 49, 53f. ; cet.s.v. *vidyā*. Cf. v. *Vāc* (sot., transc.)

Y

yāna q.s.v. Way
yoga 6, 13f., 15f., 18ff., *23*, 28f., 31,

33, 34, 37f., 41, 45f., 47, 48 ff., 53, 54f., *82*, 84, 91f., 94 n.53, 95f., 96n.54, 97, 111, 125, 132, 134, 141n.7, 148, 152f., 162f., 171f., 177f., *188f.*

Cf. vv. enlightenment & deliverance (process of —), sublimation, *vyavadāna*, consciousness (three stages of —, transfiguration of —), *dhyāna*, *vimokṣa*s, *smṛtyupasthāna*s

°*guṇa* 50

°*pravṛtti* q.s.v. *pravṛtti*

kramayoga 35, 152.

ṣaḍaṅga° 45f.

dhyāna° 86, 88, 182n.69

adhyātma° 52

svadhātusthāna° 161

sphere of — 38, 46f., 49f., cet. s. vv. *arūpa* (sphere of —), *dhyāna* (sphere of —)

— doctrine & *Sāṃkhya* 89 ; 96n 54, 182n.69

— theism q.v.

ERRATA

	instead of	*read*
p.3 l.14	3),	3 ; AV. IX, 2, 5b ; 15, 24a ; etc.),
p.4 n.6, l.2	AV:	AV.:
p.5 l.17	Vāc	Vāc,
p.8 n.13, l.3	level)	level)''
ibid., l.4	*sarupāḥ*	*sarūpāḥ*
ibid., l.5	*ekarupāḥ*	*ekarūpāḥ*
p.9 l.18	(i.e	(i.e.
p.11 n.20, l.6	*ṣad*	*ṣaḍ*
p.19 l.7	ätman	ātman
p.20 l.27	elementary	elemental
p.20 l.28	crossening	coarsening
p.21 n.7, l.2	*tiṣṭhati*	*viṣṭhitaṃ*
ibid., l.3	named	recited
p.24 l.15	paralleled	parallel
p.24 l.16	*atmeti*	*ātmeti*
p.25 ll.22, 24	on the	at the
p.25 n.15, l.4	also Taitt.	also AV. IX, 15, 19cd ; Taitt.
p.26 l.5	rüpa	rūpa
p.33 n.23, l.1	DEUSSEN'S	DEUSSEN's
p.34 l.19	designed	designated
p.34 n.24, l.10	*bïja*	*bīja*
p.36 l.1	i.e. the	i.e. in the
p.36 ll.16, 30	elementary	element
p.38 l.2	unified with the unified	united with the unified
p.38 l.26	unto	onto
p.39 l.5	one),	)
p.46 l.29	(29).	(28).
p.49 l.14	*plane*	plane
p.54 l.22	teacher'',	teacher'' (VIII),
p.56 n.1, l.6	extra-individual	extra-individual,
p.59 l.23	On the	At the
p.62 n.13, l.1	373f.,	323f.,
p.64 l.26	and applied	and was applied
p.69 l.18	*arūpa),*	*(arūpa),*
p.73 n.10, l.5	*kāy*a-doctrine	*kāya*-doctrine

	instead of	read
p.78 l.22	*dharmajñānakṣanti*	*dharmajñānakṣānti*
p.81 l.4	(p.213f.)[29],	(p.213f.)[29].
p.81 l.6	on	at
p.84 l.20	*tathatä.*	*tathatā.*
p.84 n.36, l.1	saṃprasāda	samprasāda
ibid., l.2	*saṃprasādo*	*samprasādo*
ibid., l.3	*adhigacchatīha.*	*adhigacchatīha.*
p.86 l.16	*manuṣyasua*	*manuṣyasya*
p.87 l.19	ksetrajña	kṣetrajña
p.106 l.19	elementary	elemental
p.116 l.30	designed	designated
p.119 l.10	on	at
p.149 n.20	S-P, p.	S-P, pp.
p.160 n.31, l.3	other it	other: it
p.163 l.28	jñeyavṛttis	jñeyāvṛtis
p.165 n.38, l.2	*Anagāmin*	*Anāgāmin*
p.168 l.29-30	*lakṣanas*	*lakṣaṇas*
p.169 heading	SAMVṚTI-	SAṂVṚTI-
p.171 n.46, l.21	*pratityasamutpanna*	*pratītyasamutpanna*
p.172 n.49	p.550	p. 550.
p.175 l.1	supression	suppression
p.178 l.19	elementary	elemental
p.179 l.1	svalakṣṇa	svalakṣaṇa
p.179 l.26	(st.	(stt.
p.185 l.6	*aśraya-*	*āśraya-*
p.186 n.72, l.13	*tesām*	*teṣāṃ*
p.191 l.14	q.v.v.	q.vv.

Printed in the United States
by Baker & Taylor Publisher Services